Working Women

Working Women

An International Survey

Edited by

Marilyn J. Davidson

University of Manchester
Institute of Science and Technology, UK

and

Cary L. Cooper

University of Manchester
Institute of Science and Technology, UK

JOHN WILEY & SONS

Chichester · New York · Brisbane · Toronto · Singapore

Copyright © 1984 by John Wiley & Sons Ltd

Library of Congress Cataloging in Publication Data:
Main entry under title:

Working women

  Bibliography: p.
  Includes index.
  1. Women—Employment.   I. Davidson, Marilyn J.   II. Cooper, Cary L.
HD6053.W639   1984   331.4′09172′2   84-3645

ISBN 0 471 90459 7

British Library Cataloguing in Publication Data:

Working Women—an international survey.
  1. Women—Employment
  I. Davidson, Marilyn J.   II. Cooper, Cary L.
  331.4′09172′2   HD6053

ISBN 0 471 90459 7

Phototypeset by Input Typesetting Ltd, London
Printed by Page Brothers, (Norwich) Ltd.

Contents

Contributors   vii
Introduction   ix

Part I   Women at Work in Six EEC Countries

1.   Women at Work in Great Britain
     Betty Lockwood and Wilf Knowles 3
2.   Women at Work in Ireland
     Henry Murdoch 39
3.   Women at Work in The Federal Republic of Germany
     Beate Hesse 63
4.   Women at Work in Holland
     Tineke de Rijk 83
5.   Women at Work in Italy: Legislation—Evolution and Prospects
     Maria Vittoria Ballestrero 103
6.   Women at Work in Greece: The Sociological and Legal Perspectives
     Loukia M. Moussourou and Sophia Spiliotopoulos 123

Part II   Women at Work in Three European Countries

7.   Women at Work in Sweden
     Jeannie Scriven 153
8.   Women at Work in Finland
     Kaisa Kauppinen-Toropainen, Elina Haavio-Mannila and Irja Kandolin
     183
9.   Women at Work in Portugal
     Maria do Carmo Nunes 209

Part III   Women at Work: the Two Superpowers

10. Women at Work in the USA
     Laurie Larwood and Barbara A. Gutek 237
11. Women at Work in the USSR
     Lynne Attwood and Maggie McAndrew 269

Index   305

Contributors

Marilyn J Davidson
Editor
Research Fellow in the Department of Management Sciences, University of Manchester, Institute of Science and Technology, Manchester, UK

Cary L Cooper
Editor
Professor of Organizational Psychology, Department of Management Sciences, University of Manchester, Institute of Science and Technology, Manchester, UK

Lynne Attwood
Women in Eastern Europe Group, CREES, University of Birmingham, Birmingham, UK

Maria Vittoria Ballestrero
Professor of Labour Law, Faculty of Economics and Commerce, University of Genova, Genova, Italy

Maria do Carmo Nunes
Department of Employment, Ministry of Work, Lisbon, Portugal

Barbara A. Gutek
Professor of Psychology and Executive Management, Claremont Graduate School, Claremont, USA

Elina Haavio-Mannila
Professor, Institute of Occupational Health, University of Helsinki, Finland

Beate Hesse
Federal Ministry for Youth, Family Affairs, and Health, Bonn, West Germany

Irja Kandolin
Social Scientist, Institute of Occupational Health, University of Helsinki, Finland

Kaisa Kauppinen-Toropainen
Social Scientist, Institute of Occupational Health, University of Helsinki, Finland

Wilf Knowles
Assistant Chief Executive of the Equal Opportunities Commission, Great Britain

Laurie Larwood
Head of Department of Management, University of Illinois, College of Business Administration, Chicago, USA

Betty Lockwood
Former Chairman of the Equal Opportunities Commission, Manchester, UK; Member of the House of Lords

Maggie McAndrew
Women in Eastern Europe Group, CREES, University of Birmingham, Birmingham, UK

Loukia M. Moussourou
Social Researcher, Panteios School for Political Science, Athens, Greece

Henry J. P. Murdoch
Director of Personnel, ANCO—The Industrial Training Authority, Dublin, Eire

Tineke De Rijk
Professor of Labour Relations, IVABO, Amsterdam, Holland

Jeannie Scriven
Administrator, University of East Anglia, Norwich, UK

Sophia Spiliotopoulos
Attorney and Counsellor of Law, Law Offices, Athens, Greece

Introduction

During the past decade there have been large increases in the number of women entering employment throughout countries of the West. In the mid-1970s the majority of these countries introduced laws directing that, as well as equal pay for equal work, women should have equal access to employment (Cooper and Davidson, 1982).

However, obvious distinctions between male and female employment still abound in these countries—though they vary from one country to another—and the difficulties in implementing the legislation are further compounded by the effects of the recession.

The purpose of this book is to examine the position of women at work in a representative cross-section of developed countries in the West (including the United States) and for comparative reasons also include the position of women in one country in the East, namely the USSR. Therefore, the differences between working women from one country to another as well as the major problem areas being common to almost all of the countries, will be highlighted. These problem areas include the fact that women's employment is mostly concentrated in certain industrial sectors and certain low-status, low-pay job categories; there are serious deficiencies in education, vocational guidance, and training for females; and family life (marriage, motherhood), whether an actual or potential interruption in working life, has an influence on women's careers (Davidson and Cooper, 1983).

The book is divided into three sections. In Part I we present chapters from six EEC contributors: Great Britain, Ireland, The Federal Republic of Germany, Holland, Italy, and Greece. Here we also assess the influence of the European Courts over the establishment of equal opportunities at work for women in these countries.

The second part of the book includes a selection of three other Scandinavian and Western European countries: Sweden, Finland, and Portugal. The inclusion of the situation of Swedish women at work was of particular importance taking into account this country's reputation of being a pioneer for women's rights.

Having identified the characteristics of working Western European women, we turn our attention to the position of women at work in the USA and the USSR—the two superpowers. The USA have by far the strongest legislation in the West pertaining to equal opportunities for women in the form of Affirmative Action Policy. Thus, we are able to examine the effects of this legislation, its advantages, disadvantages, and loopholes. Finally, we present a picture of working women in the USSR, the first country in the world to declare the equality of men and women, and to commit itself to a series of policies to ensure this equality. Interestingly, although Soviet women are more active in the economy and in a wider range of occupations than their counterparts in any other country in the world, like Western countries, female workers are still concentrated to some extent in low-status, low-pay, 'feminine' occupations.

REFERENCES

Cooper, C. L., and Davidson, M. J. (1982). Attitudes of European working women. *Leadership and Organisational Development Journal*, **3** (5), 30–32.
Davidson, M. J., and Cooper, C. L. (1983). Working women in the European Community—the future prospect. *Long Range Planning*, **16** (4), 49–54.

Part I

Women at Work in Six EEC Countries

Women at Work
Edited by M.J. Davidson and C.L. Cooper
© John Wiley & Sons Ltd

Chapter 1
Women at Work in Great Britain

The Baroness Lockwood
The House of Lords, Westminster

and

Wilf Knowles
Equal Opportunities Commission, Manchester, UK.

INTRODUCTION

The 1981 Census of Population showed that 9.37 million women (aged 16–59) in Great Britain were working or actively seeking work, giving an economic activity rate of 60.9% (Table 1.1).

Table 1.1 *Economic characteristics of people usually resident in Great Britain (1981).*

	Women aged 16–59	Men aged 16–64
In employment		
Full-time	35.3%	79.0%
Part-time	20.9%	0.9%
Out of employment	4.7%	10.5%
All economically active	60.9%	90.4%
Approximate numbers	9.37 million	15.16 million

Source: *Occupation and Population Census Survey Monitor,* CEN 81 CM57, tables E, F.

Those classified here as part-time exclude anyone who works part-time in a second job in addition to working full-time elsewhere. Thus there are about 3.35 million people at working age who are only employed part-time, of whom 95% are women. It can be seen from Table 1.1 that women constituted about 38% of the labour force of working age in 1981.

The *General Household Survey* of 1980 included statistics on working mothers, and these indicated that the proportion of mothers at work increases according to the age of the youngest dependent child in the household (Table 1.2).

Table 1.2   *Women aged 16–59 with dependent children (1980, Great Britain)*

Age of youngest dependent child (years)	Married women			Non-Married		
	Full-time	Part-time	ALL	Full-time	Part-time	ALL
0–4	6%	23%	30%	16	16	31
5–9	14	48	62	21	41	62
10 or over	28	43	71	36	25	62
All	16	37	54	26	27	54

Source: *General Household Survey*, 1980, table 5.7.

Thus over half (54%) of all women aged 16–54 with dependent children are at work: among non-married women with children (single, widowed, divorced, and separated) this splits half full-time and half part-time, for married women with children a greater proportion work part-time (37%) than full-time (16%).

Three basic facts can therefore be established for women aged 16–59:

(1) in 1981, the economic activity rate for women was *60.9%*
(2) in 1981, women made up *38%* of the labour force;
(3) in 1980, *54%* of all women with dependent children were at work.

The New Earning Survey (NES) shows that the average gross hourly earnings of full-time female employees has remained about 74% of that of men since 1976 (excluding overtime effects). The differences from year to year in the NES figures mainly reflect the effect of changes in the timing of some major pay settlements.

Table 1.3 *Average gross hourly earnings, excluding overtime, of full-time employees aged 18+ whose pay was not affected by absence; women's as a percentage of men's*

1970	63.1	1979	73.0
1975	72.1	1980	73.5
1976	75.1	1981	74.8
1977	75.5	1982	73.9
1978	73.9		

Source: *Employment Gazette*, October 1982, table 5.

While some of the differences in the relative earnings of men and women can be accounted for by payment systems which incorporate features such

as shiftwork premia, bonus payments, and seniority and long-service incre-
ments, the major factors affecting women's pay are job segregation, the
under-valuation of those jobs which are regarded as traditional women's
jobs, and the pattern of women's working lives.

JOB SEGREGATION

A higher proportion of female employees than male employees are in the
service sector: 50% of male employees are in services, 71% of female full-
time employees, and 88% of female part-time employees (hence 78% of all
female employees) (Table 1.4).

Table 1.4 *Employees in employment in Great Britain, September 1981 (thousands)*

	Men	Full-time	Women Part-time	All
Service industries	6058	3740	3294	7033
Production	5798	1453	434	1888
Agriculture, forestry, and fishing	279	61	31	92
Totals	12,135	5254	3759	9013

Source: Census of Employment results for 1981, *Employment Gazette*, December 1982, table
5.

The main groups of production industries with female employees (all types
of jobs) are shown in Table 1.5.

Table 1.5

	Female employees	Women as percentage of all employees in industry
Food, drink, tobacco	254,000	40%
Electrical engineering	222,000	33%
Clothing and footwear	200,000	76%
Paper, printing, and publishing	164,000	32%
Textiles	145,000	46%

Source: Census of Employment for 1981, *Employment Gazette*, December 1982.

Thus over half of the female employees in production are found in these five
main industry groups.

The services sector, where women are concentrated, covers the main industrial groups shown in Table 1.6.

Table 1.6

	Female Employees	Women as % of all employees in industry
Professional and scientific services[1]	2,476,000	69
Distributive trades	1,511,000	56
Miscellaneous services[2]	1,493,000	59
Insurance, banking, and finance	689,000	53
Public administration	582,000	38
Transport and communication	282,000	20
All services	7,033,000	54

Source: Census of Employment Act 1981, *Employment Gazette,* December 1982.
[1] Includes all jobs in the education, and medical and dental, services.
[2] Includes all jobs in catering and entertainment establishments, hotels, laundries, garages, hairdressing, etc.

Recent information on occupational distribution confirms that strong occupational segregation still exists, and a Department of Employment research project on 'Equal Pay and Opportunities', concluded that job segregation was the major factor in the restricted success of the Equal Pay Act (1970). (Snell *et al.*, 1981).

Table 1.7   *Women's Occupations*

In 1979, women accounted for 39% of people in employment. In the following occupations, employing around at least 40,000 women, the proportion of people in employment who are women was higher than 39%

Domestic staff, school helpers	98.9%
Secretaries, typists, receptionists	98.5%
Retail shop cashiers	97.9%
Counter and kitchen hands	95.0%
Nurses, nurse administrators	92.0%
Clothing workers in processing, making, and repairing	89.5%
Shop assistants, shelf-fillers, petrol attendants	84.5%
Bar staff, waiters	84.5%
Telephonists, radio and telegraph operators	83.8%
Hairdressers, barbers	82.1%
Cleaners, caretakers	79.4%
Office machine operators	76.9%
Hospital orderlies, ambulance staff	73.5%
Cooks, chefs	69.9%
Welfare workers	68.0%
Clerks	66.4%
Pharmacists, radiographers, therapists	62.9%
Teachers (other than in higher education)	62.4%
'All other' in painting, repetitive assembling, product inspection, packaging and related	59.9%

Repetitive assemblers of metal and electrical goods	59.6%
'All other' in professional and related in education, welfare, and health	59.0%
Inspectors, viewers, testers, packers, bottlers, etc.	57.6%
'All other' in catering, cleaning, and other personal service (including launderers)	55.3%
Textile workers: processing, making, and repairing	50.4%
'All other' in professional and related supporting management and administration (including managers, PAs, and TU officials)	49.7%
Supervisors of clerks and civil service executive officers	47.9%
Managers of hotels, clubs, etc, and in entertainment and sport	40.9%

Derived from the 1979 Labour Force Survey (GB). Reproduced by permission of the Controller of Her Majesty's Stationery Office. © Crown Copyright.

It is clear that further progress towards equal pay as a reality will continue to be limited until positive measures are taken to eradicate job segregation, in relation both to separate occupations and promotion structures or gradings within an occupation, whereby women are clustered in the lower levels of an organization.

POSITIVE ACTION PROGRAMMES

While recognizing the detrimental effects upon women of job segregation, most commentators have found it difficult to suggest practical ways of introducing into organizations positive action programmes which will overcome the effects of past discriminatory practices, help to remove existing attitudinal barriers, and provide women with the necessary training and counselling without which the elimination of structural impediments will have little effect. Indeed, the Department of Employment (Snell *et al.*, 1981) draws particular attention to some difficulties which might face any attempt to legislate for positive action.

However there is a danger that further legal intervention would not be acceptable to employers or unions, or indeed to many individuals, and could provoke hostility and resentment. The strong negative reactions of management in the one organization which considered positive discrimination in training and the often hostile reactions of male workers and unions to the idea of women moving into men's jobs suggest that any move towards affirmative action on the American model (or what they may see as preferential treatment for women) might be extremely unpopular in the workplace, especially in a time of high unemployment and particularly if imposed from outside rather than jointly agreed.

A number of possible mechanisms for making certain forms of positive action a legal requirement are currently under consideration, but in the present circumstances, where the development of positive action is optional, who can take the initiative or apply the necessary pressure? In our view, there are four main sources of stimulus—the organizations themselves, who can see the potential benefits of utilizing fully the skills and talents of women employees; the trade unions representing the women employees; the women themselves, either through their trade unions or as pressure groups; and the Equal Opportunities Commission (EOC).

An increasing number of organizations, in Great Britain are now describing themselves as 'Equal Opportunity Employers' and many include statements to this effect in their job advertisements and recruitment literature. Such statements usually indicate that positions with the organization are open to applicants regardless of sex, ethnic origin, or disability, but most organizations rarely move on from this very basic starting point to introduce programmes designed to redress the detriment caused by past discrimination and to provide positive guidance and assistance for the development of women's careers. Indeed, cynics will argue that many organizations use the 'Equal Opportunity Employer' label as a means of indicating good intent without actually going beyond mere acquiescence with the law. That organizations can mount positive action programmes of varying degrees of comprehensiveness, given the will and commitment to do so, is illustrated by the fact that such diverse groups as the Wellcome Foundation, Sainsburys, Westland Helicopters, Rank Xerox, Abbey National, GEC, HM Treasury, the GLC, IBM, the Civil Service, the National Westminster Bank, the West Yorkshire Metropolitan County Council, and the Midland Bank have taken the initiative and are at different stages in the development of various forms of positive action programmes.

The Equal Opportunities Commission has been very active in trying to stimulate the development of positive action through discussions with organizations, the establishment of joint projects, research, and the sanction provided by its formal investigation powers. The Commission co-funded with the National Council for Civil Liberties the major piece of positive action work so far completed in Great Britain, that being the comprehensive programme undertaken at Thames Television, London. The Commission has also recently completed a project with British Petroleum, and has funded a consultancy project with the Haringey Local Authority which is nearing completion! Currently, the Commission is financing research into the development of positive action in British Rail, and is undertaking a project with North West Gas.

The need for positive action has been endorsed by the Trades Union Congress (TUC) and, as a result of discussions at a conference on positive action, in November 1980 and at the 1981 TUC Women's Conference, the General Council has drawn up a series of recommendations for positive action. The TUC booklet rightly draws attention to the inadequacy of a mere statement of policy on equal opportunity and states that:

It must be backed by an equal opportunity programme, detailing the steps which management and unions need to take to implement its aims. And there must be the necessary joint machinery to formulate the programme, ensure its implementation and monitor its progress.

Valuable information and practical advice on developing positive action programmes is also available in a National Council for Civil Liberties booklet (Roberts *et al.*, 1981). If a programme of positive action is to be effective, it has to be designed to meet the requirements of the particular organization for which it is intended, and it is therefore difficult to describe a detailed programme. It is usual, however, for a project to consist of two phases, the first phase being an investigation of the current situation in the organization. This investigation will normally commence with a statistical analysis of the workforce by sex, grade, length of service, qualifications, promotion rate, and pay. There will then follow a series of interviews with management, supervisors, trade union officials, and the women workers, the objective being to assess the differing perceptions of existing barriers to women's career development and the prevalent attitudes within the organization. Recruitment advertising, application forms, interviewing procedures, training opportunities, and promotion criteria and procedures are all examined, and this phase concludes with the preparation of a report with recommendations for action. Phase 2 of the exercise begins when the recommendations of the report, in full or part, are acted upon and a programme of implementation is developed. The project undertaken at Thames Television provides one of the best available models for the implementation of a positive action programme, and current developments within the company are based upon the following programme:

(1) The appointment of an Executive Director with overall responsibility for:
  (a) The formation of a Company Positive Action Committee comprising representatives from management, women's committee, union and non-union staff, who will progress and develop the Positive Action Project.
  (b) The introduction of training courses for management on equal opportunities with emphasis on training for personnel management staff.
  (c) The development of a Code of Practice for interviewing evolved through training.
  (d) The provision of more detailed monitoring on womens' position within the company, covering: job applications; appointments; promotion.

(2) The encouragement of the awareness of training opportunities by dissemination of the relevant information and career counselling.
(3) Careful examination of recruitment procedures with reference to job descriptions and job advertisements to avoid unintentional discrimination in these areas.
(4) An analysis of the merits of a regular staff appraisal system.
(5) The extension of child care assistance and counselling information to all staff who fulfil the relevant criteria.

   Because of restrictions upon staff resources and finance, it is not possible for the Equal Opportunities Commission to undertake or support as many positive action projects as it would wish, and it must therefore rely to a great extent upon the initiative being taken by organizations introducing their own schemes for reacting to pressure from the trade unions or women employees.

THE EDUCATION SYSTEM

While job segregation manifests itself, of course, in the employment situation, it often has its roots in the educational system, as can be seen from the examinations statistics in Tables 1.8 and 1.9. Females are still segregated in the Arts, and males in the Science subjects, both at school and university.

Table 1.8   *GCE Advanced-Level results, summer 1980*

	Boys			Girls		
	Entries	*No. of passes*		*Entries*	*No. of passes*	
English	19,033	13,572		42,267	30,665	
Mathematics (pure and applied)	54,757	36,398		19,264	13,346	
Physics	40,720	28,778		9,727	6,856	
Computer science	2,051	1,536		576	379	

Source: DES Statistics of School Leavers, CSE and GCE, England (1980). (NB: these figures are for England only).

Moreover, a recent report entitled *New Technology and Employment* (1982) has highlighted the fact that this gender segregation is likely to cause staff shortages in the new technology jobs in the future:

There are likely to be increased employment opportunities for computer staffs, technicians, equipment maintenance staff and machine fillers. But the numbers of backroom jobs—secretarial jobs, cashiers etc are likely to stagnate and the decline, if not immediately, then in a few years' time [the banking and financial industries].

Table 1.9 *Home students admitted to UK universities, by subject (as at October 1982)*

	Men	Women
Education	295	759
Medicine, dentistry and health	3,144	3,078
Engineering and technology	9,303	986
Agriculture, forestry, and veterinary science	853	520
Science	13,302	6,566
Social, administrative, and business studies	9,818	7,971
Architecture and other professional and vocational subjects	759	531
Languages, literature, and area studies	3,007	6,687
Arts other than languages	3,120	3,766
Totals	43,608	30,876

Source: UCCA *Twentieth Report* (1981–2).

The concluding summary of the report contains the following comment:

Obviously policy conclusions are that continuous improvement in the educational services is required and that training and retraining facilities are needed to remedy critical shortages, e.g. in electronic engineering at all levels, computer programming, system analysis, and maintenance. (*New Technology and Employment*, 1982).

One only needs to compare these 'critical shortages' with the examination entry figures and results to conclude that the education system is simultaneously failing to prepare pupils to meet sufficiently industry's future demands, while continuing to educate girls for traditional roles. There should be no historical or innate-aptitude reasons for a male/female ratio of 1536/379 A-level passes in computer science (see Table 1.8) and yet it is clear that this 'new' area of study is already displaying the male bias associated with physics, engineering, and technology. If any discernible future employment growth is to require the type of skills described in the MSC report quoted above, then job segregation is going to become even more apparent unless schools take positive action to increase the numbers of girls studying computer, technological, and 'hard' science subjects.

Schools which do not provide equal access for both sexes to the full range of available subjects are acting unlawfully, but the school situation mirrors the employment scene described earlier. It is not sufficient to remove the structural barriers to equal opportunities unless such measures are accompanied by positive action to redress the effects of previous discrimination and to provide guidance, counselling, and support to encourage girls and women to look beyond the traditional employment boundaries. It is difficult to provide extensive compensatory education programmes for girls who have made the 'wrong' subject choices, but as part of a national publicity campaign designed to raise the awareness of teachers, girls, and parents, the Equal Opportunities Commission has produced a *Changing Course Information Pack* (EOC, 1982a) giving details of courses available for post-A-level students. In view of the difficulties associated with changing courses at a later stage, it is becoming increasingly important for girls to ensure that they make the correct option choices, and to assist with this the Equal Opportunities Commission has produced a *Curricular Options Information Pack* (EOC, 1982c), which provides guidance for girls of 12 and 13 years of age, and also for their parents.

The importance of schools taking the initiative at the pre-option stage and providing girls with specific encouragement to consider studying non-traditional subjects, supported by up-to-date information about employment trends and how job content is changing rapidly, cannot be over-stressed because in our experience such encouragement and information is often unavailable. It is equally important that schools should provide similar encouragement and information for girls' parents, that there should be effective liaison between the schools and the Careers Service and that Careers Officers should be as aware and as supportive as the school staffs. The difficulties which can arise when one or more of these groups, or a potential employer, is unsympathetic or unaware of the changing situation, are described graphically in *Sidetracked*, a report of the problems met by some girls who wanted to study non-traditional subjects in school or enter non-traditional areas of employment (Bennet and Carter, 1982).

TRAINING

Obtaining information about the availability of training for, and take-up of the training by, different categories of workers is very difficult, and it is not always possible to differentiate between lack of available training, lack of encouragement for a particular group of workers to avail themselves of the training, or disinterest on the employee's part. However, training plays an important part in potential career development, and there are significant indications that women often do not receive the same encouragement to commit themselves to a course of training as do male employees, even if they are not actively discouraged.

The 1975–6 National Training Survey provides the most recently available information about training, and it is sufficiently detailed to enable certain conclusions to be drawn (Elias and Main, 1982). It is clear from this report that full-time male employees receive more training than their female counterparts, and female part-time workers fare even worse than full-time women workers. While just under one-third of male full-time workers had received some full-time on-the-job training during working hours, the equivalent figure for full-time women workers was around 25% and only one part-time woman worker in ten came into this category. Comparable figures for paid part-time on-the-job training are over a quarter for full-time male employees, around 13% for full-time women employees, and only slightly over 3% for women part-time workers. These figures indiciate not only the lack of training provided for full-time women workers compared with their male counterparts, which is very likely to have a detrimental effect upon future career prospects, but also the low status associated with the skill requirements of part time work (Elias and Main, 1982).

A significant improvement in women's training opportunities, particularly in relation to non-traditional skills, is urgently required and one encouraging trend in the last year has been the increase in the number of training courses being mounted for women with the specific objective of enabling women to train for employment in areas in which discrimination in training schemes is permissible under section 47 of the Sex Discrimination Act (1975) (SDA) for designated training bodies, and the process for obtaining designation is descibed in an Equal Opportunities Commission leaflet entitled *Positive Discrimination Training Scheme's* (EOC, 1981a). There are now 64 such courses available, ranging from managerial effectiveness and accountancy to heavy goods vehicle driving and carpentry. In addition to these courses provided by individual training bodies, the Manpower Services Commission (MSC) organizes a variety of special courses for women, including basic 'Wider Opportunities for Women Courses' (WOW) designed for women returning to work after a considerable gap, higher-level courses for women aiming to return to work at supervisory or managerial level, and courses for those returning to work in areas related to new technology. The MSC also provides courses for women aiming to develop a career in management, and courses designed to introduce women to skills training. In addition, grants are provided through the appropriate Industrial Training Board to encourage employers to take on girls as technician trainees in the engineering industry, for the management training of women in the clothing industry, to train women and girls as clothing mechanics or in work study, and for women training for hotel management. Scholarships are also provided for women for a university production engineering course. Although every organization's positive action programme should include training and retraining courses to enable women to equip themselves for promotion into grades in which women are under-represented or for transfer into areas of work which have been regarded traditionally as male preserves, an extension of the provision of special training courses for women by individual training bodies and by the MSC is essential. Positive action programmes are voluntary, and it will be a long time before such programmes make a significant impact upon job segregation beyond the confines of the limited number of organizations willing to develop such initiatives. Furthermore, an increase in non-traditional training and re-training opportunities for women currently out of paid employment is required, and the MSC and individual training bodies can make a significant contribution to extending the scale of such provision.

UNDER-VALUATION OF 'WOMEN'S' JOBS

While the eradication of job segregation will ultimately enable more women to obtain employment in areas currently regarded as the prerogative of man, this is a long-term solution which depends not merely upon ensuring that employment practices comply with the legal requirements of the Equal Pay Act and the Sex Discrimination Act. The move towards the elimination of job segregation depends also upon the willingness of employers to undertake positive action programmes; the provision of more encouragement, guidance, and counselling for girls at the pre-option stage in school; and the extension of non-traditional training and re-training courses for women. Even when taking the most optimistic view, it is unrealistic to anticipate significant developments within the next few years, as a period must elapse during which the voluntary efforts of those organizations really concerned with the problem can begin to take effect, and the changing practices in schools can bring forward more women with the training and skills to demand non-traditional forms of employment. Even when the movement towards the greater integration of men and women in the work force does gather pace there are still likely to be some areas of employment which are predominantly, if not totally, male or female.

Women currently employed in 'women's jobs' have not been assisted to any significant degree by the 1970 Equal Pay Act because they cannot provide a male comparator with whom to claim equal pay on the basis of work which 'is of the same or a broadly similar nature' or because their work has not been equivalent in accordance with the requirements of the Act.

It was in order to make practical provision for women who were in employment situations not covered by sections of the Equal Pay Act that the Equal Opportunities Commission (EOC) recommended a change in the Equal Pay Act to allow for equal pay for work of equal value. This was in January 1981 and the Commission's recommendations were subsequently used by the European Court of Justice in its judgment of 6 July 1982 in the infringement proceedings against the British Government. This judgment required the British Government to establish machinery which would enable workers to claim equal pay for work of equal value thus complying with the requirement of the European Equal Pay Directive, and two points of the judgment were of paramount importance. Firstly, in order to comply with the judgment, it would not be sufficient simply to amend the existing form of words in the Equal Pay Act; it would be necessary also to 'endow an authority with the requisite jurisdiction to decide whether work has the same value as other work after obtaining such information as may be required' (Para. 13 of the judgment). Secondly, the authority thus endowed must be empowered to make a decision even when the employer disagrees: '. . .where there is disagreement as to the application [of the concept of equal value] a worker must be entitled to claim before an appropriate authority that his [sic] work has the same value as other work and, if that is found to be the case, to have his [sic] rights under the Treaty and the Directive acknowledged by a binding decision' (Para. 9 of the judgment). 'The implementation of the Directive implies that the assessment of the "equal value" to be "attributed" to particular work, may be effected notwithstanding the employer's wishes' (Para. 13 of the judgment).

Following the judgment of the European Court of Justice, the EOC intensified its work relating to the introduction of equal pay for work of equal value, and published a consultative document (EOC, 1982b) outlining its proposals for the implementation of the judgment. Basically the document proposed that the Equal Pay Act should be amended to provide for a worker or workers to claim equal pay for work of equal value, and that such claims should be heard before an Industrial Tribunal. In considering applications under the amended legislation, tribunals would undoubtedly dispose of cases which could be dealt with on the basis of 'like work' or of a valid existing job evaluation study as they would do at present. If, however, the application would require a comparison between jobs which cannot be undertaken on the present 'like work' basis, the EOC proposed that the tribunal should have access to an Equality Officer to carry out an assessment of the jobs brought for comparison. It was felt necessary to introduce into the implementation scheme a specialist group of persons with particular experience of job evaluation to undertake the necessary assessment because it was clear that industrial tribunals do not possess the expertise to do so; that their procedures would make it difficult for them to undertake job comparisons; and because it would be undesirable for the specialist process of analysis, comparison, and evaluation to be turned into adversarial proceedings. The tribunal would consider the report and recommendations of the Equality Officer; hear representations from the applicant and the respondent; and consider in particular arguments from the respondent in relation to a possible material difference. The tribunal would then give its decision and, where appropriate, make a monetary award.

The EOC proposals were founded on the belief that an applicant or applicants who claim equal pay on the basis required by the European Court are entitled to a fair hearing of their application and to a speedy determination of it, as are 'like work' applicants at present. There is no reason why their right to a determination of their application, and their enjoyment of that right, should be made conditional on negotiations and discussions with other parties. Indeed, any implementation scheme which contained such a provision might well come in for adverse criticism itself, whether before the European Court or some other court.

At the beginning of 1984 the Equal Pay Act was ammended to include the concept of equal pay for work of equal value bringing many more women within the scope of the legislation, and allowing for previously excluded comparisons such as those between women operatives and men maintenance workers, clerical staff and shop-floor workers, typists and technicians, etc. The complementary effect of women being able to claim equal pay for work of equal value and the development of positive action in educational institutions and by employers to eradicate job segregation should lead to a narrowing of the income differential between men and women.

WOMEN'S WORKING LIVES

In 1961, 30 per cent of all married women in Great Britain were in the labour force (that is, working or actively seeking work). By 1981 this proportion had risen to 50 per cent. This remarkable growth in the labour force has occurred during a period in which full time employment declined by two million and registered unemployment rose by almost three million. Yet, this rise in women's labour force participation has not been accompanied by any major revolution in terms of the division of non-paid work within the home. Most women have primary responsibility for the care of children and for domestic work in the household. How have women managed to combine their role as wage earner with family and domestic responsibilities? Do their careers or job prospects suffer as a result? How do women allocate their potential working lives between these responsibilities? Where does part time employment fit into the picture?

The above is a quotation from the introduction to a recent research report by the University of Warwick Institute for Employment Research on *Women's Working Lives* (Elias and Main, 1982) and poses a series of questions which should be of the utmost concern to all who are interested in developing true equality of opportunity between the sexes.

Figures 1.1 and 1.2 show the distribution of types of work history patterns by the average length of each pattern and by the average number of main changes of occupation within each employment period. From Figure 1.1 it is clear that a pattern of continuous employment has been the norm of the vast majority of men, with three-quarters of all men in the sample used having worked continuously since leaving school. The pattern for women which emerges from Figure 1.2 is quite different. Only about 20% of the women in the sample had worked continuously since completing their full-time education, and it is reasonable to assume they are younger than the average for the sample on the basis that the average employment period for this group is 11 years. Twenty-three per cent of the women in the sample were currently out of the labour force, having their first break in employment, while a further 23% were back at work, having experienced one break in their employment.

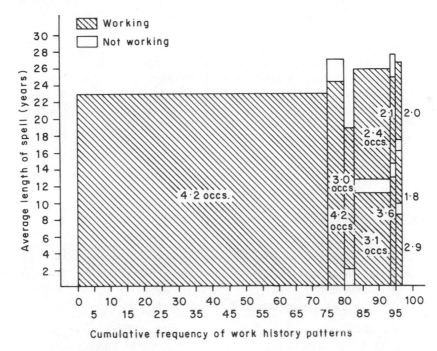

Figure 1.1. Work history pattern—men (*Source*: Elias and Main, 1982. Reproduced by permission of the Institute for Employment Research, University of Warwick.)

One interesting conclusion which can be drawn from these tables relates to the rate of occupational change. The female group which is most similar to the male average in terms of the average amount of time spent in the labour force is the group of women who have returned to work after one break in employment, and this group has an occupational change rate of 3.8 changes, compared with the male rate of 4.2 changes.

When examining the work history patterns of women in the sample by age group, two interesting points emerge. Firstly, from the age of 35 onwards the women's work history patterns show a profile in which the only significant variation is the shortening of the first complete spell out of employment. The length of this period has decreased from an average of around 14 years in the 55–59 age group to an average in the region of 5 years for the 25–34 age group. Secondly, it should be noted that in the 25–34 age group, 35% (the largest group within the cohort) of the women on the sample are out of the labour force after one spell of employment. This is often a period of career progress and consolidation, a time when first and second promotion opportunities often occur or, in the earlier year, when professional postgraduate training is reaching its peak. It is a waste of high potential if the investment

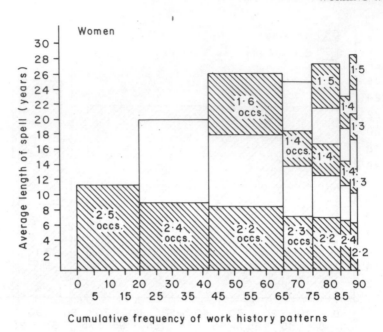

Figure 1.2 Work history pattern—women (*Source*: Elias and Main, 1982. Reproduced by permission of the Institute for Employment Research, University of Warwick.)

which might (should) have been made in earlier training for women is to be lost during this period out of employment (see the section on Part-Time Work for comments on 'skill-downgrading' as women return to the labour force). It is therefore encouraging to note that the National Westminster Bank Ltd has taken positive action to overcome this problem by introducing an experimental re-entry scheme, and that some other employers are now considering similar schemes.

In the summary of the University of Warwick's research findings, Elias and Main (1982) draw attention to the following points:

(1) Nearly all women aged 16–59 worked upon completion of their full-time education. Breaks in their employment are associated with child-bearing. One third of all women aged 35–54 are in employment after only *one* break in their working lives. One woman in twelve in this same age group has never experienced a break in her employment record, but one in six is currently not working following an initial period of employment upon completion of full time study. Two thirds of all women have only had one break in their employment record.

(2) Younger women have been taking a shorter spell out of employment for child-bearing, than did older women.

(3) Apart from the influence of family formation, discontinuous work history patterns are also associated with particular first occupations. Women whose first job upon completion of full time education was in an unskilled manual occupation are

more likely to have experienced a broken work history than women whose first job was non-manual.

(4) On average, men *and* women make about four major occupational changes during their working lives.

Day care

More mothers work now in Great Britain than at any other period during peace-time. In the decade 1961–71 the proportion of mothers with young children who were in paid employment increased by 63%, a trend which is expected to continue. Recent projections also show that the biggest increase in the total labour force is expected to be in the growth in the employment of married females. This increase in the economic activity rate of married women has created an enormous demand for child care facilities.

As long ago as 1965 it was estimated that as many as one million mothers required day care places for their under-5s and that more than a million mothers required out-of-school and holiday care for their over-5s. The most recent survey, conducted in 1974, discovered a similar level of demands; 64% of mothers desiring some form of day care for their under-5s. Another survey of three inner city areas in London found that 90% of mothers wanted day care for their 3- and 4-year-olds and 73% for their 2-year-olds.

Meanwhile the local authority target figures for day care places remains 8 per 1000 under-5s, the priority waiting lists alone stood at 12,601 in 1976, and the local authorities are under no obligation even to assess the total level of demand in their area. The total estimated number of under-5s in any form of care in 1973, including those placed with childminders, was one million. This represented 29% of the total 0–5 age group. Yet almost all of even this limited provision is part-time. Full-time care in a local authority day nursery was available for only 0.7%. The 1974 Occupation and Population Census Survey (OPCS) found that only a third of mothers wanting day care for their children had actually been able to find any.

The above figures relate to England and Wales only. This is because Scottish statistics are largely incompatible with those for south of the border. However, the Social Science Research Council publication *Co-operation in Pre-School Education* demonstrates that the shortfall in places, and the problems which derive from the different forms of provision, are as acute in Scotland as in the rest of Great Britain.

This huge gap between supply and demand has clear and disturbing implications in that many women who want to work are unable to do so for lack of child care facilities. The 1974 *General Household Survey* showed, for instance, that as many as 35% of women who were prevented from working by the need to look after children would wish to return to work earlier if suitable day care provision were available, a finding which is borne out by the marked increase in the economic activity rates of women whose youngest child is over school-age. Forty-six per cent of women with children between 5 and 15 are economically active, but only 20% of those with children under 5.

What these statistics show is that a third of all mothers of pre-school children cannot in practice enjoy educational, training, and re-training opportunities because of inadequacies in our child care system.

In Great Britain there is no coherent or systematic provision for the day care needs of families with pre-school children. The limited provision which does exist is essentially a by-product of policy commitments in other areas—by the Department of Education and Science, which provides nursery education for 3–5-year-olds, and by the Department of Health and Social Security (DHSS) whose local authority day nurseries provide care for those under-5s who meet its definition of priority children.

The responsibility for provision for the under-5s is thus shared by two Departments of State whose objectives and overall areas of responsibility are very different. This has created considerable variation in the type, the duration, and the availability of the care offered by the two Departments and has hindered the development of a systematic policy.

A unified administrative structure would go some way towards eradicating the social divisions between the children of those who are at present deemed to be in need of social services support, the children of working parents, and those who currently receive the advantages of nursery education. It could also ensure that central government funding earmarked for day care provision for the under-5s as a group would not disappear into the social services budget and 'priority only' provision.

Local authority social services departments provide some 26,000 day nursery places for children aged from a few months to 5 years. These places are available for the whole working day and for 50 weeks a year; but they are allocated on a priority basis, which usually means in practice that the children of two-parent families where both parents want or need to work or study are excluded. We have already seen that even the priority waiting list for these places stood at over 12,000 in 1976. The unit cost of one of these places is in the region of £985 per annum.

It is therefore clear that local authority day nurseries cannot today meet the needs of all working parents. For them to be able to do so, the number of places would need to be increased dramatically and the basis on which they are allocated would need to be revised.

The DES provides nursery education in nursery schools and classes for some 490,000 children in England and Wales and 26,000 in Scotland. However, this is available only between 9 a.m. and 3.30 p.m.; most children attend for only a morning or an afternoon session; the provision is closed during the school holidays and 63% of places are for 'rising 5s' in primary schools.

Children's centres are a relatively new development within the general category of state provision for the under-5s. They combine the aims and facilities of the day nursery and the nursery school or class-the two functions of 'caring' and 'educating' which have traditionally been regarded as separate and separable. They are jointly funded and administrered by local authority social services and education departments, and are staffed both by teachers and nursery nurses.

Voluntary and community organizations already provide a substantial proportion of pre-school care. This is largely due to the playgroup movement. The 1974 CPCS survey, which was the last comprehensive survey of this area, found that 19% of pre-school children went to playgroups as compared with 11% attending nursery education or day nurseries.

The shortfall of places in the state and voluntary sectors has inevitably led to extensive use of private forms of care. As a full-time form of provision which clearly meets the first major need of families where both parents, or the sole parent, works, the most widely used of these private forms of care is childminding. Exact figures are unavailable due to the reluctance of minders to register, as they are obliged to do so by law, with the local authorities; but current estimates suggest that as many as 100,000 children are placed with minders every year.

However, the 1974 OPCS survey found that only 3% of mothers wanted childminding for their children and that of those mothers using minders 73% would have preferred some other form of care. The problem of women being 'tied' to their employer because of the existence of a nursery is a real one, but could be minimized if facilities were developed jointly by employers, unions, and local authorities. Such joint ventures would be particularly useful on industrial estates where there are a number of small companies each unable to support a creche of its own.

In rural areas, where the population tends to be scattered and travelling distances great, there are considerable practical difficulties in providing adequate and viable child care facilities. Here, jointly funded employment-based nurseries could play a key part in developing facilities.

In order for women to have genuine equality of opportunity, and in order for them to develop their full potential in education and employment, a positive and comprehensive day care programme is essential. (For a fuller analysis of the day care situation see 'I want to work . . . but what about the kids? (EOC, 1978).

PART-TIME WORK

The secondary analysis of the 1975/76 National Training Survey (NTS) conducted by Elias and Main (1982) provides a great deal of information

about part-time work, and the following quotation from the report summar-
izes the recent development of this area of employment:

Part time employment has been, and most probably will continue to be, the main
area of employment growth. From 1971–78, the number of part time jobs in Great
Britain expanded by more than one million, over 30 per cent, while full time employment fell by 400 thousand. From the limited information we have on such employment
trends in the post–1978 period, it is evident that the main impact of the recent
recession has been reflected in a decline in full time jobs.

The growth of part time employment throughout the last decade has been associated
with the growth of the economy in those sectors in which part-time workers are
concentrated, principally distribution and miscellaneous services [see Table 1.10].

Table 1.10 *Proportion of women in part-time employment in selected industry orders,*
1971–78

Industry order	Percentage of women in part-time jobs		
(1968 SIC)	1971	1976	1978
Agriculture (1)	39.4	42.4	35.4
Food, drink, and tobacco (3)	31.3	34.1	35.6
Engineering %7–12)	19.3	21.0	20.4
Textiles, clothing (13–15)	15.0	20.0	20.2
Other manufacturing (16–19)	20.0	24.5	23.9
Distribution (23)	41.7	50.4	50.4
Insurance, banking, finance (24)	25.3	28.7	30.9
Professional, scientific services (25)	42.6	47.0	47.7
Miscellaneous services (26)	46.8	57.0	57.8
Public administration (27)	25.4	25.1	25.4
Whole economy (1–27)	33.2	39.8	40.2

	Percentage distribution of women in part-time jobs by sector		
Manufacturing (3–19)	17.0%	13.5%	13.1%
Services (22–27)	80.1%	83.8%	84.5%
BASE = 100% (thouands)	2757	3646	3679

Source: Annual Census of Employment, 1971, 1976 and 1978. Reproduced by permission of
the Institute for Employment Research, University of Warwick.
Note: This table refers to female employees in employment only, and excludes employees in
private domestic service, family workers, and HM Forces. Part-time workers are defined
as those working for not more than 30 hours per week.

The occupational distribution of part-time female employment is very
different from that of women in full-time jobs, while the distribution of
women in both part-time and full-time is different from the occupational
structure of full time male employment. It is clear from Figure 1.3 that there

is a concentration of women in part-time jobs in 'other personal services', while the majority of women's full-time jobs are in the clerical and secretarial area. In contrast, craft and operative jobs dominate male full-time employment. This occupational distribution of part-time work raises the important question of whether or not women in part-time employment have to adjust to a significant mis-match between, on the one hand, their skills, qualifications, and experience and, on the other hand, the knowledge, experience, and skills required to perform their job satisfactorily. Table 1.11 relates occupational distribution and employment status to school-leaving qualifications.

Table 1.11 *Qualifications and labour force status, women aged 35–44 years*

Occupational category	With school-leaving qualifications		Without school-leaving qualifications	
	Full-time	Part-time	Full-time	Part-time
1. Managers and administrators	2.8	0.7	2.7	0.3
2. Education professions	35.1	19.5	2.1	1.6
3. Health professions	16.6	14.5	6.4	5.2
4. Other professions	4.7	0.3	0.9	0.7
5. Engineers, scientists	–	–	–	–
6. Technicians, etc.	1.9	1.0	0.2	0.1
7. Clerical occupations	17.9	18.8	19.9	10.7
8. Secretarial occupations	9.1	17.2	9.0	6.9
9. Sales representatives	0.6	1.3	1.5	2.7
10. Other sales occupations	5.7	12.2	0.9	4.6
11. Supervisors	4.1	0.7	5.3	0.7
12. Foremen/women	0.6	–	2.3	0.2
13. Craft occupations	0.6	–	1.3	0.5
14. Skilled operatives	0.3	0.7	5.6	3.6
15. Other operatives	2.8	5.0	21.0	11.6
16. Security, skilled personal service	0.3	2.3	5.1	3.0
17. Other personal service	1.6	12.9	10.4	40.1
18. Other occupations	–	0.3	0.1	0.1
19. DK/NS/NA	–	0.3	0.3	–
BASE (= 100%)	319	303	1274	1513

Note: The group 'with school-leaving qualifications' is defined to include anyone with a pass in any type of school-leaving examination (eg. GCE 'O' or 'A' level, CSE—all passing grades, school certificates, matriculation, Scottish Leaving Certificate).
Source: Elias and Main (1982). Reproduced by permission of the Institute for Employment Research, University of Warwick.

It can be seen from the Table 1.11 that there is a higher incidence of school-leaving qualifications among the women employed in the education and health professions than among those women within the categories of 'other

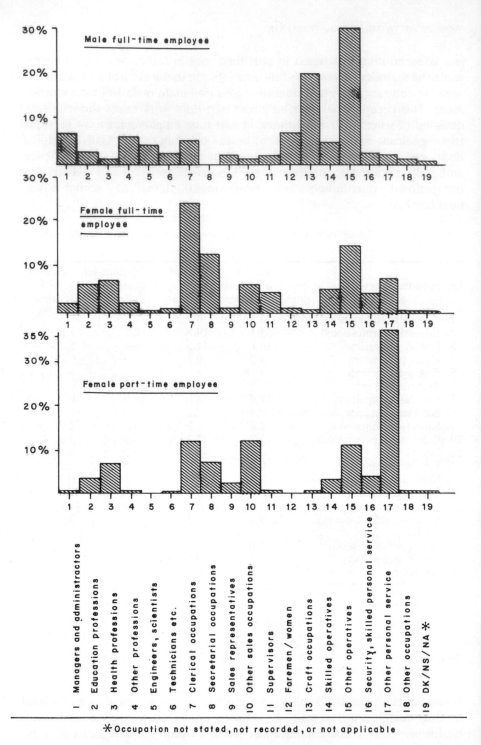

Figure 1.3 Occupational distribution by employment status and sex (*Source*: Elias and Main, 1982. Reproduced by permission of the Institute for Employment Research, University of Warwick.)

operatives' and 'other personal services'. However, the major differences in the occupational structure of full-time and part-time work are still in evidence within the group of women with school-leaving qualifications. Qualified women fill a significantly higher proportion of part-time posts in the secretarial, other sales, and 'other personal service' groups than do qualified full-time workers, while for women without a school-leaving qualification there is a significant concentration of part-time workers in the 'other personal service' occupations. The report by Elias and Main (1982) shows that most full-time women employees who hold post-school qualifications work in non-manual occupations. Those with university degrees or diplomas are concentrated in the professions, and it is not surprising that 91% of those with teaching qualifications are in the education professions, and 86% of the women holding nursing qualifications are in the health professions.

However a quite different pattern of qualification distribution emerges when examining the range of part-time occupations. Within the category of 'other personal service' there are 4% of those part-time workers with teaching qualifications, 8% of part-timers with nursing qualifications, 16% of part-timers with clerical and commercial qualifications, nearly 28% of the part-time workers holding 'other UK or foreign qualifications', and one-third of all the women part-times with Ordinary National Certificate (ONC) or Ordinary National Diploma (OND) qualifications. While it is reasonable to expect that a proportion of the ONC and OND qualifications could be relevant to work within this category, it is difficult to relate the other qualifications to the job requirements within this occupational group. It therefore appears that there is a substantial degree of 'skill downgrading' among a significant proportion of qualified women who are working part time, and, as the report says, the analysis 'suggests yet again that some women in part time jobs have accepted a compromise between their desire to work part time and the type of work for which they are qualified' (Elias and Main, 1982).

In the summary of the University of Warwick research findings, Elias and Main (1982) draw attention to the following points:

(1) Part-time employment is associated with family formation. For all employed women aged 30–59 years, *well over half* work less than 30 hours a week.
(2) Two out of five of all women in part-time employment work in low-paid, low-status, low-skilled, or unskilled occupations such as catering assistants, cleaners, waitresses. Among women in full-time employment, only one in 14 works in this occupation group.
(3) There is evidence of 'skill-downgrading' as women return to the labour market. Among women working part-time in the low-skill or unskilled personal service occupations, one woman in five had a full-time job in a more highly skilled occupation group 10 years earlier. Further, 4% of

part-timers with a teaching qualification are in this low-status, low-paid group, as are 8% of part-times with a nursing qualification, and 16% of those who have clerical and other commercial qualifications.

(4) Only one woman part-time employee in five belongs to a union, compared with two out of every five women who are full-time employees and nearly one-half of all men. Of men and women in full-time jobs, the most highly unionized occupational group is the education profession. Two-thirds of all men and women in full-time jobs in these occupations belong to a union, but only about one-third of part-time teachers are union members. For women in all part-time occupations union membership rates very low.

JOB SHARING

A recent development in the structure of working patterns has been the increase in job sharing, a subject which is well covered in the booklet *Job Sharing: Improving the Quality and Availability of Part-time work* (EOC, 1981c). Job sharing, as a variation in the structure of a person's working week, should not be confused with the government's scheme for 'job splitting).

A comparison of job sharing and job splitting

The features common to job sharing and job splitting are, first, that each involves the division of one full-time post between two employees; and second, that this division makes part-time work available in a job which is normally full-time. This superficial similarity invites a fuller comparison between the two.

A key factor in ensuring comparable terms and conditions of employment for job sharers is for their employment to be for at least 16 hours a week. All of the following statutory rights are contingent upon employment for 16 hours or more a week; after 13 weeks employees have the right to a minimum period of notice according to their length of service, and to receive from their employers a written statement of their main terms and conditions of employment; after 1 year employees have the right to protection against unfair dismissal and to entitlement to compensation or reinstatement in the event of this; after 1 year they have the right to redundancy pay, and for women, to maternity pay and maternity leave.

Employees who work for less than 16 hours but more than 8 hours per week cannot qualify for these statutory employment rights until they have completed 5 years' continuous service with their employer and those who work less than 8 hours a week cannot qualify at all.

In its publication, *Job–sharing: Improving the Quality and Availability of*

Part-time Work (EOC, 1981c) the EOC urges prospective job sharers to ensure that they are employed for at least 16 hours a week so that they qualify for full employment protection.

The job splitting scheme requires only that each partner shall be employed for a minimum of 15 hours a week, which is insufficient to entitle the job splitter to the protection outlined above. The stated intention behind this minimum is to give employers maximum flexibility in working out patterns for full-time work. Although certain conditions attached to the job splitting scheme, namely that the total hours worked and the duties performed by the two incumbents must be broadly comparable to those of the original full-time post, may ensure that job splitters work for more than 16 hours a week, there are fears that the 15-hour minimum may lead to abuse.

The pro-rata apportionment of contractual benefits is an essential ingredient of job sharing, for only thus can the arrangement offer conditions of employment which are comparable to those enjoyed by full-time employees. In a properly arranged job share paid holidays, bank holidays, paid sick leave, and parental leave are all available to both partners on a pro-rata basis. Job sharers should also have access to training and promotion in the same way as their full-time counterparts.

The job splitting scheme offers no guidance on the apportionment of contractual benefits, and there is concern lest job splitters be subjected to the disadvantages so often found in the more usual forms of part-time working. It is regrettable that the problems of entitlement to an occupational pension have been given so little attention. It appears that there are no plans to introduce the necessary modifications to pension schemes, yet the exclusion of part-time employees, or the calculation of the pension according to final salary, may well prove a disincentive to people who might otherwise regard job splitting as an attractive means of easing into retirement.

The EOC's job sharing booklet has suggested that part-timers should be admitted to pension schemes on the same basis as full-timers, and that pension entitlement should be calculated pro-rata according to highest earnings over 20 years. The booklet also includes a model pro-rata agreement which clearly sets out how contractual benefits can be apportioned to job sharers.

In the event of one job sharer leaving, the EOC booklet has suggested that the vacant half-post is first offered to the remaining partner so that their job would become full-time; if this is not acceptable the vacant half-post can then be advertised in the normal way. It is also possible to include a clause to the effect that if no suitable part-time recruit can be found the post will be advertised as full-time and the remaining job sharer employed part-time either in a supernumerary position or in other comparable part-time employment. In organizations where job sharing has been introduced specifically as a work-sharing measure, the aim has been to offer one of the job sharers the present post full-time, and for the other partner to be moved into another full-time post, after a specified period of time as job sharers.

Under the job splitting scheme employers are obliged to keep the post split and filled with eligible recruits: if one partner left the post before the end of the 12-month period, employers would not be able to adopt the procedure suggested by the EOC nor to increase the hours of the remaining employee without forefeiting the grant.

This brief comparison of job sharing and job splitting reveals that the latter lacks many of the safeguards for part-time workers which job sharing provides.

Eligibility to join the job splitting scheme

Whereas job sharing is frequently initiated by existing or prospective employees, in the job splitting scheme the initiative rests substantially with the employer who may only offer split posts to designated recruits. These include: wholly unemployed people who are receiving unemployment or supplementary benefit; existing employees who are under formal notice of redundancy; and incumbents of the full-time posts which are being split.

The designation of specific categories of people eligible to join the scheme necessarily exclude others, and the requirement that wholly unemployed recruits be in receipt of either unemployment or supplementary benefit denies many women access to the scheme.

One group of women who are completely excluded are those who have opted to pay the married woman's reduced rate of National Insurance, and who, in consequence, are ineligible to receive unemployment benefit. The justification for their exclusion is that the scheme has been designed to ensure that no more is paid in grants than has been paid in benefits. Many of these women will have been working for several years before they have become unemployed, and in some cases the loss of their income may have resulted in their husbands needing to claim means-tested benefits. Thus in many instances their exclusion rests on a false premiss, but even if this were not so, it is unreasonable to subject them to a detriment which did not exist when they opted to pay the reduced rate.

Other groups are potentially excluded because they are seeking part-time work. The apparently illogical exclusion from part-time work of those who want part-time work arises because eligibility for unemployment benefit generally rests upon the claimant's availability for full-time work. Because it is more often women than men who have domestic commitments which cannot be combined with full-time employment, it is women who will be lessly likely to be able to use the job splitting scheme as a means of getting a job.

This brief review of the conditions of eligibility shows that disproportion-ately more women than men are excluded from the job splitting scheme. The exclusions derive from residual discrimination in the payment of benefits.

Job sharing and job splitting are not necessarily synonymous. Job sharing has the potential to bring the employment conditions of part-time workers up to the level of those enjoyed by their full-time counterparts, and it would be unfortunate if job sharing were to be brought into disrepute through being confused with job splitting.

MATERNITY AND PATERNITY PROVISION

Maternity leave was introduced by the Employment Protection Act of 1975 and came into effect in 1977. The main provisions concerning a woman's right to reinstatment after childbirth are contained in the Employment Protection (Consolidation) Act 1978, but these were substantially amended by the Employment Act 1980. The current provisions are set out below.

Maternity rights: the current situation

The conditions attached to maternity provisions are complex, and it is easier to consider separately a woman's employment rights and her rights under the National Insurance Scheme.

Employment rights

The maternity provisions of the Employment Protection (Consolidation) Act 1978 and of the Employment Act 1980 are the minimum rights the law guarantees and are available only to women who satisfy certain conditions. However these minimal rights can be, and often are, considerably improved by contractual arrangements negotiated at individual work places.

1. Unfair dismissal

Pregnancy is not fair grounds for dismissal, and the legislation protects a woman from unfair dismissal on account either of pregnancy itself, or of some other reason which can be shown to be connected with her pregnancy. However, as with all instances of protection from unfair dismissal, a woman has to work for her employer for 1 year before qualifying for this protection. Since October 1980, someone working for a concern which employs fewer than 20 people has to wait 2 years for protection against unfair dismissal. The dismissal of a pregnant woman can, however, be fair if pregnancy makes her incapable of doing her job properly, or if a law prevents her from carrying out the work to be done. A woman who would have qualified for the right to pay, and reinstatement if she had remained at work, will retain that right even though she has been fairly dismissed. (The most frequently encountered example would be that of a radiographer, whom statute prevents from performing her normal duties, and who may be fairly dismissed, but who would nevertheless retain any right which she may have to return to work after the birth.) However, an employer has a duty to try to find alternative work for her during her pregnancy, on terms and conditions not less favourable than those of the original job. (Thus a radiographer could be assigned duties which did not involve exposure to radiation.) Only when an alternative position can be shown not to exist can the woman be fairly dimissed.

2. Time off to attend ante-natal care

All women are allowed reasonable time off work, with pay, to receive ante-natal care. There are no service conditions to be fulfilled, but the ante-natal visits must be authorized by a doctor, health visitor, or midwife. Employers have the right to demand proof, such as an appointment card, of all appointments except the first.

If an employer unreasonably refuses time off to attend ante-natal appointments a woman can bring a complaint against her employer before an Industrial Tribunal. Compensation may amount to the payment which she would have received had the request for time off been granted.

3. Maternity pay

A woman who has worked for the same employer for 16 or more hours a week for 2 years from the 11th week before the expected date of confinement, or for less than 16 hours but more than 8 hours a week for 5 years from the 11th week before the expected date of confinement, is entitled to claim maternity pay from her employer. Women who work for fewer than 8 hours a week cannot claim maternity pay. The right to maternity pay is *not* dependent upon a woman's intention to return to work.

Maternity pay is payable for 6 weeks after the woman stops work prior to the birth, and is paid at a rate of 90% of her basic weekly wage minus tax, National Insurance contributions, and the maternity allowance. (The maternity allowance is deducted even when a woman does not qualify for it.) In order to claim maternity pay a woman must remain in employment up to the beginning of the 11th week before the expected date of confinement. (A woman who is ill but has obtained a medical certificate, or who is on holiday according to her contract of employment is technically still in employment and can claim.) A pregnant employee does not have to finish work at the 11th week before the baby is due, but can stay at work as long as she feels able to do so. She must, however, give her employer 21 days notice of her intention to stop work and claim maternity pay. Before making any payments the employer has the right to request a medical certificate giving the expected date of confinement.

Payment can be made either weekly, monthly, or as a lump sum. The employer can reclaim from the maternity pay fund the amount paid to the woman plus the employers' National Insurance contribution. The maternity pay fund is financed by the employment protection allocation which forms a part of the employers' National Insurance contribution.

If an employer fails to pay an employee the maternity pay to which she is entitled she may seek redress from an Industrial Tribunal. If the employer is unable to pay she may apply directly to the fund for payment (EOC, 1982d, page 5).

4. Maternity leave and the right to return to work

A woman who has worked for the same employer for 16 hours or more a week for 2 years from the 11th week before the expected date of confinement, or for between 8 and less than 16 hours a week for 5 years from the 11th week before the expected date of confinement, may be entitled to return to work with the same employer at some time after the birth. A woman who works less than 8 hours a week has no right to return to work. A woman may take a maximum of 11 weeks before the birth and 29 weeks afterwards, but she may of course take less than this if she wants.

If her employer has five employees or fewer, and does not find it reasonably practicable either to give her the same job back or to provide suitable alternative employment she can be fairly dismissed. In larger concerns a woman can be offered 'suitable' alternative employment. The terms and conditions of this alternative job must be 'not substantially less favourable than those of the original position'. The employer is not obliged to tell the woman she is not going to get her old job back, but if she wants to contest the employer's decision before an Industrial Tribunal, the employer would have to prove that it was 'not reasonably practicable' to reinstate her in her previous post.

If a woman has been employed in circumstances where protective legislation has prevented her from working while pregnant, or has been otherwise fairly dismissed because no alternative work was available, she is credited with having been in employment up to the 11th week before the expected date of confinement, and will be entitled to return to work provided that she can meet the service condition. If this is the case, she too must comply with the notification procedure described below.

5 The notification procedure

In order to have the right to return to work after maternity leave the employee must notify her employer on three separate occasions of her intention to return to work. *Failure to do so will result in the loss of the right to return.*

(a) The first notification must be given *in writing* to the employer 3 weeks before the employee intends to stop work. A woman has to inform her employer that she intends to stop work prior to the birth of a child and that she intends to exercise her right to return to work after a period of maternity leave.

The employer has the right to ask for a certificate of expected confinement. (As this notification is required at the same time as the claim for maternity pay has to be made the two can be done together.)

(b) After the birth an employer has the right to request a written confirmation of a woman's intention to return to work. This confirmation may be requested in a letter from an employer at any time after 49 days after the expected date of confinement. Any woman receiving such a request, and who intends to return to work, *must* reply *in writing* within 14 days. Failure to reply will result in the loss of the right to return. The employer's request, which must also be written, should also contain a warning of the loss of rights arising from a failure to reply.

(c) The employee must give a final *written* notification of her intention to return to work 21 days before the date upon which she intends to start work again.

Extension of the 29-week period

There are three situations in which the 29-week period of leave after the birth can be extended:

(a) The employee may delay her return by up to 4 weeks if she is ill regardless of whether or not the illness is connected with the pregnancy. A medical certificate must be produced. The employer must be notified before the end of the 29-week period that the leave is to be extended. This extension can only be used once per pregnancy.

(b) The employer may delay the return of the employee by up to 4 weeks. The employer must notify her of this intention before the 29th week, give a new date for her return, and state the reason for the delay. The employer is not specifically limited to doing this only once.

(c) The return to work may be postponed (if there is some interruption of work (e.g. a strike) and the return may be delayed until it is reasonably practicable to resume work.

Summary of information necessary to claim employment-related rights

(1) The expected date of confinement. (Confinement means the birth of a living child, or the birth of a child whether living or dead after 28 weeks of pregnancy.)
(2) The date on which the 11th week before the expected date of confinement begins. ('Week' means a period of 7 days beginning with midnight between Saturday and Sunday.)
(3) The length of time spent working for the *present* employer as at the beginning of the 11th week before the expected date of confinement.
(4) The number of hours worked per week for the 2 years prior to the 11th week before the expected date of confinement, or for the 5 years prior to the 11th week before the expected date of confinement.
(5) The number of employees at the workplace.

National Insurance benefits
1. Maternity Grant
The contribution conditions for the Grant were abolished in July 1982. From 4 July 1982 a residence qualification is the sole condition for eligibility. A mother-to-be will have to be living in Britain for at least 26 weeks out of the 52 weeks prior to confinement. There will be exceptions to this residence qualification for women serving in the forces, wives of men in the forces, women whose employment causes them to work abroad, and women whose husbands work abroad.

2. Maternity Allowance

The Maternity Allowance is a weekly payment available to women for 11 weeks before the baby is due and for 7 weeks after it has been born. Entitlement depends upon the fulfilement of certain contribution conditions; these are:
(1) the claimant must have paid Class 1 or Class 2 National Insurance (NI) contributions on earnings of at least 25 times the lower weekly earnings limit;
(b) the claimant must have paid or been credited with Class 1 contributions, or equivalent Class 2 contributions, on earnings equal to 50 times the lower weekly earnings limit in the relevant tax year.
Special credits may be available to women whose contribution records are

inadequate for reasons, for instance, school-leavers, students, trainees, apprentices, divorcees, and widows.

The current rate of the Allowance is £25 per week (November 1982 figures). A proportion of this standard rate is available to women whose contribution records are insufficient to qualify for the full amount. The Allowance must be claimed in *the 3-week period from the 14th to the 17th week* before the baby is due.

Women receiving Maternity Allowance are credited with National Insurance contributions for the weeks during which they receive benefit (except for any weeks when they receive maternity pay from their employers: the employer makes the NI payment for those weeks). Because of this crediting, and the way in which relevant tax and benefit are defined, it is possible for a woman to qualify for the Allowance for a subsequent birth occurring within 2 years of the first, even though she may not have paid any NI contributions between the two confinements. The Department of Health and Social Security advises women of the contribution years relevant to any claim for the Allowance.

The involvement and interest of men in the birth of their children is rarely acknowledged. As recently as 1969 a Private Member's Bill to introduce 7 days of statutory paternity leave was described by an opponent as 'grotesque', 'an incitement to a population explosion', and 'an absurdity' (*Hansard*, 1979). However, fathers are increasingly demonstrating their desire to participate in the birth and care of their children. Although there are no national statistics on the father's attendance at the birth a number of research studies have shown that their presence at the delivery is becoming a rule rather than the exception in many hospitals (Oakley, 1979). Perhaps more significantly, many fathers take time off work when a child is born. A survey has found that 81% of the women questioned recorded that their partners had taken an average of 7 days off around the time of the birth, yet only 13% of the relevant fathers had had access to special paid leave for this purpose (Daniel, 1980). The majority had taken part of their annual paid holiday and the second-largest group had taken unpaid leave, thus either restricting the opportunity for a family holiday later in the year, or foregoing income at a time of heavy demand upon the family finances.

Apart from the need to relieve the mother of her share of the domestic activities of the household during the later stages of pregnancy, such assistance will be essential in the period immediately after the birth. The mother may either remain in hospital for up to 10 days of return home to rest; in Daniel's (1980) survey, it was found that 44% of mothers had only the father to help them in the first month after the birth and 7% had no-one at all to assist them.

During the first 6 months of a child's life there are virtually no child care facilities other than those provided by the immediate family. After that a limited number of social services day nursery places are available to social priority families. Thus, despite the fact that men undertake the most overtime and shift work when their children are young, a number of studies have shown that fathers are the primary form of child care when mothers of very young children return to work (Moss, 1980). However, even if there were not this *need* to provide care for their children, fathers should, if they so desire, have the same *opportunity* as mothers to be involved in the early care of their children.

The present government have 'recognized the value' of paternity leave provision, but have suggested that 'this is a matter best left to individual negotiation and collective agreement', (*Hansard*, 1980). For a fuller discussion of benefits and leave around the time of childbirth see *Parenthood in the Balance* (EOC, 1982).

EFFECTS OF THE LEGISLATION

The main objective of the Equal Pay Act (1970) was to equalize rates of pay, not earnings, whilst the Sex Discrimination Act (1975) was intended to provide the legal basis for the equal treatment of men and women. It was never envisaged that these pieces of legislation would secure total equality for women in respect of equality of pay and working conditions. Nevertheless, the removal of job segregation and the achievement of higher earnings for women are the essential targets for the foreseeable future.

The Department of Employment Research Report by Snell *et. al.* (1981), concluded that on the criterion of meeting the objectives as set out in the legislation itself, the two Acts have been reasonably successful. The researchers reported that women have made tangible gains as a result of the Acts, particularly with respect to pay—the vast majority of women in the organizations studied being entitled to, and having received, some increase in their rates of pay as a result of the Equal Pay Act. With regard to the Sex Discrimination Act, it was reported that most overt forms of discrimination in employment had disappeared, and some job opportunities which had previously been restricted to men were now available to women.

The Equal Pay Act and Sex Discrimination Act may therefore be assessed as being largely successful in respect of the limited objectives of the legislation itself, but the Department of Employment research concluded that it cannot be said to have had much success in achieving equal pay and opportunities in the wider sense, and Snell *et al.* (1981) indicated seven problem areas which their investigation had revealed:

(1) The number of women not in practice covered by the Equal Pay Act. The high incidence of women in the organizations studied who were not entitled to equal pay suggest that on a national scale a large number of women may fall outside the terms of the Act altogether.

(2) The extent of lawful underpayment of women despite the Equal Pay Act. Many women in the organizations studied received less than they might have done because of employers' minimizing strategies or, because of the method of implementation used, were paid less than their skills and job levels merited and less than a comparable man would have been paid.

(3) The number of either clear-cut potential cases of non-compliance with the Equal Pay Act, which women (and sometimes employers and unions) failed to identify and/or act on.

(4) The difficulties of maintaining the gains made in pay as a result of the Equal Pay Act given the large number of *de facto* women's grades and men's greater bargaining power in most organizations.

(5) Women's continuing lower pay relative to men's even where employers complied with the Equal Pay Act. Because women were in the lower-graded jobs within organizations and in lower-paid industries generally, women remained less well paid however fair the payment system.

(6) The extent of continuing job segregation despite the Sex Discrimination Act. Job segregation was in many cases the outcome of the way in which established structures, practices and attitudes interacted to restrict indirectly women's opportunities, often unintentionally, rather than the result of unlawful behaviour.

(7) The number of cases of direct (and possible indirect) discrimination which would have been unlawful under the Sex Discrimination Act but which were not recognized or taken up by the women involved nor by the unions in the work-place.

In can be seen that only two of these 'problem areas' (the third and seventh) relate to potential unlawful acts, and the failure here is not caused by the legislation itself but is due to a lack of awareness, or the will to act. The other problems lie outside the scope of the present legislation and will only be dealt with by a combination of positive action, as described earlier, and amendments to the legislation. In 1981 the Equal Opportunities Commission presented the Government with proposals to amend the Equal Pay and Sex Discrimination Acts which were designed, *inter alia*, to eliminate the majority of the problems described above.

The major impact of both the Equal Pay Act and the Sex Discrimination Act has been through individual cases, ranging from comparatively straightforward equal pay decisions to complex complaints of indirect discrimination, with some cases requiring referral to the European Court of Justice. A summary of the most significant decisions between 1976 and 1981 is available from the Equal Opportunities Commission in their publication entitled *Towards Equality: A Casebook of Decisions on Sex Discrimination and Equal Pay (EOC, 1982f)*.

CONCLUDING REMARKS

It is clear that the legislation in Great Britain, in its current form, has not been, nor is likely to be, effective in creating and then maintaining true equality of opportunity in employment, and the findings of the Department of Employment researchers, '. . . suggest that stronger action is needed on both the voluntary and legislative fronts to be effective' (Snell *et al.*, 1981). In order to enable the improvements brought about by the current legislation to form the basis for further development, it must be recognized that legal intervention can be fully successful only when complemented by changes in attitudes. Strategies to change attitudes are necessarily long-term, and it is not possible to bring about change in the work-place in isolation from the educational practices which precede employment and the traditional sexual division of labour in relation to paid employment and domestic/family rearing roles. These and other factors impinge upon equality of opportunity at work, and while the law has a central place in bringing about change, the impetus for increasing awareness and developing attitudes must come from a sustained consciousness-raising campaign. There must be increased pressure for change, through both stronger and more comprehensive legislation and greater voluntary effort, and the pressure must be sufficiently vigorous and determined not only to achieve short-term improvements but also to sustain the continuous expansion of true equality of opportunity in the work-place.

Apart from the moves to introduce into the Equal Pay Act the concept of 'equal pay for work of equal value', as previously described in detail, there is no indication that the British government will act to implement the EOC's further proposals for ammendments to the legislation.

Although the Equal Pay Act was limited in its scope and effect it did have considerable effect upon women's pay, but in many instances this appears to have been a 'once and for all' result, with an actual regression following upon the first impact of the Act. The maintenance of the gains achieved in pay as a result of the Equal Pay Act is one of the 'problem areas' referred to in the research quoted above. While this problem may be partially resolved by the introduction of 'equal pay for work of equal value' and by the EOC's proposals for the introduction of the concept of the 'notional man', the extension of the formal powers of the Central Arbitration Committee to allow it to investigate and make amendments to collective agreements where discrimination in practice remains despite modifications to remove 'women's grades', and greater trade union pressure, it is probably through the combined long-term effects of legal action, positive action and the de-segregation of jobs that the wage differential will be narrowed significantly and the gains thus achieved maintained.

REFERENCES

Bennet, Y., and Carter, D. (1982). *Sidetracked*. Equal Opportunities Commission, Manchester.

Daniel, W. W. (1980). *Maternity Rights: the Experience of Women*. Policy Studies Institute, No. 588.

Elias, P., and Main, B. (1982). *Women's Working Lives*, University of Warwick Institute for Employment Research, Warwick.

EOC (1978) *I Want to Work . . . But What About the Kids*? Equal Opportunities Commission, Manchester.

EOC (1981a). *Positive Discrimination In Training Schemes*. Equal Opportunities Commission, Manchester.

EOC (1981b). *Proposals to Amend the Equal Pay and Sex Discrimination Acts*. Equal Opportunities Commission, Manchester.

EOC (1981c). *Job Sharing—Improving the Quality and Availability of Part-time Work*. Equal Opportunities Commission, Manchester.

EOC (1982a). *Changing Course Information Pack*. Equal Opportunities Commission, Manchester.

EOC (1982b). *Consultative Document: Equal Pay for Work of Equal Value*. Equal Opportunities Commission, Manchester.

EOC (1982c). *Curricular Options Information Pack*. Equal Opportunities Commission, Manchester.

EOC (1982e), *Parenthood in the Balance*. Equal Opportunities Commission, Manchester.

EOC (1982f). *Towards Equality: A Casebook of Decisions on Sex Discrimination and Equal Pay*. Equal Opportunities Commission, Manchester.

Hansard (1979). Commons, 31.1.79, col. 1496.

Hansard (1980). Commons, 18.7.80, col. 731.

Moss, P. (1980). 'Parents at Work', in P. Moss and N. Fonda (eds), *Work and the Family*. Temple Smith, London.

Manpower Services Commission (MSC). *New Technology and Employment*. MSC, Sheffield.

Oakley, A. (1979). *Becoming a Mother*. Martin Robinson, Oxford. 'Husbands Becoming Fathers'—paper presented at a symposium on the impact of children on marriage, Central Middlesex Hospital, London.

Roberts, S., Coote, A., and Ball, E. (1981), *Positive Action for Women: the Next Step*. NCCL, London.

Snell, M. W., Glucklich, P., and Poval, M. (1981). 'Equal Pay and Opportunities', Research Paper No. 20, Department of Employment, April.

Women at Work
Edited by M.J. Davidson and C.L. Cooper
© 1984 John Wiley & Sons Ltd

Chapter 2
Women at Work in Ireland

Henry Murdoch
AnCO-The Industrial Training Authority of Ireland, Dublin

INTRODUCTION

Nearly one-third of Ireland's labour force of 1.15 million is female. They tend to be young, mainly in traditionally female employment, and are inadequately represented in managerial and skilled occupations. They dominate secretarial-type work and part-time work. Their average earnings are less than most of their male counterparts. They tend to drop out of work to marry and raise their family, and have difficulty re-entering the labour market.

There is no one reason for this. It is caused by a mixture of tradition, custom, perceptions, values, and opportunities or the lack of them. What it does represent is a waste of a national resource and an under-utilization of potential skills, which are sorely needed in these difficult economic times.

Who is to blame, and what is being done about it? Well, as in any complex social problem, there is not any one government, political, or social system to blame. We are all to blame, if that is the right word, in our values and perceptions and in the barriers we have erected consciously or unconsciously. But then a lot has been achieved in removing barriers, over the last decade especially, as will be described later.

It is important, in removing the barriers to greater and more effective participation of women at work, that we do not destroy the better side of the values which have stood the community well over the centuries. For example, while recognizing the value of married women at work, we must also retain the value we place on the freely chosen decision of a married woman to remain at home, working in the home.

The world of work is changing in Ireland as it is throughout Europe (see Chapters 1–9). Ireland has developed from a mainly agricultural base to the present time when industry and the services sector are predominant, as can be seen in Table 2.1.

Ireland's accession to the EEC in 1973 widened its market base and the economy developed excellently, notwithstanding a recession in 1975, until

Table 2.1   *Proportion of the labour force according to major sector*

Sector	Percentage of Labour Force		
	1961	1971	1981
Agriculture	36	26	16
Industry	24	31	31
Services	40	44	52

the recent recession, since when, in line with our European partners, unemployment has been increasing significantly and was expected to reach some 200,000 (17%) by the end of 1983.

It is against this background that this chapter reviews the position of women at work in Ireland, where the need for employment creation is paramount. In the future the whole structure of work will change. Employment in agriculture is predicted to decline further, while industry will remain fairly constant and the services sector will need to develop significantly. The talents and untapped resource of women will need to be utilized if this is going to be achieved.

The last decade, starting with the establishment of the Commission on the Status of Women in 1970, saw a whole range of legislative and other actions taken to remove many of the barriers to women at work, and to help them participate on equal terms with men in the political, social, cultural, and economic life of the country. Much has also been done to promote the education and training of women and to broaden their horizons away from traditional female occupations. But much still needs to be done.

The social influence on women at work are enormous. Influences in relation to the responsibility of women for their children's up-bringing are major, as are attitudes towards women at work, the organization of work, and the whole taxation and social welfare system as it differentiates between women, single and married. More about that later.

Newly established organizations, such as the Employment Equality Agency, have a major role in acting as a catalyst to ensure the removal of the remaining barriers to the full participation of women. But there is only so much that legislation or agencies can achieve in this field; the major advances can only be achieved by advances in our own attitudes, both of men and women.

LEGISLATION FOR WOMEN AT WORK

An historical context

The seventies saw a number of significant changes and developments take place for women in Ireland. By the end of the decade, with the impetus gained from International Women's Year in 1978, the principle of equality for women had been raised as one of the major issues of our time.

The publication in May 1973 of the Report of the government-appointed Commission on the Status of Women marked the first official statement of the position of women in Ireland within the educational, economic, social, legal, and political spheres. This report formed an invaluable basis for discussion and policy formation for the rest of the decade.

The Commission's Report contained 75 recommendations and 24 suggestions designed to eliminate all forms of discrimination against women in the fields of employment, social welfare, education, taxation, property, and in all areas in central and local administration. Overall responsibility for coordinating the follow-up action on the Report was assigned by the government to the Minister for Labour.

In the mid-seventies, Ireland's first equality legislation was passed, preceded in 1973 by the removal of the marriage bar. This was a legal bar to the recruitment of married women to the Civil Service, or to their retention after marriage. It is also existed in the Local Authorities and Health Boards and had also been the dominant practice in private industry.

In 1974 the Women's Representative Committee was established. Its terms of reference were to monitor progress towards the implementation of the recommendations of the Commission on the Status of Women and to make submissions on the legislative and administrative reforms which would enable women to participate in all spheres of life on equal terms with men. At the end of 1979 the Committee reported that only 38 of the 75 recommendations had been implemented by the relevant government departments by the end of 1978. While a further 15 were partially implemented or still under consideration, 20 had not been implemented at all. In addition, of the 24 suggestions for action by voluntary organizations, 10 had been fully implemented, 10 had been partly implemented, and only two areas had not received any attention. The Women's Representative Committee was disbanded in 1979 as the Council for the Status of Women became established. The Council now represents 35 major national women's organizations.

The objectives of the Council for the Status of Women are:

(1) to provide liaison between government departments and women's organizations;
(2) to press for the implementation of the Report of the Commission on the Status of Women;
(3) to provide educational and development programmes for men and women aimed at giving women the opportunity of participating fully in the social, economic, and political life of Ireland;
(4) to consider any other legislative proposals of concern to women; and
(5) to examine and combat cases of discrimination against women.

In 1983 responsibility within government for the Council for the Status of Women passed from the Department of Labour to the Minister for State with Special Responsibility for Women's Affairs (in the Department of the Prime Minister—Taoiseach).

Employment equality legislation

Substantial legislation has been introduced over the past 10 years with specific reference to women at work, dealing particularly with employment equality, equal pay, and maternity protection. Ireland as a member of the EEC participated in formulating an EEC Directive which made it obligatory to introduce specific equality legislation.

The Employment Equality Act, 1977 makes it unlawful to discriminate on grounds of sex or marital status and also provides for the establishment of an Employment Equality Agency. It is unlawful to discriminate on the grounds of sex or marital status:

(1) in recruitment for employment;
(2) in conditions of employment (other than remuneration or a term relating to an occupational pension scheme);
(3) in training or in work experience; or
(4) in opportunities for promotion.

Under the Act it is unlawful for an employer to have rules or instructions which discriminate on the grounds of sex or marital status. While the Act is aimed primarily at eliminating discrimination by employers, it also makes unlawful discrimination in activities which are related to employment, such as discrimination by organizations concerned with the provision of training courses, as well as placement and guidance services provided by employment agencies. Admission to membership and to benefits provided by trade unions and employer organizations are covered by the provisions of the Act. The Act also prohibits the display or publication of discriminatory advertisements.

The employment equality agency

The Employment Equality Act (1977) provided for the establishment of an Employment Equality Agency with responsibility for promoting equality of opportunity in employment between the sexes generally. The functions of the Employment Equality Agency are broadly:

(1) to work towards the elimination of discrimination in relation to employment;
(2) to promote equality of opportunity between men and women generally;

(3) to keep under review the working of the Employment Equality Act, 1977, and the Anti-Discrimination (Pay) Act, 1974 and to make recommendations for any amendment of these Acts which are necessary.

The enforcement functions of the Employment Equality Agency in the public interest may be summarized as follows:

(1) For the purpose of carrying out its functions the Agency may conduct formal investigations into any matter in relation to employment and where it discovers conduct which contravenes the Act or the Anti-Discrimination (Pay) Act, 1974 it will have power to issue a non-discrimination notice which, if not appealed to the Labour Court, must be complied with.
(2) The Agency is empowered to seek a High Court Injunction in respect of persistent discrimination.
(3) The Agency has the sole right to initiate proceedings in cases of:
    (a) discriminatory advertisements;
    (b) pressure on persons to discriminate;
    (c) general policy of discriminatory practices.
(4) The Agency may also refer a case to the Labour Court on behalf of an individual where it would not be reasonable to expect an individual to refer the case (e.g. because of the complexity of the case or because of the individual's fear of retaliation).

Equal pay

The Anti-Discrimination (Pay) Act 1974 aims to ensure that men and women receive equal treatment in regard to pay. It does this:

(1) by establishing the right of a woman to equal pay for like work; and
(2) by providing the means for the enforcement of that right.

The right to equal pay means that a woman has the right to be paid the same rate of remuneration as a man who is employed on like work by the same employer or an associated employer. Disputes may be referred to an Equality Officer in the Department of Labour.

Maternity protection

The purpose of the Maternity Protection of Employees Act in 1981 is to provide maternity protection for employees who are expecting a baby. It does so by giving them certain legal rights, the main ones being:

(1) the right to take maternity leave;

(2) the right to take additional maternity leave;
(3) the right to return to work;
(4) the right to take time off from work for ante-natal and post-natal care
     in accordance with Regulations made under the Act;
(5) the right to protection of their jobs during maternity leave, additional
     maternity leave, and time off for ante-natal and post-natal care.

Disputes or appeals concerning these rights may be referred to a Rights
Commissioner or to the Employment Appeals Tribunal. The Department of
Social Welfare is responsible for payment during maternity leave for
employees who fulfil the required contribution conditions.

In general, under the Unfair Dismissal Act 1977, the dismissal of a woman
is deemed unfair if it is caused by the pregnancy of the employee or related
matters. The remedies include reinstatement, re-engagement, or
compensation.

STATISTICAL PICTURE OF WOMEN AT WORK

Women in the labour force

The proportion of women in the Irish work force has remained constant over
the past two decades at approximately 28%—one of the lowest levels in the
EEC and well below the EEC average of 36%. The many reasons for this,
both historical and social, must be seen in the context of an unemployment
rate currently running at 16%. Generally speaking, the pattern of women's
employment in Ireland is similar to that of other western economies with
two notable exceptions; namely participation rates by age and marital status.

A Labour Force Survey carried out in 1979 indicated that Ireland had
1.174 million females aged 15 years and over; while over half of these women
are married, in the working age groups this rises to three-quarters in many
cases. When this fact is viewed against a background of a strong tradition in
Ireland for married women to be solely engaged in home duties, it is perhaps
easy to understand the low participation of Irish women in the work force.

A significant change, however, has been the increase in the proportion of
working women who are married, as can be seen in Table 2.2. Though still
one of the lowest in Europe, the participation rate of married women in the
Irish work force has increased considerably, i.e. from 14% in 1971 to 31%
in 1981, and the indications are that this trend is likely to continue.

If we look at the proportion of women in the labour force classified according
to age group it is clear that half of those in the younger age group are at
work and that this proportion drops considerably as they get older (Table
2.3).

Table 2.2   *Women in the labour force by marital status*

Marital status	1971	1979	1981
Single	77	66	64
Married	14	28	31
Widowed	9	6	5

Note: Women as a proportion of the total work force remained at 28% for the years outlined.
Source: Census of Population, 1971; Labour Force Survey, 1979; Sample Census of Population, 1981.

Table 2.3   *Women in the labour force by age group*

	Age group				
Year	15–24	25–44	45–64	65+	All Ages
	%	%	%	%	%
1979	54	29	22	4	29
1981	53	34	24	5	30

Source: Labour Force Survey, 1979; Sample Census of Population, 1981.

In addition, fertility rates in Ireland are high; far greater than in other EEC countries. A summary measure of fertility in any year is the total fertility rate, i.e. the average number of children which a woman would have in her lifetime. Completed family size in Ireland declined from 3.95 in 1966 to 3.78 in 1968, increased to 3.98 in 1971, and fell steadily to 3.24 in 1978. The average annual decline in total fertility over the years 1971–8 was 2.9% per annum (Blackwell, 1982). Although the fertility rate has declined, the actual birth rate has not decreased significantly as there has been an increase in the lower age of marriage of women in Ireland generally. The high fertility rate makes it harder for women to participate in the labour market.

Where women work

The work force in Ireland is still largely segregated by occupation and by industry, with women concentrated in lower-paid occupations and in a limited range of industries.

Industrial breakdown

A comparison between 1961, 1971, and 1981 shows the shifting dominant industrial groups in which women have been employed. In 1961 agriculture was one such group, but this was no longer the case in 1981. In 1961 Personal Services was one of the industrial groups where a high percentage of women were located. It was not as important in 1981. The dominant industrial groups for all three periods have been manufacturing and commerce. Between 1961 and 1981 professional services as an industrial group has become increasingly significant for women (see Table 2.4).

Table 2.4   *Percentage of women at work classified by industrial group*

	1961	1971	1981
Agriculture, forestry, and fishing	15	9	4
Mining, quarrying, and turf production	0.06	0.1	—
Manufacturing industries	22	23	19
Electricity, gas, and water supply	0.2	0.4	—
Building and construction	0.3	0.6	1
Commerce	17	17	16
Insurance, finance, and business services	2	4	6
Transport, communication, and storage	2	4	3
Public administration and defence	3	4	7
Professional services	18	23	31
Personal services	18	13	9
Other industries or industry not stated	2	2	3

Source: Census of Population, 1961, 1971, and Sample Census of Population, 1981.

The single largest area of female employment is professional services—mainly nurses, nuns, and teachers—where 31% of women workers are employed.

Occupational breakdown

The single largest occupational grouping of women workers is in the clerical area, followed by professional and technical occupations, as can be seen in Table 2.5.

Table 2.5   *Women at work—occupational groups*

Occupation	Percentage of all women at work	Percentage of all workers in group
Clerical workers	28	71
Professional/technical workers	21	47
Service workers	15	56
Commerce/insurance/finance	13	34
Producers/makers/repairers	12.5	15
Agricultural workers	6	9
Transport/communication workers	3	13
Labourers/unskilled workers	0.4	2
Others	1	8
Total	100	28

Source: Labour Force Survey, 1979.

Women form over two-thirds of the work force in the clerical area, over half of service workers, and almost half of professional and technical workers, but only 15% of producers and makers.

In all the major sectors of Irish manufacturing industry, female participation is low at managerial and supervisory levels according to an AnCO Manpower Survey carried out in 1981 (see Table 2.6). This survey also showed the dominance of women in the professional, administrative, and clerical categories. Women also predominate as production operatives in the clothing and footwear industries but not so in the other industries. Clothing and footwear also had the highest category of women in the usually male-dominated jobs in management and technology. However, in all the other industries women accounted for a very low percentage of technologists, technicians, and skilled workers. The areas within the industrial sector where women are concentrated were identified in the 1979 Annual Report of the Employment Equality Agency as: 'areas where pay is traditionally low, skills appear to be undervalued, job mobility and promotion non-existent and training opportunities severely limited'.

Female earnings and hours of work

Despite the Legislation enacted in 1974 to establish the right to equal pay for like work, women tend to earn less on average than men. The ratio of average female to average male weekly earnings declined from 0.51 in 1966 to 0.47 in 1969, increased to 0.52 in 1975, and increased again to 0.59 in 1981 (Blackwell, 1982). The relative disparity between male and female earnings is greater in the case of weekly earnings, as the average work week is 5.6 hours shorter for women than for men.

Men tend to have greater access in their jobs to overtime and in addition, up until quite recently (February 1983), there were legal restrictions on women working at night. Applications for women to work at night can now be submitted to the Minister for Labour for approval, although the Minister is still entitled to apply conditions.

In addition, as already mentioned, women tend to be clustered in a narrow range of occupations and industries generally requiring lower skills and consequently commanding lower wages.

It is clear from Table 2.7 that in all industrial sectors the hourly earnings for women were lower than for men. The lowest were IR£1.85 for a woman and IR£2.84 for a man; the highest were IR£2.96 for a woman and IR£3.95 for a man. The lowest earnings for women were in the clothing and footwear sector where women are highly represented at all levels.

Table 2.6   *Occupational profile of men and women at work in major sectors of Irish manufacturing industry*

Industry	Job title	Male (%)	Female (%)	Total
Textiles	Managers, supervisors	94	6	1,516
	Technologists	95	5	114
	Technicians	66	34	243
	Professional, administrative, clerical	34	66	1,304
	Production operatives	69	31	8,743
	Other workers	84	17	1,404
Clothing and Footwear	Managers supervisors	68	32	2,351
	Technologists	63	37	126
	Technicians	65	35	412
	Professional, administrative, clerical	26	74	1,474
	Other production operatives	12	88	16,883
	Other workers	51	49	969
Food, Drink, Tobacco	Managers, supervisors	94	6	7,178
	Technologists	90	10	488
	Technicians	75	25	1,064
	Professional, administrative, clerical	59	41	12, 231
	Production Operatives	70	30	22,132
	Other workers	89	10	11,214
Engineering	Managers, supervisors	95	5	11,857
	Technologists	98	2	837
	Technicians	96	4	3,097
	Professional, administrative, sales	—	—	—
	Clerical	46	54	11,341
	Production operatives	65	34	25,633
	Other workers	91	9	5,218
Chemical and Allied Products	Managers, supervisors	94	6	4,135
	Technologists	90	10	404
	Technicians	75	25	921
	Professional, administrative, clerical	50	50	4,764
	Production operatives	60	40	14,849
	Other workers	81	19	3,876
Printing and Paper	Managers, Supervisors	90	10	2,274
	Technologists	94	6	33
	Technicians	77	23	70
	Professional, administrative, clerical	52	48	4,022
	Production operatives	41	59	4,457
	Other workers	91	4	2,022

Source: AnCO Manpower Survey, 1981.

Table 2.7   *Average earnings per hour (IR£)*

Industrial sector	Men	Women
Textiles	2.88	1.95
Clothing and footwear	2.84	1.85
Drink/tobacco	3.83	2.96
Food	2.95	2.33
Metals and engineering	3.16	2.23
Chemicals	3.86	2.34
Printing and paper	3.95	2.47
Mining/Quarryturf	3.16	2.02
Miscellaneous	3.34	2.09
Total manufacturing	3.70	2.17
Total transportable goods industries	3.19	2.16

Source: Irish Statistical Bulletin, September 1982; figures relate to December 1981.

Women in decision-making occupations

A study carried out by the Commission on the Status of Women in 1972 showed that 4.9% of top professionals and 4.9% of managers were women. There are a number of contributory factors, including the narrow skill profile of women at work generally, the perceptions of women at work, and their own expectations. Another contributing factor may be the bar in the public service, which until 1973 prohibited married women from continuing in employment.

In her article reproduced in a recent Irish publication entitled: *Power Conflict and Inequality,* Rudd focused on women's involvement in the more formal structures of society, and concluded that women remain, at best, 'on the margins of the power elite' (Rudd, 1982). While making the point that it would be reasonable to expect that women would be proportionately represented at the decision-making levels of the employment structures in which they are involved, she noted many instances where the reverse was true: e.g. the Nursing Council in 1981 was made up of 12 women and 11 men controlling a nursing profession dominated 90% by women.

In the public service the majority in the clerical grades are women, and yet in 1981 there were no women Secretaries or Deputy Secretaries of a government department, and of 80 Assistant Secretaries only one was a woman. The situation in local administration was not much different. There were no women county or city managers and few women in the higher grades of local administration (Rudd, 1982).

The boards and councils governing state-sponsored organizations are usually composed of elected or nominated members and the chief executive of the company. In April 1980 the Council for the Status of Women published a booklet entitled *Who Makes the Decisions,* in which it examined the composition of the boards of 75 state-sponosred bodies. Just 10% of the members of these boards were women; i.e. 79 out of a total of 824 members. Forty-four of the organizations had no women at all on their boards.

In an examination of representation of women on the boards of 15 private companies the position was little different. Only 2 out of 194 board directors were women, despite the fact that the particular companies employed a substantial number of females, (Rudd, 1982).

Women and trade unions

Women are inadequately represented in the power structures of trade unions in Ireland despite high union membership. The Irish Transport and General Workers Union estimated in 1980 that out of more than a quarter of a million women employees in the Republic 63% were members of trade unions. Women make up 31% of the membership of general unions, 51% of membership of white-collar unions and 9% of craft and other unions. In some of the white-collar unions, they form a substantial majority, e.g. in the Irish National Teachers Organisation some 70% of its members are women (ITGWU, 1980).

key positions in unions. There are very few female union officials; they are under-represented numerically on the Executive Councils of all unions with the exception of the Irish Women Workers' Union; and the overall representation of women on executives of unions affiliated to the Irish Congress of Trade Unions is 20%.

Trade unions have a considerable role to play in influencing the organization and structure of work, and consequently the role that women play in them must be of fundamental importance to their increased participation in the work-place generally.

THE SOCIAL INFLUENCES ON WOMEN AT WORK

There are many social factors influencing the position of Irish women at work. In addition there are influences which determine the kind of work women undertake in the labour force. For example, the education which women receive is of great significance in making women available for work of a particular nature. There are also many factors which determine whether or not women will actually undertake paid employment at all—for example, the cultural value system in relation to women's perceived role as wives and mothers is a major influence in this respect.

The responsibility of women for child care

As has already been seen, a very high proportion of Irish women in the working age groups are married. Most of these women have children. Social values assign major responsibilities for caring for those children on the mother and consequently, in the absence of adequate child care facilities, it is not surprising to find that large numbers of women drop out of the work force between the ages of 25 and 30, the main childbearing years.

Hence women are likely to leave the labour force either temporarily or permanently at a time when they are likely to be eligible for promotion and salary increases. The largest Irish Trade Union, the Irish Transport and General Workers Union (ITGWU), holds the view that the extent to which Irish women's earnings improve in the future will be dependent partly on the extent to which:

(1) they can remain in the work force during these particular years, and
(2) society can recognize that absence from the work force during child bearing and child-rearing years must not be penalized (ITGWU, 1980).

Although many mothers do not wish to take up paid employment, many more would be available to the labour market if adequate child care facilities were available. Existing facilities for working mothers are private—they consist of childminding in an individual's home, in creches, and day nurseries. These facilities are not recognized by the State and are not accountable to any statutory authority. There are some day centres run by Health Boards, but they provide a service only for disadvantaged children or for children of single parents who need to work for financial reasons.

This inadequacy has been recognized by the Task Force on Child Care Services which recommended to the Minister for Health in 1980 that the situation be remedied with particular reference to the need for standards to ensure that the quality of the service is maintained at a high level and that the interest of the children involved is safeguarded.

But even if adequate child care facilities were to be provided, there still remains the fact that women are generally assigned a traditional role in Irish society in relation to caring for their children. This is changing, however, and even the change is a potential source of stress, particularly for women, as extra burdens are placed on them due to the requirements of fulfilling two roles, as mother and worker (Redlich, 1978).

Women and education

It has long been recognized that education has a significant impact on determining the type of work which we undertake. The Employment Equality Agency (EEA) in Ireland has the general function of promoting equality of opportunity between men and women in relation to employment. It was in recognition of the importance of education in determining access to, and achievement in, employment, that the Agency initated and maintained an interest in a major research project undertaken by Professor Damien Hannan and his colleagues in the Economic and Social Research Institute (Hannah *et al.*, 1983).

This study was commissioned to investigate the sex differences in the provision, allocation, and student choice of subjects in second level schools, and represents the most comprehensive treatment of this topic to date. It is likely to have a major impact on the education policy in Ireland for some time to come.

While it is not possible here to do justice to the scope and extent of this investigation it is important to note, as highlighted in the Summary Report (EEA, 1983), that 'the extent of sex differentiation is deeply institutionalised in the ideological and cultural presumptions underlying the education system'. In its commentary on the research findings, the EEA referred to the 'hidden curriculum' which influences the provision and choice of subjects, and which reflects the attitudes and values which are dominant in society and clearly reflected in schools.

More specifically it referred to generally accepted assumptions as to what is considered to be appropriate to girls and boys on the basis of sex-stereotyped perceptions:

These assumptions are in general widely shared by teachers, principals, parents and pupils. They are reflected in implicit, taken for granted distinctions which are made between girls and boys. They are found also in the expectations which most parents have for their children and in the expectations and self attitudes of students themselves. (EEA, 1983).

There are no legal or administrative barriers to the education of girls in Ireland. In fact, the participation rate for girls at second level is significantly higher than for boys. By 1980, for example, two-thirds of the female, compared to only half of the male, cohort went on to take the Leaving Certificate examination. There is, however, a significant difference (highlighted in the Summary Report already referred to) in the take-up rate by girls of specific maths, science, and technical subjects, which in turn limits their further education, training, and employment opportunities. The report further indicated that girls are slightly less likely than boys to go to third level education and more likely to take short courses prior to employment equipping them for segregated non-manual positions within the labour market.

In its commentary, the Employment Equality Agency indicated that considerable change in the educational system is required if it is to redress the persistent inequalities in terms of girls' career prospects and to prepare boys and girls equally for rapidly changing employment circumstances.

Attitudes towards women at work

A major influence on the participation of women in the labour force is the value system in Irish society with regard to married women working. There have been a number of studies undertaken which looked at this issue.

One of these examined attitudes towards women in relation to employment opportunities. A range of topics were looked at which could influence women's own attitudes towards working. One of the main findings of the study (Fine-Davis, 1977) was that traditional sex role attitudes are associated with a belief that men and women have different tasks to undertake; in other words a belief in male and female stereotypes. The study suggests that there is some evidence to indicate that attitudes are changing. The overall finding in relation to the employment status of married women was that the employed married woman has asserted her individuality and autonomy in the context of a now supportive social environment.

Another investigation of attitudes towards women at work made particular reference to married women. This study (King, 1976) showed that many of the attitudes people held were negative in relation to married women. For example, they were regarded as most often absent and late. In general, the view of the respondents was that married women are different from other workers in their attitudes and behaviour at work. An interesting result was that even married women themselves regard themselves as different from other workers. The study indicates that the major determinants of attitudes towards married women at work may be factors outside the workplace, e.g. married men with children hold less favourable attitudes towards married women working than do married men without children. In addition, over 45% of all groups, except married women, believe that a married woman's place is in the home.

It cannot be doubted that the influence of attitudes, either one's own or one's peers, determine to some extent a married woman's likelihood of participating in the labour force. Yet other factors—such as her financial situation, the kind of skills she has, and whether or not she has children—may outweigh these influences to the extent of her taking up a paid job.

The organization of work

The actual structure of work in terms of the number of hours a day a person is expected to work, and the actual times, can facilitate, or make it difficult for, women with children to participate in the labour force.

The changing structure of work in Ireland—with increasing flexitime, flexible working arrangements, working from home, and part-time work—all help women with children to participate in the labour force. Although no accurate statistics are available, it is estimated that 7% of the work force is part-time and that 90% of these workers are women (NiMhurchu, 1983). However, some of these women would work full-time hours if adequate child care facilities were available.

One of the disadvantages of part-time work is that there is often inadequate protection available within existing legislation; for example, in order to benefit from maternity protection legislation a woman has to work a minimum of 18 hours per week.

The traditional structure of full-time work in Ireland can make it very difficult for women with children to participate in the labour force. Domestic and family responsibilities are often inconsistent with the requirements for travelling and being available for overtime of the full-time job (Callender, 1983).

Traditional work structures are as much a function of the requirements of the industry as of the assumption of the unpaid woman at home. But traditional work structures are changing. New technology is fast changing many jobs from 'doing' jobs to 'thinking' jobs, where location and availability will not be as important as previously. These changes could have a profound beneficial effect on increasing flexible job opportunities for women.

Taxation

A major grievance of women in the seventies was the continuing discrimination against married women in the tax code. Major changes were, however, introduced in 1980 as a result of a Supreme Court decision (Dublin, unreported, No. 1435p). On 25 January 1980 the Supreme Court held in the case of Francis Murphy and Mary Murphy v. Attorney General that Sections 192–198 of the Income Tax Act 1967 were repugnant to the Constitution in so far as those sections deemed all income of a married woman living with her husband to be the income of her husband, and as a result of this decision a new system of taxation of married couples was introduced by Section 18 of the Finance Act of 1980 commencing 6 April 1980. This new system of income-splitting gives all married couples, whether with one or two incomes, double the personal tax-free allowance and tax bands enjoyed by single people. As far as married women in paid employment are concerned, income splitting is generally more advantageous than being taxed as a single person. In most families, though not all, the wife will benefit directly or indirectly from the new system, and in some cases the additional family income could contribute towards enabling women to seek employment outside the home, given that the high cost of child care arrangements presently prevents many women seeking employment, who might otherwise wish to do so.

However, income splitting has not removed all anomalies in the tax code. For example the tax-free allowance payable to people employing 'housekeepers' is still only available in a limited range of circumstances and at a very unrealistic level (ITGWU, 1980). In addition anyone obliged to pay for child care, whether by employing somebody in the home or by using facilities outside the home, is not able to offset the cost against tax.

Income splitting has not removed the anomalies in the income tax code as far as all working women are concerned. For example, the tax allowance for mortgage interest relief varies from IR£2000 for a single parent (the same as a single person), to IR£2900 for a widow, to IR£4000 for a married couple. The 1983 Finance Bill proposed classifying separated spouses in the same way as married couples; in this way separated people may also benefit by income splitting. All employees in Ireland taxed under the Pay As You Earn provisions claim to bear an unequal share of the national tax burden in relation to, e.g. self-employed, farmers, etc. and have expressed their dissatisfaction through their trade unions, through demonstrations, etc. A government-appointed Commission of Taxation in its 1982 Report made many recommendations regarding the overall tax structure, which are still under government review.

Social welfare

As with the taxation system, single women without dependants are regarded in the same way as their male counterparts. However, there are many anomalies or formal inequities within the social welfare code in relation to married women or women with dependants.

An EEC Directive requires member-states to eliminate sex discrimination in social security matters by the end of 1984. The principal area of discrimination which is tackled by the EEC Directive is that which applies to married women, particularly those working outside the home (Fitzgerald, 1983), in which case the implementation of the Directive will bring about an improvement in the status of working married women with regard to social welfare in Ireland.

The following current inequities are among those expected to be resolved shortly.

(1) Most of those who work less than 18 hours a week are not insured at the full rates. As most part-time workers are women, women are worst affected by this fact.
(2) Unemployment and disability benefits are paid at a lower rate to married women.
(3) Unemployment benefit is paid for a shorter period of time to married women.
(4) Only in limited circumstances are married women eligible for unemployment assistance.

(5) The concept of dependency in the social welfare code discriminates against women in that married women are automatically considered to be the dependants of their husbands. This is the case whether or not the wife is earning an income in her own right.

While some of the major formal inequities in our social welfare code will be resolved by December 1984, there still remains much to be achieved in this area. For example, entitlement to unemployment benefit is related to a married woman's considered availability for work; i.e. her availability can be queried where she has children and enquiries are made about her child care arrangements. Her entitlement to injury benefits and invalidity pensions is also related to the status of her husband, irrespective of whether or not she is dependent on him.

These and other issues (not necessarily related to women—i.e. widowers and deserted fathers are not entitled to the same allowances as their female counterparts), are the subject of continuing debate concerning reform of the social welfare code in Ireland.

TRAINING FOR WOMEN

Training is all about the acquisition of skill, knowledge, and motivation. It is a powerful tool to help match people to jobs and is particularly relevant to redressing imbalances in society, whether as a result of discrimination or otherwise. It is of particular relevance to women. It has been and continues to be, of particular relevance to women in Ireland, particularly because of the impact of AnCO, The Industrial Training Authority.

AnCO was established by legislation in 1967 in order to raise to the highest international standard the skill level of the Irish work force, male and female, from operative to general manager. Training is regarded as an essential element of an overall manpower policy aimed at increasing employment opportunities for all. Training can and does overcome many of the problems faced by women in participating actively in the labour market, or in returning to work after or during child-rearing.

Briefly stated, AnCO provides training in its own training centres which are located around the country, and through its External Training Division offers a flexible training resource by contracting external trainers and facilities to meet specific training needs in regional areas. In addition AnCO provides a Training Advisory Service to industry. Since 1975 AnCO has actively pursued a policy of equalizing training opportunities for women. AnCO's policy on training for women is in summary:

(1) To increase the skill level of the female workforce:

(a) of unemployed women through training in a wider range of skills and for more highly skilled work;

(b) of employed women through advice to industry.

(2) To work systematically towards the full integration of men and women in training.

(3) To develop appropriate training solutions to problems which women encounter in the work force.

(4) To deal with the particular problems of women who wish to return to work after a break in employment.

In 1975 the situation in AnCO with regard to women was as follows:

(1) only 10% of AnCO trainees were women;

(2) the majority of these women trained in a narrow range of courses (hairdressing, clerical, sewing);

(3) there were no female craft apprentices.

AnCO aimed to correct this by increasing the number of women trained, increasing the range of training, dealing with special problems which women have, and carrying out relevant research. By the end of 1981 the situation had improved significantly as follows:

(1) 29% of AnCO trainees were women;

(2) 16% of these trained on traditionally male courses;

(3) 38% of junior management trainees were women;

(4) there were 49 girl craft apprentices, and a further 19 qualified female craftpersons.

Employment equality legislation provides for special training programmes for women in areas where female participation is particularly low. AnCO has responded with special programmes. A more detailed description of these and other initiatives can be found in a report published by the European Centre for the Development of Vocational Training (CEDEFOP, 1979).

AnCO special programmes

Craft apprenticeship for girls

In 1975 there were no girl apprentices. A National Review of Apprentices was held in this year, and the future training of girl apprentices was highlighted. As a result of this, a Programme for the Training of Girl Apprentices was introduced to integrate girls into apprentice training for the skilled trades.

All publicity material was altered to emphasize that apprenticeship courses were open both to boys and girls, and a special brochure directed specifically at women and girls was introduced, giving information on craft apprenticeship. In addition, a programme of visits to schools around the country was established. Sessions cover career planning, with particular reference to non-traditional careers for women and consideration of apprenticeship as a career option.

AnCO itself reserves a number of apprenticeship training places each year for girls, and another major state-sponsored organization is now doing likewise.

Return to work training

There has, as already indicated, been a marked increase in the numbers of women seeking to return to paid employment. As job seekers, women returning to work may be more out of touch with the work force than other categories of unemployed. In addition, the majority of them have to plan and co-ordinate two jobs: one in the work force and one in the home. To meet the specific training needs of women making the transition back to paid employment, AnCO introduced a Return to Work course. This is an orientation course which covers life, social, and career planning skills. A period of work experience is an essential part of the course. It is run both in AnCO training centres and in external locations around the country. In addition, a number of programmes to extend the Return to Work course to disadvantaged women have recently been piloted by AnCO.

Women into engineering

Due to the limited numbers of women in the engineering industry, a radical new programme to train adult women for semi-skilled engineering occupations was piloted in 1981 in one training centre, and was extended to six centres in 1983. This programme combines intensive recruitment and placement with the training phase. The training phase includes Return to Work training and Introduction to Industry, after which the women continued training on one of the engineering courses on offer at the training centre.

Women into management

Although women comprise almost one-third of the work force in Ireland, only 4% of managers are women. This imbalance pointed to the desirability of a special training provision for women to enable them to break through to management positions and the Management Training for Women programme was set up. This programme concentrates on recruitment of trainees, motivation and confidence-building, and placement in employment on completion. The response to this programme is so great that women now represent 38% of AnCO's junior management trainees, and are securing relevant employment on completion of the courses.

Pre-school care

The increasing numbers of married women in the work force in recent years has intensified the need for facilities for the care of children of pre-school age. Trained personnel to staff pre-school centres are an essential element in meeting this need. As a result of this, AnCO set up a 9-month course in pre-school care to provide training for those who wish to pursue a career caring for children up to 5 years of age. This course has proved extremely popular and more recently, a course to train women to set up their own play-group/crèche was introduced.

Initiatives for women in employment

A recent follow-up study of women who had trained for traditionally male occupations carried out by AnCO indicated that there were no major practical obstacles to training women for what could be termed non-traditional occupations (Whyte, 1983). The difficulties arise, however, when it comes to seeking and obtaining employment. The findings indicated that the subsequent employment take-up rate was due largely to 'pioneer' women, i.e. independent and highly motivated women. It showed that the difficulties associated with non-traditional employment for women go much deeper than limited employment outlets for their skills, and that in reality the situation is far more complex and culturally bound. An important conclusion highlighted the fact that 'attitudinal barriers which inhibit women in their choice and pursuit of a wider range of occupations than are currently 'open' to them, must be recognized as an integral feature of any attempts to achieve a more equitable distribution and to eliminate structural discrimination in the labour market'.

The report recommended that the potential of women to be trained and re-trained in non-traditional skill areas should be promoted amongst employers, and that they should be encouraged to initiate positive strategies giving opportunities for women to train for jobs of higher levels of skill and responsibility. As a result a programme of positive action in companies has been developed by AnCO, although it is still at an early stage. The programme has two phases. The first phase includes a strategy for raising employers' awareness of the female work force as a personnel resource, and to offer practical techniques which firms can use to introduce positive action. This phase was approached through a series of workshops for personnel/

training managers in industry at various locations around the country, and the distribution of a quarterly newsletter to industry.

It is hoped to interest and involve a number of firms in the second phase, which involves AnCO personnel acting as consultants to individual firms on the design and introduction of positive action strategies.

The first programme undertaken under the second phase—the traineeship—was within AnCO itself. The broad objective of this programme was the training for upward mobility of talented staff at lower levels, to categories of jobs where access had previously been limited. In general, it involved the training of female secretaries to a variety of jobs at the professional training level, as training advisers and instructors. This programme is currently being reviewed. AnCO also collaborates on a consultancy basis with companies on similar-type programmes of positive action for women.

Training has a major role to play in preparing women for employment, in helping them return to work, and in improving and proving their skills so that they can obtain and retain better jobs. It is also a key in redressing imbalances. Much progress has been made in Ireland in the last decade but much more needs to be done.

SUMMARY

The participation of women in the Irish labour force has remained fairly static at 28% and is one of the lowest in the EEC. The participation of women at work is affected by a strong tradition in Ireland for married women to be solely engaged in home duties, although this is changing—married women's participation in the female labour force increased from 14% in 1971 to 31% in 1981.

Women in Ireland tend to be concentrated in lower-paid occupations and in a limited range of industries. There has been a significant shift away from personal service and agriculture in recent years and an increase in participation in professional services. Women are predominant in clerical work, where they constitute two-thirds of the work force. Women earn less than men generally. They are under-represented in the main decision-making roles at work, whether as managers or board directors, and in trade union affairs.

Overall this represents a waste of a national resource and an under-utilization of potential skills. This has been recognized by successive governments, and in recent times the necessary framework, legislative and social, has been established to effect the changes which are necessary.

A whole range of legislation has been enacted in the 1970s to influence equal pay, employment equality, and maternity protection. An Employment Equality Agency has been established with specific statutory functions, but also as a catalyst to effect change. There is a very active Council for the Status of Women.

These developments have increased the awareness of the major social influences affecting the decision of women to work and the types of work available to them—whether it concerns the social attitudes on women's responsibility for child care, the major influence education has, women's own attitudes to work and the attitudes of others as well. It is also recognized that the taxation and social welfare systems have influences on women at work, and changes are taking place on both these fronts.

There is also increased awareness in Ireland that training can be a powerful weapon to redress imbalances in women's participation in the labour force. Considerable progress has already been achieved in increasing the skill level of women, in widening job opportunities through training, and in assisting women back into the work force either during or after child-rearing. Special initiatives have also been taken to improve opportunities for women at work and to obtain better recognition of them as a key personnel resource within companies.

However, much more needs to be done. There is only so much that can be achieved by legislative action and by agencies, statutory or otherwise. The world of work is changing with the impact of high technology and more flexible working arrangements, all of which will increase the opportunities for women in Ireland to have a more active participation in the work force. But the whole community, men and women, must desire change to take place if it is to happen.

ACKNOWLEDGEMENTS

Special thanks are due to Christine Whyte and Candy Murphy in the Research and Planning Division, AnCO. I also wish to acknowledge the extensive background material prepared by Lucy McCaffrey, External Training Division, AnCO and Bernadette Barry, Researcher, AnCO.

REFERENCES

AnCO (1981). The Industrial Training Authority. *National Manpower Survey*. AnCO, Dublin.
Anti-Discrimination (Pay) Act, 1974. Explanatory Booklet, Department of Labour, Dublin.
Blackwell, (1982). *Digest of Statistics on Women in the Labour Force and Related Subjects*. Report for the Employment Equality Agency, Dublin.
Callender, (1983). 'Women at work, can society cope', in *Trade Union Women's Forum: Topical Issues for Women at work*, pp. 23–33. Trade Union Women's Forum, Dublin.

CEDEFOP (European Centre for the Development of Vocational Training) (1979). *Equal Opportunities and Vocational Training, Training and Labour Market Policy Measures for the Vocational Promotion of Women in Ireland*. Berlin.

Central Statistics Office (1979). *Labour Force Survey*.

Central Statistics Office (1982). *Irish Statistical Bulletin*, **LVII** (3), September.

Central Statistics Office (1961). '*A Profile of the Demographic and Labour Force Characteristics of the Population*'. Sample Analysis of the 1961 Census of Population.

Central Statistics Office (1981). *Sample Census of Population*.

Commission on the Status of Women (1971). Interim Report on Equal Pay. Stationery Office, Dublin.

Commission on Taxation (1982). *First Report, Direct Taxation*. Stationery Office, Dublin.

Commission for the Status of Women—Report of (1972). Stationery Office, Dublin (December).

Council for the Status of Women (1980). *Who Makes the Decisions*. CSW, Dublin.

Employment Equality Act, 1977. Explanatory Booklet, Department of Labour, Dublin.

Employment Equality Agency (1983). *Schooling and Sex Roles, Agency Commentary, Recommendations and Summary Findings of Report*. EEA, Dublin.

Fine-Davis, (1977). *Attitudes Towards the Status of Women: Implications for Equal Employment Opportunity*. The Department of Labour, Dublin.

Fitzgerald, E (1983). 'Sex discrimination and social welfare', in *Trade Union Women's Forum: Topical Issues for Women at Work*, pp. 15–20. Trade Unions Women's Forum, Dublin.

Hannan, Breen, Murray, Watson, Hardiman, and O'Higgins (1983). *Schooling and Sex Roles, Sex Differences in Subject Provision and Student Choice in Irish Post-Primary Schools*. ESRI Paper No. 113, Dublin.

Irish Transport and General Workers Union (1980). *Equality for Women, A Discussion Paper presented to Annual Delegate Conference*. ITGWU, Dublin.

King, (1976). *Attitudes to Women at Work, with particular reference to Attitudes Towards Married Women*. AnCO, Dublin.

Maternity Protection of Employees Act, 1981. Explanatory booklet, Department of Labour, Dublin.

McCarthy, E. (1978). 'Women and work in Ireland: the present, and preparing for the future', in MacCurtain, M. and Donncha O Corrain (eds), *Women in Irish Society, The Historical Dimension*, pp. 103–117. Arlen House, Dublin.

NiMhurchu, 'Part-time workers', in *Trade Union Women's Forum: Topical Issues for Women at Work*, pp. 7–12. Trade Union Women's Forum, Dublin.

Redlich, P. (1978). 'Women and the family', in MacCurtain, M. and Donncha O Corraind (eds.), *Women in Irish Society, the Historical Dimension*. Arlen House, Dublin.

Rudd, J. (1)82). 'On the margins of the power elite: women in the upper echelons', in Kelly, M., O'Dowd, L. and Wickham, J. (eds), *Power Conflict and Inequality*, pp. 159–170 Turoe Press, Dublin.

The Women's Representative Committee (1976). *Progress Report on the Implementation of the Recommendations in the Report of the Commission on the Status of Women*. Stationery Office, Dublin.

Wickham, A. '*Women, industrial transition and training policy in the Republic of Ireland*', in Kelly, M., O'Dowd, L. , and Wickham, J. (eds), *Power Conflict and Inequality*, pp. 147–158. Turoe Press, Dublin.

Whyte, C. (1983). *Blue-Collar Jobs and Women—Summary Report*. AnCO, Dublin.

Women at Work
Edited by M.J. Davidson and C.L. Cooper
© 1984 John Wiley & Sons Ltd

Chapter 3
Women at Work in the Federal Republic of Germany

Beate Hesse
Ministry for Youth, Family Affairs and Health, Bonn, West Germany

INTRODUCTION—A STATISTICAL OVERVIEW

Female participation in the labour force

In the Federal Republic of Germany there has been a continuous increase in the number of female wage-earners in recent years, in spite of there having been only slight changes in the residential population. While there were only 9.6 million women among the wage-earners in 1967, the numbers had risen to 10.5 million in 1980. Applied to the female residential population of employable age of between 15 and 64 years this means a participation of 50.2%, i.e. roughly every second woman of employable age works today. Owing to longer training periods and the introduction of flexible earlier retirement within the old age pension schemes (annuity insurance) the increase in the number of working women is to be found among those between the ages of 25 and 60.

The situation of the family is a determining factor in the attitude of women towards work. Due mainly to economic reasons the highest rate of women working is to be found among unmarried women. As the number of unmarried, divorced, and widowed women working has been relatively high and constant for quite a while, the rate of *married* women working is the decisive factor that determines the total participation of women in the labour force.

It has been ascertained that the attitude of married women towards work has changed tremendously during the last two decades. In 1961 only 37.0% of the married women between the ages of 20 and 60 participated in the labour force; in 1980, however, this had risen to 48.9% i.e. the activity rate of married women working increased in this period by over 30%. Particularly high increases were to be found among the 25–50 year-old women, i.e. during the age span when children are being born and brought up. Indeed, the activity rate of married women with children under the age of 18 was only 33.2% in 1961, rising to 41.9% in 1980. Although women with larger families are less likely to work, more important than the number of children, is the net income of the family, which in general refers to the net income of the husband. This means that when the income of the family is low, more women work despite having many children.

The 'divided' labour market

In spite of the increasing participation of women in the labour market, their position is still markedly different compared to that of men, so one still has to refer to a 'divided' labour market. Hence, the labour market is divided in the three following ways: (1) work patterns; (2) job segregation; and (3) job status.

Work patterns

It was agreed in the collective pay settlements in 1980 that there would be a regular working week of 40 hours for about 94% of all German employees. Differing from this, the actual average working week for women is 33.3 hours and for men 41.9 hours (Clasen, 1981). Shorter working hours and part-time work is to be found nearly exclusively among women. In 1980, of the 3 million part-time work contracts offered, 89% were filled by women and 11% by men. Therefore, about 30% of the employed women work part-time, i.e. less than 40 hours per week (Statistische Bundesamt, 1981). Owing to the fact that the work-load in the family is still distributed unevenly, for many women part-time work allows them to combine a family with work. Therefore, it is not surprising that the number of part-time workers is highest (55%) among married women with children, and lowest among those that are not married and have no children. Besides the duties towards the family, the economic situation of the women determines the amount of part-time work, i.e. even if there are no children to be cared for, the number of married women working part-time increases with rising family income (Hofbauer, 1981).

The work pattern of married women is also in many cases characterized by having had to interrupt work once or repeatedly. Hitherto, the general rule has been that, out of three women, one woman would withdraw permanently from the labour force after the birth of the first or second child, the second woman would interrupt her employment, and the third woman would stay on at her job. Nowadays, the first group is increasingly becoming smaller, in favour of those women who want to return to work after a certain period away. The period of the break has also become shorter. Two out of three women planning to return to work interrupt their employment for only 1–5 years, 12% for 6–10 years, and 20% for more than 10 years. Fifty per cent of all those wishing to return want to go back to work after a break of less than 5 years. Moreover, according to the microcensus of 1974, 41% of the women took up part-time work after the break. Out of those women returning to work as part-timers, only 51% took up employment that corresponded to their training, whereas 85% of the fully employed women had done so (Yohalem, 1982).

Job segregation

A breakdown of the structure of the labour force along gender lines shows clearly that most of the working women (58%) are employed in the service sector. In the producing sector the women fill almost one-third of all workplaces, whereas they make up just half the labour force in the consumption goods industry and only one-quarter of the capital goods (investment) industry (Institut für Arbeitsmarkt, 1981).

There are fields of trade and industry in which far more than 50% of the employees are women. At the top end there are the private households, with 97% being women, and then the health and veterinary services, and the clothing industry (both with 75% female employment), and finally the retail trade, with 64% of employees being women. In other branches of industry and trade, though, the women are badly under-represented as, for example, in the construction industry, in the energy industry, in the water supply service, and in mining. There are no fields of work where men are as heavily under-represented (except in private households) as the women are in the above-named branches. At the same time the working women are found in greater concentration in a comparably smaller number of employment sectors compared to their male counterparts. Fifty-one per cent of the working women are to be found in only seven out of 46 sectors, namely: retail; agriculture and gardening; the leather, textile, and clothing industry; health and veterinary services; electrical engineering; the civil service; and education (Institut für Arbeistsmarkt 1981).

The relatively narrow employment range of women is more or less preprogrammed by the present distribution of girls to the jobs they are trained in. There are a number of jobs that are taken up nearly exclusively by girls, for example as secretaries, typists, audiotypists, datatypists (proportion of women 97%), as doctors' assistant, medical-technical assistant, and masseurs (proportion of women 93%), and as educators, social workers, educational sociologists (proportion of women 81%). Forty per cent of the girls are to be found in only four so-called 'typical female' occupations, whereas 40% of the male trainees are to be found in at least 10 different occupations.

Job status

Women in the Federal Republic of Germany are still to be found predominantly in the lower-status jobs. Managerial positions are only rarely occupied
by women. A survey done in 1979 for the private sector revealed that only
2% of all managerial positions were occupied by women.

Every few years the microcensus also asks questions concerning work
content. In the last survey, from April 1980, only 2.2% of the women,
compared to 6.8% of the men, classed themselves as having to do managerial
work for most of the time. Yet a comparison with the figures from 1976
shows that the situation has hardly changed in recent years (predominantly
dealing with managerial duties in 1976: women 2.0%, men 7.0%) (Wirtschaft
und Statistik, 1982).

Even in fields where women provide a large percentage of the labour
force, such as the textile and clothing industry or in the health service, they
are still found in positions of dependence rather than in positions at the top
end of the scale, which are predominantly filled by men.

The consequences of the divided labour market

The difference in status between men and women in the labour market is
most obvious in the wages and salaries differentials, as well as in the greater
way unemployment affects women.

Pay differentials

In 1982 the average gross hourly earnings in industry was DM11,33 for female
workers and for male workers DM15,60—the gross hourly earnings of women
was thus 27.4% lower than that of men (in 1950 the difference was 36.2%).
For decades the monthly salaries of women employees have been about one-
third below that of the men (1982: 32.2%; 1950: 38.2%). This difference can
partly be explained by the shorter regular working hours (part-time work).
That the situation is worse for the female employees can be clearly illustrated
by examining the salary bracket figures; thus, 54.2% of the women are placed
in the lowest salary bracket IV and V compared to only 14.6% of the male
employees. In the highest salary bracket only 7.6% of females are to be
found, as opposed to 38.0% of the male employees.

Unemployment

Between 1976 and 1982, in absolute figures, more women were not in employment compared to men. Certainly the recession has led to increasing unemployment among men. Nevertheless, taking into account their activity rate

in the labour force, women are still worse hit by unemployment than men (annual average rate of unemployment in 1982: women 8.6%; men 6.9%). In addition there is the so-called hidden reserve of women, i.e. women that are not to be found in the unemployment statistics because they have not registered as unemployed. Among these women, research indicates that a high percentage wish to return to work; three-quarters of them want to work as part-timers and of those registered as unemployed, 80% are looking for full-time employment (Statistisches Bundesamt, 1983).

MEASURES TO IMPROVE THE SITUATION OF WOMEN IN THE LABOUR FORCE

In recent years it has been brought to the attention of the federal government, the state governments, the trade unions, and women's organizations, that it is necessary to try and change this divided labour market. Numerous activities have been initiated which have brought about some beneficial changes. While measures to reduce these deficits have been introduced to some degree in most fields, discussion will be focused on the following four most important areas: (1) general and vocational training; (2) further education/training; (3) affirmative action; and (4) the family/work conflict.

General and vocational education

Equality of opportunity in education and training is essential if women are to have equality in their later working life. As far as it concerns the participation of girls in education (primary, secondary modern, and grammar schools) there are no longer any qualitative differences between girls and boys. Only among the school-leavers of secondary and vocational schools with the requisite qualifications for higher and professional education is the percentage of girls still below that of boys (in 1981: 46.4%). At the same time, it can be said that this difference has continuously been reduced in recent years (Bundesminister für Bildung und Wissenschaft, 1982).

The situation for the girls in secondary schools also seems to be qualitatively better—i.e. from the point of view of performance and achievement. Quite clearly fewer girls than boys fail to move up into the next higher form; in many cases the average grade of the girls in their final reports is better than that of the boys. However, in secondary schools the girls are traditionally oriented towards foreign languages as opposed to natural sciences and technical subjects, which tend to be chosen by the boys. This tendency can be quite clearly observed at university level. The engineering departments, economic departments, mathematics and natural sciences, as well as the schools of medicine, are still dominated by male undergraduates training for professions which allegedly offer a career and job security. A higher percentage of women, however, can be found in the educational sciences, in the teaching profession, and in the social sciences/social work fields in which the unemployment rate for graduates has increased immensely in recent years.

Recently, various efforts have been made to direct girls and women, before they enter the job training market, into visualizing a more atypical job and therefore choosing school and university subjects other than the usual traditional 'female' ones. An important role in this is played by the subject 'Arbeitslehre' (work/career-oriented subject) which has been introduced in the past few years in all states at all secondary modern, technical, and comprehensive schools, and in Niedersachsen also in secondary modern schools.

In particular, the practical training that is an obligatory part of the syllabus can be decisive for the future choice of employment at an early stage. Consequently, the federal government has turned to the state governments (which are responsible for education) and has come down in favour of introducing practical training within the syllabus at all secondary schools, and also (if possible) at grammar schools. In addition, it especially welcomes those initiatives of the states that aim at having more girls participate in technical and natural science classes.

In the Federal Republic of Germany, *vocational training* takes place predominantly within the context of a *dual* system, i.e. in individual organizations/firms, and for the more theoretical side of the training in a technical college. For some jobs (e.g. jobs within the health services) training is possible as a full-time student at a technical college. However, even within this dual training system the main fields of training for jobs with good prospects are still under-represented by female trainees. Although the number of female apprentices has increased more than that of the male ones since 1975, the proportion of girls in the dual system was only 38.6% in 1981. One of the reasons for this is that the firms that have the vacancies for the apprenticeships registered at the 'Bundesanstalt fur Arbeit' (Federal Office for Employment) quite often expressly ask for a male apprentice. Only about 25% of all apprenticeships are offered to men *and* women, against 25% only to women.

Apprenticeships in the production field are as a rule offered only to men. On the other hand, apprenticeships in the service sector are only offered to women. Accordingly, 85% of all female apprentices are to be found within the service sector. The training opportunities for young women are consequently quantitatively and qualitatively restricted (Bundesminister für Bildung and Wissenschaft, 1983).

It has therefore been the declared goal of the federal and state governments for some years to expand the job spectrum for women and to make a greater number of apprenticeships accessible to them. The federal government has financed for this purpose a number of pilot schemes. It is the aim of these schemes to encourage firms that take on apprentices to train women in jobs hitherto dominated by men, and to interest young women in industrial and technical apprenticeships. The girls participating in these schemes are trained for jobs such as skilled workers in the chemical industry, fitters and welders, and female tool-makers. This pilot scheme by the federal government, combined with some states initiating plans for affirmative action, has increased the willingness of firms to train young women in industrial and technical jobs. Also, reservations on the part of the women themselves and their parents were removed with the help of the pilot schemes. As a result, the number of female apprentices in the traditional male occupations rose from 11,500 in 1977 to 41,300 in 1981. This means that, in the academic year 1981/2, 6.3% of all the female apprentices were trained in these types of occupations, compared to 2.0% in 1977.

Although the figures do not in fact mean a breakthrough, they do show a widening of the hitherto narrowly restricted job market for young women. Consequently, it is now important to continue with this development and to remove its special pilot status, allowing it to become the normal course of events.

As by far the largest number of young women (over 75%) will be found in the foreseeable future in one of the traditional female occupations, the federal government is going to look into what the future prospects for these women are. This research is supposed to lead to greater public awareness of the fact that there is a need for change, and of the possibilities of changes within the traditional framework of female occupation. The questions raised are whether changes in the national training programme are necesary, how the split along gender lines in the labour market can be overcome, and what measures have to be implemented to further affirmative action on behalf of working women.

In connection with the improvement of the job opportunities for women there have been quite controversial debates in the federal government for some time concerning the maintenance of the special health and safety standards in industry for women. Some believe that these health and safety standards for women are one of the main obstacles against implementing equal opportunity. Indeed, out of 451 recognized training fields, 33 are closed to women because of safety regulations (mainly jobs in the building and construction trade). The trade unions, though, are as yet not prepared to give up the special health and safety standards for women.

Further education training

Further education/training courses offer an opportunity to catch up on qualifications in order to satisfy the continuously changing demands of the job

market, and to promote one's career. They therefore especially offer women
a possibility of reducing deficits incurred during their initial training, and to
reduce their disadvantages in comparison with men.

Taking into account the double burden for working women, it must be
seen as a positive achievement that according to a survey of 1979, 17% of
the working men, but at least 14% of the full-time employed women, have
taken part in further vocational training. However, the women working part-
time are a special problem; in this group only 8% took part in further training
programmes. Further, it appears that the tendency to take part in further
training courses rises proportionally with the level of education already achieved. This implies, though, that those women who would benefit most from
further training are the least likely to take advantage of it.

In the Federal Republic of Germany numerous institutions deal with
further education/training and re-training. The main instrument to support
further vocational training has been the 'Arbeitsforderungsgesetz' (Labour
Promotion Law), which was passed in 1969. Due to this legislation, the costs
of a course are paid for, and in certain conditions a grant towards the living
costs is given. In recent years this has encouraged more women to enrol on
these courses. While in 1974 only every fourth participant in these training
courses was a woman, in 1980 every third participant was female.

Nevertheless, since 1980 the percentage of women has not risen and
remains at 33%. Due to the higher unemployment rates of women, surely
they ought to be over-represented rather than under-represented in the
measures introduced according to the 'Arbeitsforderungsgesetz'. The reason
for the stagnating participation rate of women has not yet been examined in
detail. But this development must be viewed as being connected with the
cuts in further training and specifically the cuts in the grants introduced in
1980, which were necessary due to the worsening financial situation of the
public budget. Consequently, both women's organizations and trade unions
are now demanding that the cuts in further education/training should be
reversed. Even so, despite these cuts, one main goal of the 'Arbeitsfoderungsgesetz' is still effective. It stipulates specific measures which are intended to
help women re-enter the labour market after having left to have a family.
For this particular group of women who wish to return to work, the federal
government has introduced a number of non-fee-paying pilot projects aimed
at developing training courses for the needs of women with children. As the
time span during which women interrupt their work life has become shorter,
more and more women are returning to work while their children are not
yet totally independent. Three-quarters of those returning to work wish to
work part-time, therefore one of the demands as regards further training is
to offer more courses on a part-time basis. According to the 'Directorate on
Women's Affairs' of the Federal Ministry for Youth, Family Affairs and
Health (Bundesministerium für Jugend, Familie und Gesundheit) the instru-

ments of the 'Arbeitsfoderungsgesetz' must in future be directed towards training women in hitherto atypical occupations, especially in the commercial and technical fields. About four-fifths of the female course participants introduced because of the Arbeitsfoderungsgesetz get further training in the traditional female-dominated service sector. In addition, due to the increased used of new technology, the demand for widening the range of further training for women grows increasingly. In fact, pilot schemes carried out by the federal government have shown that women who get the qualifications for a job as adults, are adaptable and are also capable of further education/ training in other fields because the traditional female ones (Bundesminister für Jugend, Familie und Gesundheit, 1980).

These schemes have also shown that the measures necessary to reintegrate a woman successfully into the labour market are more work-intensive the longer the woman has been away from work. Therefore, the 'Directorate on Women's Affairs' has initiated a survey on 'Contacts with the working world *during* the family phase'. It is supposed to look into whether and how women, who drop out of work for a longer period of time, can possibly keep up on what they were originally trained for during this time at home. As part of this survey the possibilities offered by the different firms and administrations (e.g. replacing someone in cases of illness or holiday, flexible working contracts or participation in courses of further education) are being recorded. The same goes for schemes that are offered by the private sector (e.g. industrial administration and institutes for further education). Hence, the future looks brighter with new measures being tried and tested with the help of firms, administrations, and institutes of further education.

Affirmative action

Despite the previously discussed discrimination against women in secondary and further education, there is no doubt that the level of education of German women has risen in recent years. Generally, more and more women are gaining qualifications and the problem of having no formal qualification at all is one which lies mainly with the older female generation. In 1981, two-thirds of women aged 60–64 years had no formal qualifications compared to only one-third of the female 20–24 year-olds. Moreover, the number of working women without formal qualifications has reduced even more with three-quarters of working women aged between 25 and 35 years having qualifications of some kind. Also, between 1970 and 1978, the percentage of female graduates made up of working women 30–35 years old, doubled—from 5.1% to 11.7% (men to 15%) (Hesse, 1982).

In spite of the increased level of education attained by women, as previously mentioned in the introduction to this chapter, they are still discriminated against at work in terms of pay and salary. There is a strong discrepancy between this and the way they caught up in training and qualifications. A survey on the wage and salary discrimination against women was not so much a problem of direct income discrimination but rather its main cause could be found in the so-called discrimination in the work-place. This type of discrimination involves women having fewer opportunities for advancement than men and 'women still get given work that does not correspond with their education, qualifications and work experience' (Langkau, 1979).

Because women are to be found far more often than men in so-called dead-end jobs that do not offer any career prospects, employees are more hesitant to invest in further training for women than for men. Prejudice, and a certain fear of taking on risks, are evident when it is a question of investing in the career of women. This is true both for the private sector and for the public sector.

The fact is that women still clearly have fewer opportunities to promote their careers than men, despite improved levels of education. This has started a debate on plans for affirmative action (positive discrimination) for women in the Federal Republic of Germany. When considering which schemes for positive discrimination should be implemented, certainly the USA and Sweden seem to be able to offer ideal models (see Chapters 7 and 10). In these countries special plans for affirmative action on behalf of women have been drawn up and implemented for some years. Thus an inquiry by a select parliamentary committee, set up by the 'Deutsche Bundestag', said in its report on 'Women and Society', published in 1980, that the measures that were taken to improve the training and the job situation for girls and women in accordance with the "Affirmative Action Plans" were right and should be tested and tried'.

The term 'affirmative action for women' means that specific activities in the public and in the private sector are offered to women to give them more opportunities in terms of getting a job, and of gaining promotion. Thus, the firms and the administrations will have to report on how the jobs are distributed along gender lines and on what possibilities for further education and for promotion are offered to women. These analyses will be the basis for projections and schedules which will determine what positions are to be filled by women and during what sort of time-scale. The aim of the affirmative action programme is to open up a wider range of jobs for women and to offer them better job opportunities at all levels of the hierarchy. Included in these plans are the places of work and the places of training.

To promote the idea of positive discrimination on behalf of women in the Federal Republic of Germany the 'Directorate on Women's Affairs' in the Ministry for Youth, Family Affairs and Health, has been very active. Contacts have been made with some receptive firms from different fields of industry, and talks have begun on how the existing capabilities of the female work force could be better used. Some firms have stated in writing, what measures they intend to introduce to advance the careers of women. These plans, made by the firms on a voluntary basis, intend for example to train and employ more women in atypical fields of work, to offer better further training opportunities and hence improved promotion prospects, to offer them jobs that were previously the reserves of men and, generally, to see to it that the atmosphere in the firm is more pro-women. To support this the 'Directorate on Women's Affairs' intends to develop special courses for further training of executives and personnel managers in the private sector. These will deal with the question of how to improve the situation for women on the job market and how to remove the prejudice towards employing women. It is to be hoped that these plans and programmes will emphasize the main problems and issues, and consequently influence other firms to follow suit.

As regards the public sector, the federal state of Hamburg has already been active. There, the Senate has decided to give preference to women when filling jobs that offer good prospects, especially in those fields in which they have hitherto been under-represented. That a woman has to be just as qualified for an advertised post as a male applicant—as in the above outlined activities of the private sector—is a self-evident prerequisite. The different departments of the Hamburg Senate have been asked to propose measures which could contribute to achieving parity for women. To make it easier for women to advance professionally, special courses for further training are to be developed. On all these measures the different departments are to report every second year.

Affirmative action on behalf of women on the job and in the labour market is of increasing importance, especially if viewed against the background of the intensifying use of new technology. A scientific survey by the Batelle Institute in 1980 came to the grim conclusion that of the jobs favoured by the microelectronics industry (predominantly technical jobs and those of the computer industry), 95% were 'male' jobs, while of those endangered and most threatened to be lost (predominantly of the commercial kind and engineering draughtsmen) 53% were traditionally jobs for women (Dostal, 1981). It can be observed that in the past women were often pushed into newly developed routine jobs (which developed during the industrial automation gap) and work-places characterized by monotony. In many cases this was due to the low qualifications of women, but also the internal management decisions which traditionally offered women fewer opportunities for professional advancement than men. For these reasons improvements in vocational qualifications and changes in the decision-making structure of organizations will be of central importance in the future. What is evident is that without affirmative action the existing discrimination against German women will worsen. The 'Directorate on Women's Affairs' has commissioned a project that is to develop strategies for further training of women working in fields

that are particularly badly threatened (banks, insurance and precision engineering). The survey is to focus mainly on the decision-making structures of
the firms which come into play when a post is to be filled by either a man
or a women, when a man or a woman is to be selected for a further training
course, etc. Technical innovations do not as such have a negative or positive
effect, but only as a consequence of internal decisions made by the firm.

Incidentally, the increasing mechanization of industry and trade may also
have positive effects on the work opportunities for women. The difference
between physically exhausting (difficult) work done mainly by men, and the
physically less demanding work done predominantly by women, has been
diminished with the technological developments. Thus, technological developments may in principle have a favourable effect on female jobs.
Concerning this issue the trade unions are now demanding changes aimed at
assisting women and insisting that they be actively implemented.

The family work conflict

The opportunities for women on the labour market depend, in the main,
on their responsibilities *vis-à-vis* the family. Therefore higher vocational
qualifications do not generally mean the same career opportunities for women
as for men. Thus, it is not enough to focus all efforts solely on the improvement of the vocational qualifications and the status of the women in the workforce, when debating on how to increase the career prospects of women. The
aim must be to take into consideration the family ties and to give these more
priority at work. This is emphasized by the fact that increasingly fathers are
becoming interested in participating just as intensely as the mothers do in
the care and the education of their children. For this, though, the present
working conditions fail to meet these needs. So that women and men have
a better chance of combining both a job and a family, something must be
done to change the structures and the routines of the labour market. Further
avenues must be found in order to relieve a person from work so that he/she
can look after the children. Recently, more attention has been focused on
the questions of how to restructure the working day in order to accommodate
family life. Politicians, institutions, and academics have been addressing these
problems associated with the family/work conflicts.

Structuring of the working day

One measure to help women to combine family and work is to demand
more flexible working hours; however, this demand has caused considerable
controversy. In particular, the trade unions are sceptical about any measures
that plan to make the working hours more flexible.They fear that forms of
flexible working hours may serve as an instrument of rationalization by

thc personnel, and that these measures are primarily oriented to company requirements. A central demand is, therefore, to examine carefully who gains from restructuring the working day.

Flexitime

Allows the employee to decide when to start and when to end work within a certain fixed space of time. How widely flexitime has been introduced varies a lot depending on the field of work. Thus, only one in every 20 workers and one in every 25 skilled workers can profit from it, but nearly one in five qualified/managerial employees and civil servants can. In the production field flexitime has been rarely introduced and only 7% of employees have been offered it. On the whole, only full-time employees may profit from the introduction of flexitime and only 6% of part-timers are offered this scheme (Lage et al., 1981).

Restricting flexitime to certain occupations and economic sectors is not particularly satisfactory. However, it is partly practised in the production field by unskilled and semi-skilled workers. A recent survey maintained that those practising flexitime preferred having their working day thus structured, and also that many employees with fixed working hours would like flexitime to be introduced. Where flexitime has been introduced, the trade unions and the representatives of the workers' councils see to it that these are devised as favourably as possible to the employees (e.g. the possibility of transferring overtime to the following month, going to the doctor's during working hours, etc).

The trade unions are fighting the so-called 'capacity-oriented' variable working hours. This means that contracts are made with the employee in which only the number of hours within a certain period of time (e.g. a month) and the salary has been fixed. Time, place, and length of work is fixed by telephone by the employer each time at short notice. The employee has to be at the employer's disposal continuously. This form of structuring the working day (which is being practised predominantly in the retail trade) is to be criticized, especially from the point of view of the worker with a family, as it allows no flexibility whatsoever.

Part-time work

Another important form of structuring the working day is part-time work. This is mostly done as half-day morning work, and comprises 20 hours per week, from Monday to Friday, within a fixed period of time. This traditional form of part-time work is practised (according to a survey carried out by Brinkmann, 1980) by 24% of all working women. Personnel managers should also appreciate that the wish to work part-time does not necessarily just mean a half-day of work but also includes other variations. Brinkmann's survey showed that the desired average working hours compared to the actual working hours would be reduced by just 5 hours to 29 hours per week for the women, and by a good 5 hours, to 38 hours per week for the men (Brinkmann, 1980). Thus, part-time work and reductions in working hours should, from the point of view of those surveyed, go beyond what is being offered hitherto, i.e. half-day work.

An important sociopolitical and trade union demand as regards part-time work is to give this group of employees the same securities, corresponding to the scope of their work, as full-time employees have. In this context a recent verdict of the Supreme Court (Bundesverfassungsgericht) is of importance, whereby part-time workers are not to be excluded from the company's retirement schemes. There is also a demand to offer far more qualified employees part-time work. Incidentally, the trade unions see part-time work only as a sort of interim or temporary solution until further general cuts in working hours have been pushed through.

Job sharing

Quite recently the prospect of job sharing has been more widely debated. The debate was started by the 'Work Circle Chemistry' (Arbeitsring Chemie) who presented the first model job-sharing contract. This contract states that the job-sharing partners have to stand in for one another, and when one of the partners hands in his/her notice, then the other one can be given notice automatically. As the obligation to stand in for the partner is especially hard on employees with children, the women's organization of the Christian Democratic Union has submitted a different model which stipulates that to stand in for the partner should not be obligatory, but should only be a possibility. In the same vein, it should not be possible to sack someone because his/her partner has left the job-sharing relationship. The organization of the employers believe that these measures endanger job-sharing and refuse to accept them. The 'Deutsche Gewerkschaftsbund' (TUC), on the other hand, criticizes the model contracts because the risk of losing an employee is being transferred from the employer to the job-sharing partner and because of the additional risk of being fired; this they believe has not been removed from the model of the CDU women's organization either.

Job-sharing is only beginning to be practised in the Federal Republic of Germany. A survey, commissioned recently by the Ministry for Youth, Family Affairs and Health, revealed that less than 1% of organizations practise job-sharing. Some firms interpret the job-sharing scheme incorrectly and use it as a method of introducing traditional part-time working contracts whereby two workers instead of one full-time worker are employed. (They are covered, though, by the same social security and old age pension schemes as full-time employees.)

The new Christian-Liberal Federal Government has taken a positive attitude towards this model of job-sharing and is also trying to support this idea in the public sector. Furthermore, the Minister for Internal Affairs, responsible for the public sector, has published recommendations which deal specifically with the implementation of job-sharing.

Maternity leave

Since July 1979 wage-earning women in the Federal Republic of Germany have had the possibility of taking up to 4 months maternity leave in addition to the 8 weeks leave given after the birth of the child. During maternity leave they receive a substitute pay of up to DM750 per month and their job is still guaranteed. In addition, the mother does not have to pay into the pension scheme nor pay health insurance, and is insured against unemployment during this period. Ninety-five per cnt of entitled mothers accept the benefits of this maternity leave and the maternity pay. After the maternity leave 50% of the women take up work again.

Maternity leave is an important social achievement because it is a great relief to the working mother for the first few weeks, and it helps to develop the bond between mother and child. Critics, though, think that the period of leave is too short and also demand the involvement of the father. The involvement of fathers (which would be optional) would not only promote the relationship between father and child but also, at the same time, force the employers to come to terms with the men taking time off work to participate in parental duties. For these reasons one federal state has brought in a bill at the Bundesrat (second chamber) which would have provided for paternity leave for fathers. The bill, though, failed to get the necessary majority. As a consequence of this, proceedings were started by the EC Commission against the Federal Republic of Germany in this matter, based on the supposition that existing maternity leave regulations discriminate against fathers. The outcome of these proceedings is awaited with a degree of trepidation.

Obviously, special problems occur for working parents when a child is ill. For these cases a provision was incorporated into the Health Insurance Law (Krankenversicherungsgesetz) in 1974, according to which parents within the scope of the national insurance scheme can take up to 5 working days per year off work to look after a sick child no more than 8 years of age. To make up for the loss of earnings they can claim sickness benefit. However, over 90% of the mothers, but only 10% of the fathers, take advantage of this provision. The limit of 8 years of age is unsatisfactory, and in many cases the 5 days are not enough. Particularly on the part of the trade unions there is the demand first, to raise the age of the child, and secondly to increase the number of days that can be taken off work. Neither plan, though, has a chance of being realized due to the monetary situation. In addition to the above outlined provisions parents have the right to ask for domestic help for the period of a hospital stay or for a period of convalescence, on condition that the child is under 8 or handicapped and cannot be looked after by anyone else.

Child care facilities

Child care establishments to help and support the family, such as day nurseries, kindergartens, and day centres, are of central importance in enabling both men and women to combine a family with a job.

Day nurseries

These are facilities for small children up to 3 years of age. Although the number of places at the day nurseries has increased in recent years, today there are places for only 1.5% of the 1.5 million children under the age of 3. The demand is considerably higher.

Kindergartens

These are for children older than 3, up to school age. Here the offer of places is much higher; i.e. for about three-quarters of the children between 3 and 6 there is a place at a kindergarten. The opening times of the kindergarten, though, often do not coincide with the working hours of the parents, and this can cause a lot of problems. In fact, the majority of places at the kindergarten are offered only as half-day places, i.e. from 8 a.m. or 9 a.m. to noon.

Day centres

In the day centres children of school age are catered for; as in most German schools there are classes only in the mornings. In spite of the number of places at the day centres having increased, there are still not enough. Due to the lack of places at day nurseries and day centres, very strict criteria for enrolling children are applied. Preference is given to children from one-parent families or from families with special difficulties (e.g. their income is below the national assistance rate).

Company nurseries

The number of company nurseries has diminished. Owing to the risk of the development of a form of dependency on the part of the employee, the trade unions prefer the public kindergartens which are totally independent from companies and organizations. They demand the expansion of council and city child care facilities, but these are pressures which are unlikely to have any real effect due to the present unfavourable financial situation of the cities and councils.

Legal measures to implement equal rights for women in work

In the Federal Republic of Germany the demand for equal rights is anchored in the Constitution. Therefore legislation, executive power, and jurisdiction already exist as part of the present laws. People who believe they have been treated unfairly at work can take legal proceedings, appealing to the industrial tribunals and to administrative courts. Although the equal rights clause of the the Constitution has been in force for nearly 35 years, and has brought about many progressive legal decisions, the actual equality of men and women in the work-place is still far behind the constitutional demand for equality.

To make sure that all workers, both men and women, are treated equally at work, the EC adaptated legislation in the context of Labour Law which was passed in 1980. This prohibits discrimination against employees throughout all the stages of their work contracts. The EC legislation in the context of labour laws (the stipulations of which have become part of the Code of Civil Law) also regulates the burden of proof in cases of discrimination. Moreover, it stipulates that all vacant jobs to be advertised as being open to either sex and the relevant legal regulations must be displayed on the notice boards of all companies. Based on the experiences with this legislation the federal government submitted a report to the Bundestag in April 1983, which came to the conclusion that the legal situation for women in the labour market had improved due to the EC Adaptation Law in the context of the Labour Law. Since the law's enforcement some pioneering decisions have been made by the industrial tribunals.

The trade unions and the women's organizations have also taken a stand regarding this legislation, and are now demanding a tightening-up of the existing regulations. Their demands focus on changing the minimum regulations concerning job advertisements and the obligation by organizations to display the stipulations of the law on a notice board. They want these to be changed into fixed regulations, as well as wanting the burden of proof to be reversed completely and the legislation on the settlement of damages improved. However, the federal government plans to await further developments and legal decisions pending trials, before committing itself to any further changes.

FUTURE PROSPECTS

Scientific reports on future developments of the participation of women in the labour force in the Federal Republic of Fermany have forecast that in the coming years the number of women wanting to work, and those actually working, will increase. Women with children have developed similar attitudes towards work as those women without children. There are as yet no signs of this general tendency being reversed. Along with their level of qualifications, the motivation by women to work has increased. All social groups are of the opinion that if women's increasing desire to work is to be accommodated, then the creation of sufficient numbers of work-places must be given priority. Next to this, the improvement in the qualifications of women is also seen as an important future issue. The programme for further education/training and re-training of women is to be widened, especially in view of the increased introduction of new technologies. Measures which serve to improve the compatibility of work and family life should also be improved. Generally, there is agreement on the importance of implementing strategies enabling the re-structuring of the working day. On the other hand, there is still some conflict over the principal direction this re-structuring should follow: while the trade unions generally demand shorter working weeks (to be exact, a 35-hour week), the government aims at establishing more part-time work-places and the possibility of job-sharing positions. In particular, the groups involved in women's issues (e.g. the women's organizations of the political parties and the trade unions) believe that, over and above this, there is a need for more establishments that would take care of children and offer opening times which do not clash with the working hours of the parents. Finally, there have been considerable legislative changes in the Federal Republic of Germany, enabling both women and men who choose to interrupt their working life in order to bring up children to be able to keep in contact with their former work, or to participate in training for vocational re-incorporation.

REFERENCES

Brinkmann, C. (1980). *Veranderung des Arbeitsvolumenangebots bei Realisierung von Arbeitszeitwunschen.* Project No. 2–232 of the Instituts für Arbeistsmarkt und Berufsforschung der Bundesanstalt für Arbeit, Nürnberg.
Bundesminister fur Bildung und Wissenschaft (1982). *Grund und Strukturdaten* 1983.
Bundesminister für Bildung und Wissenschaft (1983). *Berufsbildungsbericht.*
Bundesminister fur Jugend, Familie und Gesundheit (1980). *Frauen '80,* p.11.
Clasen, A. (1981). '40 Stunden für fast alle', in *Bundesblatt,* Vol. 3.

Dostal, W. (1981). 'Frauenbeschaftigung im technischen Wandel', in *Beitrage zur Arbeitsmarkt-und Berufsforschung der Bundesanstalt für Arbeit*, No. 56, Nurnberg.
Hesse, B. (1982). 'Frauenforderungsporgramme—ein Instrument zum Abbau der Benachteiligungen von Frauen im Beruf', in *Berufsbildung in Wissenschaft und Praxis*, 11.
Hofbauer, H. (1981). 'Zur Struktur der Teilzeitarbeit bei Frauen', in *Beitrage zur Arbeitsmarkt und Berufsforschung der Bundesanstalt fur Arbeit*, No. 56, Nurnberg, p. 107 ff.
Institut für Arbeitsmarket und Berufsforschung der Bundesanstalt fur Arbeit, Nürnberg, Nos. 5 and 3.1 inclusive.
Lage, Dauer, Tatsachen, Entwicklungen, und Verteilung der Arbeitszeit (1981). *Forschungsbericht im Auftrag des Bundesministers fur Abeit und Sozialordnung*, Bonn.
Langkau, J. (1981), (1979) Lohn und Gehaltsdiskriminierung von Arbeitnehmerinnen in der Bundersrepublik Deutschland. *Bestimmung und Analyse des geschlechtsspezifischen Einkommensabstandes 1960–1976*, Bonn.
Statistiches Bundesamt (1981). *Stand und Entwicklung der Erwerbstatigkeit* (Series 1, No. 4.1.1).
Statistisches Bundesamt (1983). Seies 16, Nos. 2.1 and 2.2, March.
Writschaft und Statistik (1982). No. 6.
Yohalem, A. M. (ed.) (1982). *Die Ruckkehr von Frauen in den Beruf—Massnahmen und Entwicklung in fünf Ländern*, Bonn, p. 43ff.

Women at Work
Edited by M.J. Davidson and C.L. Cooper
© 1984 John Wiley & Sons Ltd

Chapter 4
Women at Work in Holland

Tineke de Rijk
Amsterdam, Holland

INTRODUCTION

May 1983. The Congress Centre in The Hague is the scene of a historical meeting. For the first time women of 83 women's organizations meet each other. There are representatives of rather traditional organizations such as the 'Nederlandse Christen Vrouwenbond' (an organization of Protestant women); the 'Nederlandse Bond van Plattelandsvrouwen' (originally an organization of farmers' wives); women groups of political parties (liberal-conservative, Christian-democratic, liberal-socialist, socialist-democratic, radical-socialist and communist parties); women of several trade unions and women of 'autonomous' feminist groups such as 'women against sexual violence'.

The central issues of this first women's conference, concerned the 'Redistribution of paid and unpaid labour'. Each organization and group participated in the preparations for this conference and supported the demand of a 'normal' working week for 25 hours with a wage sufficient to live on independently. Besides this reduction of working hours the women formulated demands regarding child care, schooling, maternity/paternity leave, social security, and tax systems.

One fact was clear to all the women who visited this conference: women have the right to work outside their homes and should not be pushed out of the labour market because of the social-economic recession.

At the end of the conference day there was a panel discussion with two men; one representative of the FNV (the largest Dutch trade union federation) and one representative of an employers' organization. Both of the men commented on the list of demands that women see as necessary for the redistribution of paid work. These comments illustrated the contradiction between wishes and reality. The employers' representative argued that the

83

demands of the 83 women's organizations were 'a list of wishes: not realistic in a period of economic recession'. He stressed that a 'regular' labour process demands a 40-hour working week. The only possibility he saw for another distribution of paid work was part-time jobs. Demands for provisions such as child care, and parental leave are 'a wish for when economic conditions improve'.

The union representative was more positive about the women's demands. The principles of the FNV have been changed in favour of women who want to do paid work. For 2 years the programme of this union federation fixed the interests of the 'employee and his family'. This term has disappeared, and the FNV includes a programme clause which focuses on the redistribution of paid and unpaid work between men and women. But the union representative had to admit that it is very difficult to realize this goal.

The result of this conference illustrates the position of working women, and women who want to do paid work in the Netherlands. Women know more and more what they want but they are confronted with more and more obstacles. Women's unemployment increases more than men's unemployment. A lot of Dutch women who search for a job are not even counted in the statistics.

The segregation between male and female identified jobs seems only to be crossed by men who enter professions such as nursing and librarianship. Part-time work has become women's work, with fewer rights than full-time work. Women still do not have the same educational level as men and have less rights to social security benefits; they pay more tax if they are married; earn a lower average wage than men; are discriminated in promotion opportunities; are not accepted in 'male-identified' jobs such as management and technical positions; and are supposed to quit their jobs when they become mothers. Even in 1983 the main reason for women leaving the labour market remains the birth of their first child. Provisions for sharing family responsibilities and paid work outside the home are insufficient.

The whole social–economic system in the Netherlands is still based on the 'average' male breadwinner with a family to support.

This chapter presents the position of Dutch working women who want to do paid work; it shows the obstacles they confront when attempting to exercise their rights to participate in the labour market; it details the equal opportunity legislation and the present provisions.

WOMEN AND PAID WORK

The definition of paid work adopted in this chapter is: 'labour on regular hours based on a labour contract and with a fixed wage'. Therefore, examples such as farmers' wives, and women who assist their husbands or children in a family company, women who do paid work at home, and women with irregular jobs, do not qualify as paid workers. These women who are not 'average' workers will be discussed in more detail in the second part of the chapter.

This section contains statistics and information on the following major areas: (1) the female participation in the work force, (2) the unemployment of women, (3) their expected participation in the future, (4) the kind of work women do, (5) the number of hours they work, (6) the wage difference between men and women, (7) the educational level of working women, and (8) the quality of women's work.

Female participation in the work force

Labour market policy in the Netherlands shows some remarkable changes of opinion where it concerns women. In the middle of the sixties the work force was too small. There was an increasing shortage of workers and the employers discovered a 'new' potential: married women. At that time it was not common in the Netherlands for a married woman, and especially a mother, to have a job outside the home. Only in cases of poverty did society accept exceptions to the norm other than the father being the major breadwinner in the family.

The employers were right in their conclusion for, compared with other industrialized countries, Dutch women showed very little inclination when it came to looking for paid work.

Table 4.1 *Participation rate of women in the total work force*

	Year	Percentage	Year	Percentage
Belgium	1961	27	1973	34
Denmark	1960	31	1973	41
Western Germany	1961	37	1972	37
France	1962	33	1968	35
Ireland	1961	26	1971	26
Italy	1961	25	1973	27
Luxemburg	1960	27	1970	26
The Netherlands	1960	22	1971	25
United Kingdom	1961	32	1966	36
Sweden	1960	30	1973	38
USA	1960	32	1973	38

Source: Social Economische Raad (1979).

Table 4.1 illustrates that in the sixties the female work force in the Netherlands increased by only 3%: from 22% to 25%. On the other hand, in Belgium the figure increased by 7%, Denmark, 10%, and Sweden 8%. Countries such as the United Kingdom, France, and Western Germany

already showed a large participation of working women (Sociaal Economische Raad, 1979).

Official government reports (one serious proposal to increase the participation of women was to give 'just-married' women a paid leave of 2 weeks—the
aim was to allow the women to become accustomed to their new status so
they could return more easily to their work-place!) could not really change
the norm that married women do not have a paid job. Companies tried to
find solutions, such as a creche for the children of female workers, special
re-training programmes for women (subsidized by the government, e.g. seamstresses and nurses), and providing transport between home and work-place.
All these efforts only resulted in a growing participation of Belgian women
in the south of the Netherlands, a main reason for the electronic industry
(Philips) and some big confectionery workshops choosing to settle there.

In the seventies this pattern of female participation changed tremendously.
The labour market policy did not influence the mothers but it did affect the
daughters. Marriage ceased to be a reason for leaving the labour market.
Indeed, there was a rapid increase in the number of women working in the
second half of the seventies and the beginning of the eighties: 1975: 27.7%;
1977: 28.6%; 1978: 29.1%; 1979: 29.7%; 1980: 30.4%. In 1982 this rate had
increased to 32%. It is, however, important to note that these statistics
indicate only the 'official' part of the female work force, i.e. all the women
between 15 and 65 years old who work more than 25 hours a week.

This increase is caused by three main factors: the higher education level
of women, the possibility of birth control and smaller families, and the fact
that more and more working women are married. In 1960 only 19% of the
female work force was married, in 1971, 38% and in 1975, 51%. However,
compared to other European countries the Netherlands still present a
different picture.

Table 4.2   *Work participation rate (percentage) of married women aged 14–65 in EEC
countries, 1975 and 1979*

	1975	1979
Western Germany	35.3	36
France	40.2	44
Italy	20.1	24
The Netherlands	15.2	20
Belgium	30.9	32
Luxemburg	20.9	21
United Kingdom	45.1	46
Ireland	13.1	14
Denmark	46.3	55
Total EEC	33.9	36

Source: Raad Voor de Arbeidsmarkt (1983)

In 1979 only 20% of all married women had a paid job as their 'main' activity (i.e. a job of more than 25 hours a week). Consequently, with the exception of the Irish (see Chapter 2 for more details), a lower percentage of Dutch married women work compared with any of the other EEC countries! This is due mainly to the fact that most married women show little interest in entering the labour market. More and more women now stop their careers not because of marriage, but rather at the birth of their first child.

Table 4.3   *Work force participation of married women, 1979: age, education level, number of children (percentages)*

Age	Basic and lower level education				Middle and higher level education			
	No. of children				No. of children			
	0	1	2	3–4+	0	1	2	3–4+
35	56.0	20.0	19.5	19.5	79.8	22.7	21.8	20.9
35	11.4	16.8	20.0	15.9	30.4	30.8	31.1	27.6

Source: Raad Voor de Arbeidsmarkt (1983).

Table 4.3 shows that the labour participation rate of married women is almost 80% for women younger than 35 years without children and with a middle or higher level of education. But for the women with a low level of education the participation rate is still only 56%. This 80% falls to 22.7% for women under the age of 35 with at least one child—the period when the children are small.

The level of education no longer remains a reason for staying in the labour force, all married women younger than 35 with one or more children show a participation rate of between 19.5 and 22.7%. After the age of 35 the participation of women with a middle or higher level of education increases but there is no return to 80%. The highest rate is 31.1%. Therefore, the age of the children forms the main indicator for the participation rate of married women.

In 1979 only 16% of all married women younger than 35, and with children younger than 4 years old, were active in the labour market. Nevertheless, there is growing support for a change from the Netherlands' model of the 'nuclear family' with the father as breadwinner and the mother as housewife. In 1979, for instance, 23% of working men maintained they would like to work part-time; but they also acknowledged the many obstacles (social security, tax system, loss of promotion chances) which hamper this wish—in reality, only 5% of Dutch men work part-time.

The general public's attitudes have also changed: in 1965, 84% of the Dutch population did not accept the idea of working mothers; in 1975 this rate had decreased to 44%. But the strongest evidence of a changing mentality is the growing intention of women to look for solutions which will enable them to combine domestic work with paid work.

Recently the 'Raad voor de Arbeidsmarkt' (1983) (Council for the Labour Market: an influential advice committee to the government) published a report with new statistics on women planning to re-enter the labour market. In the eighties, each year the total work force increases by at least 75,000 people (note that the total unemployment rate in 1983 was in excess of 800,000!). More than half of these 75,000 continue to be women, and predictions indicate that there will be a yearly increase in the number of married female workers. The total work force in 1980 was 5,434,000: 3,759,000 men and 1,675,000 women. In the next 20 years the participation rate of women will increase more than that of men.

Table 4.4   *The predictions for the increase of the workforce (no. of person)*

	Women	Married women	Men	Total work force
1980–1985	244,000	69,000	221,000	5,899,000
1985–1990	226,000	89,000	203,000	6,328,000
1990–1995	99,000	71,000	103,000	6,530,000
1995–2000	70,000	52,000	23,000	6,642,000
2000–2005	57,000	1,000	12,000	6,667,000
2005–2010	40,000	5,000	48,000	6,660,000

Note: The figure for married women is a part of the total female figure. Raad voor de Arbeidsmarkt (1983).

The age of the female work force

The fact that married women constitute a small part of the total work force is an indicator of the age of women workers; indeed, their average age is lower than that of male workers. One can assess from Table 4.5 that the highest rate for working women is found in the age group 20–24; probably the women without children. In the age group between 24 and 54 the rate has increased but is still very low compared with men's rates. In the age group 15–19 participation decreased and this is due to the higher level of education. Girls attend school longer than they did 7 years ago, but they still enter the labour market at a younger age than boys. In 1975, 45% of the total female work force was younger than 25 years; for men this rate was 18%.

The unemployment of women

In 1981, 331,660 men and 141,960 women in the Netherlands were unemployed. For 1982 these figures were 454,144 and 190,647. All those unem-

Table 4.5   *The age of the Dutch work force (percentages)*

Age	Men			Women		
	1975	1980	1982	1975	1980	1982
15–19	33.2	28.9	28.8	40.8	32.2	31.4
20–24	81.2	78.3	78.2	61.3	69.6	71.4
25–29	95.2	93.0	92.7	34.6	45.4	48.3
30–34	97.5	97.1	96.8	28.2	35.0	37.2
35–39	97.2	96.7	96.7	29.1	36.0	37.5
40–44	96.2	94.5	94.0	29.1	34.9	35.8
45–49	93.4	91.1	90.2	27.2	30.4	31.4
50–54	90.0	85.1	84.6	23.6	25.1	25.8
55–59	82.1	74.1	72.0	20.1	17.9	18.2
60–64	66.8	47.1	44.9	11.8	9.3	9.3

Source: Raad voor de Arbeidsmarkt (1983)

ployed men and women looked for a job of more than 25 hours a week. Unemployed people who worked, or wanted to work, less than 25 hours were not included in this official unemployment statistic. However, this was changed on 1 January 1983 and the limit for the unemployment statistics is now 20 hours a week. Not surprisingly, this change in definition increased women's unemployment immediately instead of the 190,647 unemployed women in the December statistics, in 1983 there were 235,140 women looking for jobs. This means that 17.2% of the total female work force is unemployed. For men the figure is 15.4%. Furthermore, a lot of unemployed women are still not registered in the statistics, especially those women who want to work less than 20 hours a week (and these probably number about 10,000).

There is another reason why it is very difficult to give an exact unemployment figure for women. In the Netherlands married women who lose their jobs have less rights than men to unemployment benefits. They only receive a benefit for the first half-year of their unemployment. After that period it depends on the income of their husband and the level of their own income as to whether they receive any benefits or not. To receive benefits one has to be registered as an unemployed person, and women stop this registration once their benefits are withdrawn.

Evidence of this practice is illustrated by the fact that of the unemployed men in 1982, 35% ceased their registration, and that for women this figure was 49%. Unfortunately, government policy relating to unemployment statistics methodology is unlikely to change and the 'truc' unemployment figures for women will continue to be hidden.

The renumeration of women's work

Until the end of the sixties, collective agreements included different wage levels for men and women who did the same work. This differences could be as high as 30%. In the Netherlands the struggle for equal pay took a very long time. At the beginning of the fifties union women demanded equal pay, but the unions refused to acknowledge the demands of their female members. Just after the war the country had to be rebuilt, and raising women's wages was not economically viable. The common belief was that even young unmarried men should earn more than women; they had to save money for their future family responsibilities!

However, in 1973, women workers in a clothing factory decided they could no longer accept the large wage differences between men and women doing the same kind of work. At first the unions would not support the women, so collectively they organized a strike. These women felt their case was supported by the European Directive of Equal Pay. The Netherlands had already signed this directive but the government was in no hurry to bring it into effect. The strike won the support of public opinion: a lot of people were astonished that women earned so little. Eventually, the unions decided to support the strike and so the 'Optilon' (the name of the factory) women forced a break in the long tradition of unequal pay between the sexes.

Hence, since 1975 there has been an Equal Pay Law: men and women should earn the same for work of equal value; but despite this law, women still earn less than men for comparable work. In 1980, for example, the 'Loon techniese Dienst' (a research office of the government with the task of controlling wage laws and collective agreements) established that employers paid women 2.8% less than men for comparable work. In fact, between 1977 and 1982 the average wage of women decreased compared to the wage level of men. In 1982 the average wage of male workers was about 23% higher than that of female workers. Certainly, there is a need to discover the reasons behind this growing difference in wage level.

While there is a lack of sound research pertaining to this problem, there are some obvious explanations; namely: the segregation between male and female occupations, the minimum wage law, the fact that part-time work is 'women's work', and the ineffectiveness of the 1975 Equal Pay Law.

The segregation between male and female occupations

The segregation between men's and women's work can be investigated both by occupations and industries. Secretaries, saleswomen, nurses, hairdressers, seamstresses (a job fast disappearing), teachers of small children, nursing assistants, cleaning women—are all occupations predominantly made up of women. On the other hand there are the male-dominated occupations: skilled industrial work, middle and higher management, conducting trains/buses, and scientific occupations; in fact all the high-status jobs.

The unions lend their strongest support to the skilled industrial workers, who are predominantly male. Unions power tends to be weaker in female-dominated sectors such as hospitals; consequently it took a long time before the union became strong enough to reach a good collective agreement concerning a decent wage. The same process occurred for librarians and occupations connected with domestic labour. Women's work just did not have the same 'status' as male-identified work.

Besides this, women tend to be concentrated in low-level jobs in most occupations. In the banking sector, for example, men and women enter with the same level of education but after 5 years men reach a higher level. This is mainly due to the internal training policy of banks: a man should have the possibility of being able to run an office; a woman, on the other hand, is seen as a temporary worker. There is even an indication that the Evelyn Sullerot's old law (when men enter a female occupation wages rise . . . and the other side of it—when women enter male occupations wages decrease) is valid. Women working in hospitals, libraries, and social work places have argued for better working conditions, and have attained collective agreements and improved training systems. But now the men are entering the very same professions and are quickly occupying the middle and higher management positions.

All in all, male-identified jobs still have a higher status than female ones; and this is indicative of the difference in wage levels between the sexes.

The Minimum Wage Law

This law ordains that each worker should earn at least a fixed mininum hourly wage. The level of this wage is indicated by the cost of living and is associated with general wage levels. In a collective agreement it is possible to be paid more than this wage, and indeed most male workers earn more than the minimum wage.

But the fact that minimum wage-earners are mostly women is not the only effect of the Minimum Wage Law; for this law has an exemption clause: if someone works less than one-third of the normal working week (i.e. about 12 hours a week) he or she is not entitled to this wage. This exemption works as a discriminatory factor against women: many part-timers have a contract with a guaranteed number of hours that is less than one-third of what is common, in the company that hires them; therefore the employer can pay any wage he wants. In stores, for example, it has become 'standard' to hire (married) women with a contract like this. Each week they can be asked to work more hours, but that does not include more rights or a higher wage.

The effect of part-time work at the wage level

For people who work less than one-third of a standard working week, the exemption clause of the Minimum Wage Law affects their income level. Part-timers who work more hours a week can earn this minimum wage or a higher sum. Still, part-time work can be seen as an indicator for the wage difference between men and women, in middle and higher (better-salaried) functions, part-time workers are rare. Part-time work is restricted to lower positions such as administrative work, cleaning, saleswomen, and nurseries. These are all female-identified jobs, and it is of little surprise that of all part-time workers, more than 75% are women. Part-time work in the Netherlands becomes more and more 'women's work', with all the well-known characteristics such as a low wage level and so on.

The Ineffectiveness of the Equal Pay Law

It is more than 8 years since the 1975 Equal Pay Law began operating in the Netherlands, and yet women still have not reached the same income level as men. Besides the segregation between male- and female-identified jobs, the exemption clause of the Minimum Wage Law, and the fact that most part-timers are women, there is growing evidence that this Equal Pay Law has many flaws.

Female union members have proposed that the effectiveness of the Equal Pay Act is influenced by two main characteristics of the law. First, the individual character of this law, whereby the person who feels he or she earns less compared with persons of the other sex doing the same or comparable work should take individual action himself or herself. The Equal Pay Law Committee then judges if this complaint is justified. To reach this decision the committee asks the employer for additional information. This means that one needs to be in a secure position to file a charge with this committee, and the employer knows immediately who it concerns. It is not possible to ask the union to contact the Equal Pay Committee and file the charges in such a way that the person concerned can remain anonymous at the information stage. Thus the union cannot take legal action, it can only support its members who do. Another aspect of the individual character of this law is that a group of workers cannot argue for equal pay; each person has to take his or her own action.

The second flaw in this law concerns the lack of severe sanctions. If the charges have been judged valid the employer is only obliged to pay the differences in wage with retroactive effect. The Equal Pay Law does not impose severe sanctions such as fines and damages. In most cases the only sanction that can be useful is publicity.

Third, the Equal Pay Law is centred on the establishment of a 'good functional classification system', but more and more it has been shown that these systems only serve to sustain the male and female job divisions. This results in 'female' jobs being found more in the lower scales compared to 'male' jobs. Taking care of children, for example, gets less 'points' in the monitoring system than a production process worker. In any company women can fight to gain more points for their particular job, but it is hard to prove that they do work comparable to men's at other places, inside or outside the work-place.

The character and the quality of women's work

Women's work is often labelled as 'light' work, i.e. less responsibility, less physical power, and lower levels of educational qualifications. In contrast, men's work, on the contrary, is by definition 'heavy'. The quality aspects of women's work are neglected far too much. Interestingly, recent research on the position of cleaning women proves that their higher rate of sickness was not caused by their family responsibilities (the common assumption) but by bad working conditions. Another indication of the low quality of women's work is the position of elderly working women. Only women with higher-ranking jobs reach pensionable age, but most elderly women have to leave the labour market before then because of bad health.

Specific aspects inherent in the quality of women's work are associated with the low educational level needed for the job. Recent Dutch research shows that women more than men occupy functions below their educational abilities and the emotional and physical demands of their jobs are often undervalued. Aspects concerning fertility and pregnancy also need to be taken into account. Still very little is known about the effects of chemicals and poor working conditions on fertility and pre-natal development. Finally, one needs to consider the effects of sexism, e.g. the traditional view that women should behave like 'women'. For women in non-traditional jobs sexism and female stereotyping can be a major obstacle in terms of career development equal to that of men.

The number of hours women work

Although there are indications that the participation rate of women in the work force is increasing, one should not become too optimistic, as other statistics indicate that more and more women share the same amount of working hours and are congregated in just a small part of the total labour market (Equal Status Council, 1980).

Table 4.6   *Average rate of the number of hours women work as a percentage of the number of hours men work in western Europe*

Country	1973	1975	1977
Western Germany	8.38	84.8	83.7
France	85.0	85.3	86.0
Italy	89.5	89.1	88.6
Netherlands	74.4	75.0	73.8
Belgium	90.0	88.8	88.7
Luxemburg	89.8	91.6	90.8
United Kingdom	71.2	70.6	68.7
Eire		76.4	76.0
Denmark		73.6	74.5

Source: Equal Status Council (1980).

Table 4.6 compares all working women, and the hours they work, with all working men. In the Netherlands one can assess that there is about 25% difference between men and women. The prediction for the eighties is one of little change, and the predicted figure for 1990 is 26.7%! So, while the number of women entering the labour market will increase, the amount of hours they actually work will not increase very much. This will be heavily influenced by women still working mainly in part-time jobs of less than 25 hours a week.

There is also a general trend for women to work increasingly in so-called 'small' jobs. This is mainly due to the 'additional' workers effect, whereby the economic recession and the unemployment of male breadwinners forces women to look for opportunities to increase the family income. Also there is a general lack of support facilities enabling women to combine family responsibilities with a paid job.

THE HIDDEN PART OF THE FEMALE WORK FORCE

The first part of this chapter concerned the 'official' part of the female work force—that is women who 'work regular hours based on a labour contract and with a fixed wage'. But there are more women who work, and employed women have other work besides their paid jobs.

Firstly it is possible to assert that most employed women need also to work at home, and consequently they have a 'double task'. It is not a coincidence that most part-time workers are married women! Secondly, many of the jobs women do are related in some way with housework, e.g. cleaning, nursing, and caring for children and the elderly. This kind of job has a long tradition of being associated with voluntary work. The idea that individuals (i.e.

married women!) should take on this unpaid work again is becoming more and more part of official government policy. Thirdly, there are the many women who are married to farmers or self-employed husbands, who increasingly have to act as unpaid assistants to their husbands. The final group of non-'official' female workers is made up of the increasing number of home industry workers. Recent research shows that homeworkers have to work very hard, under bad conditions, and for small wages.

Women who do housework

In the Netherlands there have been recent studies investigating the distribution of housework, paid work, and volunteer work between men and women. These studies were the first to prove that women, and even employed women, spend more hours doing housework than men (Stichting voor Economisch Onderzoek der 1982). Table 4.7 shows the distribution of paid work, housework, volunteer work, and other activities (e.g. sleeping, hobbies, social activities, etc.) between men and women. These figures show that women spend more time than men doing housework. Women's housework increased in the 5 years between 1975 and 1980, from 19.9% to 21%. Men's participation in household work increased too—from 7.6% to 8.1%. This was a small increase and may have been caused by increasing male unemployment. It is also notable that the number of hours women spent doing paid work stayed at the same level between 1975 and 1980, even though the female work force increased during this period. Another remarkable fact is that in 1980 women worked more than men did (women 25.4% and men 22.1%) and spent less time on 'other activities'.

Table 4.7 *Participation in paid work, housework, volunteer work, and other activities, as a percentage of the total number of hours a week; 1975 and 1980*

	Men		Women	
	1975	1980	1975	1980
Paid work	14.8	14.0	4.4	4.4
Housework	7.6	8.1	19.9	21.0
Volunteer work	1.2	1.2	1.1	1.0
Other activities	76.4	76.7	74.7	73.6

Source: Stichting voor Economisch Onderzoek der 1982.

Women who work as volunteers or in low pay jobs

Table 4.7 suggests that men and women spend about the same amount of time participating in voluntary work. But there are distinct differences between the types of voluntary work done by men and women. Most male volunteers do unpaid work in political organizations, unions, sport, and hobby organizations. This kind of volunteer work often has a high social status. Most female volunteer workers, on the other hand, can be found in nursing homes, in schools, and in company services such as home helpers. In nursing homes, for example, only 36.1% of the workers receive a salary! The others just get a small fee or nothing at all.

The organizations made up of homecare workers have (on the orders of the government) developed a 'new' category of workers—people who work less than one-third of the working week and consequently are not entitled to minimum hourly wages. Not surprisingly, this regulation has had the effect of reducing the number of 'standard' paid workers. Another recent development in government policy is that people who receive unemployment benefits now have to ask permission to carry out unpaid work, especially in the social sector. This can also threaten the position of working women, as all these developments mean that existing work is disappearing from the 'official' labour market and becoming 'grey' (with a fee as a salary) or unpaid work.

Women with self-employed husbands

Women who work in their husbands' businesses are often in poor position. They do not have individual rights to a wage, are neglected in the tax systems, and have only a very small chance of getting a disability pension if anything should happen to them. (Incidentally, this pension dates from just a few years back!) These women form yet another 'forgotten' group of female workers.

In 1977 about 160,000 women worked in family businesses. As the total female work force in 1980 was 1,675,000, these women cannot be viewed as a non-significant group. However, there is almost no statistical material outlining their position—what is available shows that, in 1977, 39,000 of the 160,000 women worked in farming and fishing; and the remainder in commerce, hotel and catering, and service industries. Moreover, the council for small and medium-sized businesses assumes that in more than half these firms women assist their husbands as unpaid workers. Finally, it is interesting to note that recent research into the position of farmers' wives has shown that their so-called 'assistance' consists of an average working week of 24 hours . . . a real part-time job!

Female home industry workers

Home industry dates back to the pre-industrial period and conjures up images of women working at home under bad conditions. Today, with the economic depression, the increasing cost of living, and the unavailability of 'real' jobs, many women are glad to earn money by working from home. The number of women doing home industry work is estimated at about 40,000 (again not a very small group) and the working conditions for these women are bad. The social security system has the provision that if a home worker earns more than two-fifths of the minimum wage, he or she is entitled to the same rights as someone with a full labour contract. Employers therefore try to avoid this situation by keeping the wages below the limit. In fact this is the only legal provision for home industry workers. They have no rights to 'days off' benefits, do not get money when they are ill, and there is no control over their work requirements. Home industry workers have to pay their own electricity costs and heating, and often buy the equipment they need, such as sewing machines and typewriters.

The women's union of the FNV (the largest Dutch trade union federation) has investigated the position of home industry workers, and found that besides the traditional kind of work women did at home (sewing, peeling shrimps, knitting, and packing), there is a 'new' kind of home industry developing which involves typing and electronic work. It is even suggested that automation will bring about an increase in the number of women working at home on small computer terminals.

Unfortunately, as the majority of these women work at home alone and lack 'fellow' worker support, they rarely complain about their working conditions. In addition, most of them would be afraid of being identified and subsequently being sacked by their employer.

THE OBSTACLES

Dutch women who attempt to exercise their right to participate in the labour market meet several obstacles, for the whole system of work is still based on the principle of a 40-hour working week and a (male) breadwinner. Anyone who works less than these 40 hours or is not a breadwinner is not entitled to the same benefits and protection. The exemption clause of the Minimum Wage Law, for example, excludes many female workers from their fundamental right to a good wage. Indeed, the ineffectiveness of the Equal Pay Law still permits discrimination on the basis of sex.

While differences in wages can be shown to exist very easily, it is more difficult to prove discrimination when it comes to opportunities for promotion. Certainly women do not reach the same ranks as men, and male-identified jobs and positions seem 'closed' to women.

External and internal labour market policies create several obstacles for women who fail to conform to the image of the 'standard' worker. Table 4.5 showed that in particular, it was the young women with small children who chose to leave the labour market. This too is caused by the lack of child care facilities. This lack, combined with the poor quality of the child care centres that do exist, is the second major obstacle faced by women.

The third obstacle is the social security system and the tax system. Both systems still openly discriminate against non-breadwinners, i.e. women.

First obstacle: labour market policy

For the purpose of this chapter, labour market policy is defined in a broad sense and includes education policy, income policy, and employment policy, while internal labour market policy is the policy within companies.

External labour market policy

Education and training policy

Women still choose to enter the more female-identified jobs compared to men. They therefore continue to perpetuate the segregation in the labour market. Education is one method of changing this pattern, and feminist organizations and political parties have addressed themselves to this issue. There have been numerous studies on the actual material used in schools, with the norm still being that of a 'nuclear' family. The attitude of teachers has also been shown to be important—a girl does not easily choose mathematics if her teacher believes that it is not feminine for her to do so. However, equal rights to education failed to bring about an equal distribution of girls and boys in various educational establishments. For example, women still frequent technical schools less than men do, and a similar picture can be found in university departments such as economics. Therefore, there is a need for an active policy to change the different subject choices made by boys and girls.

There is, however, another development in education policy. In the seventies a whole system for adult education came into being, and women started their own high school. Now this initiative has been taken over by the government and made into official policy. Besides this high school system (married women form the largest group of participants) there is a whole adult education network for different subjects, and there are special adult education systems for women.

While the government subsidizes this form of adult education, there are still problems as there is no direct relationship with the labour market. For older women it is very difficult to learn a profession, for example, and most apprenticeships are only accessible to people younger than 27 years of age. The government has its own institute for training people older than 27 for technical professions, but until recently these institutes were hardly accessible to women. Indeed, some women did not agree with this system and campaigned against this policy. Now a few women have entered these institutes and there is a government committee writing a report on how to improve this situation.

The government subsidizes other forms of education that have connections with the labour market. Companies can get money if they train new workers who were unemployed for some time. There are also some other, small, provisions for individuals to get their training paid for. For women there has been a project for re-training hospital nurses, but now there are too many nurses on the labour market.

An obstacle in the criteria for state aid in training facilities is that one has to have been officially unemployed for a certain period; and women are not always registered officially as unemployed.

New developments, again initiated by women's groups, are projects to offer guidance and training advice to women who want to enter the labour market; but these projects are still very much at the beginning phase.

Income and employment policy

The income policy is also based on the 'standard' notion of the male bread-winner. In 1983 there was still a wage difference between men and women and there was no clear policy intended to change this.

While women remain unable to reach the same income levels as men, they will never achieve economic independence. A lot of working women plainly need the financial support of their parents or husbands.

One of the central points of discussion in employment policy is the reduction of the working week. Women's organizations opted for a 25-hour working week with the aim of attaining a better distribution of paid and unpaid work between men and women. Unions supported this demand, but in practice they went ahead and negotiated collective agreements with a reduction of 4 working hours and ignored the position of the part-timers. Because of this reduction in working hours the hourly wage decreases, and this means that a part-timer earns less for the same amount of hours worked! The position of part-timers is clearly a 'forgotten' one in employment policy. They still have less rights than full-timers.

Internal labour market policy

One of the hardest obstacles for women is formed by internal labour market policy. It is very difficult to change this. Research shows that there is still a lot of discrimination in selection, schooling, and promotion of women within companies. In 1980, 64% of the employers admitted that they had a different policy for men and women. They would not select and train women for technical, commercial, or management jobs, only for lower administrative functions would they choose women over men.

The main reason given for this policy was that women are not reliable workers because they tend to leave the labour market. The Equal Treatment Law (that orders that it is forbidden to discriminate on basis of sex in selection, training, and promotion (potential workers) has the same problems as the Equal Pay Law, i.e. a law without sanctions. Investigations into the effect and influence of this law have shown that only women in good positions, and with high levels of education, send in complaints to the equal treatment commission.

Second obstacle: child care facilities and maternity leave

The key obstacle for women who want to combine paid work with family responsibilities is the lack of child care facilities in terms of quantity and quality, and there are just a handful of nurseries where one can leave a child for the whole day. Usually children go to the nursery for just a half day. At an older age there is the problem of the different school time schedules, and women with children at different schools spend much of their day collecting and waiting for their children to come out of school.

The quality of the nurseries is not regulated by law, but nursery schools do get some governmental financial assistance. However, there have been big cuts in the system of financial assistance. (Note that just 36.1% of all workers in nurseries receive a wage!) It is also permissible for anyone to start a private nursery school and make a profit from the situation.

Some companies and institutes have their own child care system (the University of Amsterdam just opened its own nursery for children of students and university workers) but it is becoming more and more difficult to keep these facilities open.

Another possibility to combine child care and work is parental leave and a commission of the Social Economic Council is preparing a report on this issue (as a result of a European directive!). However, the report will not become law immediately. Up until now there have been two laws regarding working mothers. Firstly, since 1976 it has been unlawful to sack women workers just because they are pregnant. Secondly, there is a legal maternity leave of 12 weeks. Women stop working 6 weeks before the expected birth of the child, and after the birth they are given a further 6 weeks to recover. Undoubtedly this paid leave is insufficient, and if, for example, the baby is born just 1 week after stopping work, one automatically loses 5 weeks. In fact many women stay home on sick leave after 6 weeks maternity leave.

In some collective agreements there are additions to this official maternity leave: the opportunity, for example, to work 3 months on a part-time basis. Another example of collective agreements is the clause that individuals (women and men) can take leave (mostly unpaid) when their children fall ill.

Other gaps in provisions that women consider to be obstacles to working outside their homes are the long travelling distances to and from work (the Netherlands tends to be divided into districts to live and districts to work). Inadequate public transport, short opening times of shops, the problem of getting home help if one of the parents is ill; are other facilities that form a 'standard' place on the list of demands of women.

Third obstacle: the social security systems and the tax system

Both of these systems are too complicated to describe in detail but they are both built on the notion of the male breadwinner, and married women only get unemployment benefits for half a year. After that period it depends on the husband's income whether or not they can get other benefits. After 2½ years however, they lose all rights.

On tax forms men have to report their wives' incomes and so married women do not have their own tax forms. In addition, costs mainly made to combine family tasks with work outside the home (child care, schooling) are not recognized as legitimate tax relief claims.

The only legislation which favours women is the widow's allowance; each widow over 40 years of age, and young widows with small children, receive this benefit. Widowers, on the other hand, do not get anything at all.

A thorough re-examination of the social security and tax system is now taking place. Because of the European directive, it will not be possible to continue this different treatment assigned to men and women; but the new initiatives give little hope of any real change. Nevertheless, women will get an individual right to social security benefits and one-parent families will qualify for additional benefits.

As part of the tax system, the government made a regulation imposing tax on men and women who both work (the so-called 'double-income' families). This means that women with a small income (and that is true for most female workers) will influence family income in such a way that the husband has to pay more tax. Hence, it again encourages married working women to leave the labour market. Obviously this is not a very progressive policy, and indeed it will provide additional funds to the government.

THE NEED FOR WOMEN TO ORGANIZE THEMSELVES

It is not the intention of this chapter to create an image of the Netherlands as a very old-fashioned country in relation to the problems and the position of women at work. While the statistics tend to support this impression, on an optimistic note more and more Dutch women are beginning to organize themselves into pressure groups in order to improve their position in the labour market and to fight for equal rights.

The conference in The Hague described in the opening of this chapter is one example. Another is the 'Breed Platform Vrouwen voor Ekonomiese Zelfstandigheid' (Broad organization of women for economic independence). In this committee women from different political parties and trade unions have got together in order to fight for the improved economic status of women.

In the past 7 years each trade union connected to the FNV (the largest Dutch trade union federation) has collected information about the existence of women's groups with their own facilities such as schooling, publicity, organizing conferences, etc. One of the most important effects of these women's groups is that the FNV has changed its attitude and policy so that now the 'employee and his/her family' formed the main interest of the union.

The last development in the Dutch women's movement is the creation of work collectives, whereby women form their own jobs without waiting for the government or the employers. The kind of work women do in these collectives includes technical jobs; adminstrative (doing the administration for small companies or non-profit organizations that cannot afford their own administration); nurseries (sometimes in combination with educational facilities for the mothers); clothes (selling new and second-hand clothes and making them); in printing offices; and in women's health collectives. Today, there is also a special department in the Dutch government for women's affairs, with its own state secretary. Therefore, although the situation of working women in the Netherlands is still poor, there have been signs of improvement and awareness which, until a few years ago, would have been unthinkable.

REFERENCES

Een deel van het geheel (1981). FNV report on the position of part-time workers. Amsterdam, July.

Equal Status Council (unpublished internal material) (1980).

'Feminisme en Politieke Macht. Deel 2 (1983): Herverdeling van de betaalde en onbetaalde arbeid', *De populier*. Amsterdam, May.

Raad voor de Arbeidsmarkt (1983). *Arbeidsmarktverkenning 1983*. The Hague, February.

Sociaal Economosiche Raad (1979). *Advies over de verbetering van de arbeidsmarktposition van vrouwen*. The Hague, October.

Stichting voor Economisch Onderzoek der 1982. *Verschuvivongen in de verhouding tussen betaalde en obnetaalde arbeid*. Universiteit van Amsterdam. Amsterdam, August.

Women at Work
Edited by M.J. Davidson and C.L. Cooper
© 1984 John Wiley & Sons Ltd

Chapter 5
Women at Work in Italy:
Legislation—Evolution and Prospects

Maria Vittoria Ballestrero
University of Genova, Genova, Italy

INTRODUCTION

Broadly speaking, the history of Italian legislation relating to women workers can be divided into the following periods:

(1) The first period is characterized by single-sex protective standards dealing with motherhood, working hours, and conditions. Protective legislation dates back to the first years of the twentieth century; it was reinforced under the Fascist regime.
(2) After the Second World War the provision of equality between males and females was introduced in Italian Law by the Constitution (Article 37), enacted in 1948. The post-war period is characterized by the coexistence of single-sex protective measures with the principle of equal pay and equal rights for men and women workers. But I am bound to say that the provision of equality was not actually implemented.
(3) The last period of Italian legal history begins with the Act of December 1977. The Equal Treatment between Male and Female Workers Act (henceforth ETA) has completely upset previous legislation relating to women workers. The ETA, drawn from the anti-discriminatory legislation of other countries, repeals previous single-sex protective standards, except for measures dealing with motherhood and child care (as amended by the Act of December 1971).

To date, there has been little research into the position of working women in Italy, therefore, as a member of the legal profession, in this chapter I shall concentrate largely on relevant legislative issues.

The subject-matter of this chapter is a tentative analysis of the impact of the recent anti-discriminatory legislation upon the actual conditions of women workers. However, for this purpose it seems timely to provide some information about the previous legal situation.

THE FASCIST LEGISLATION: PROTECTION AND EXPULSION OF WOMEN WORKERS

The most lasting foundations of the Italian legislation relating to women workers were laid down by the Fascist government (1922–43). The Fascist legislation includes both protective and expulsive measures.

Beginning in 1923, expulsive measures were enacted. These measures aimed to limit female employment in public services and to concentrate women into marginal employment. First of all, women were prohibited from teaching philosophy and economics in secondary school and from managing middle and secondary schools. Then, the Act of January 1934 authorized the public administration to discriminate against women in hiring. In 1938 public and private sectors were prohibited from engaging more than 10% of women. But the 1938 Act was not actually enforced. Two years later the wartime emergency imposed massive female employment.

At about the same time as the expulsive measures, important single-sex protective measures came into operation. The Act of April 1934 reformed the previous 1907 Act. The structure of protective standards remained as it was. Nevertheless, provisions were more extended and detailed now than they were before. The innovations substantially consisted of: extending the list of dangerous and unhealthy work prohibited to women under 21, including in the list morally dangerous work, and increasing sanitary measures and controls. Protective standards had a large sphere of validity. Significantly, work done at home and family work (meaning the jobs performed within a family firm) were excluded. The exceptions were designed to discourage employers from using female labour in factories. Outwork was encouraged; besides the preferential use of females in low-paid and unprotected work was explicitly theorized. Work done in the homes (outwork) was deemed to be a sort of integration of household duties.

Provisions for workers' motherhood were enforced in a separate Act. The separate protection focused on motherhood, as a central political question. The Act of July 1934 protracted the period of rest for a term of 10 weeks (1 month before and 6 weeks after childbirth). The 1934 Act also provided pregnant workers with special protective standards relating to hours and heavy work. The most relevant innovation consisted of prohibiting employers from dismissing women during the period of rest. Besides the job security guaranteed to working mothers, this Act changed the reason for the subsidy. Whereas it had been an unemployment benefit, it now became a workers' motherhood benefit.

As well as the contemporary Protection of Women and Children Act, the Protection of Workers' Motherhood Act did not apply to outworkers, domestic, or family workers. In the legislative policies and intentions of the Fascist government, single-sex protective measures were intended to discourage the massive use of female labour. Because of legal protection, the female work forces should have become 'rigid'. The less protected male work force, left 'flexible', should have become more convenient.

But actually legal protection did not introduce an additional factor of discrimination against women workers. Female participation was maintained on the same level as after the First World War. The trends of the female labour market were mainly influenced by economic events, as regards to which legal protection was hardly relevant. Job restrictions, costs related to maternity leave, and protection against dismissal could all discourage employers from hiring women. But in some industrial sectors, low-pay and underevaluation of female work continued to make hiring women attractive.

POST-WAR REFORMS: EQUALITY, UNEQUALITY AND PROTECTION

It seems unnecessary to explain the political reasons why the Republican Constitution, issued in 1948, provided general legal equality between males and females. Beside general equality, Article 37 of the Constitution runs thus:

'The working woman has the same rights and, for equal work, the same remuneration as the man. Working conditions should permit the fulfilment of her essential family function and ensure the mother and her child a special, adequate protection.'

Constitutional provisions concern equality as well as protection, as if there were no contradiction between them. However, reflecting the ideas then widespread, the Constitution focuses on women's family role rather than on their full social involvement. Anyway, for several years the highly problematic sentence of Article 37 of the Constitution was not systematically discussed. As a matter of fact, the provision of equality was not implemented. Women received less remuneration than men, even when they were engaged in the same job activities. Marriage and motherhood often meant dismissal. For married women, finding a job was as difficult as ever.

In spite of Article 37 of the Constitution, only in 1960 did a collective agreement enforce the principle of equal pay for equal work. Nevertheless, large disparities between the wages of men and women still remained. The existence of such a gap was partly due to lower female skill. But it was essentially due to the underevaluation of stereotypically female jobs.

Although conditions of inequality persisted, new and more efficient protective legislation was enacted. The Act of August 1950 reformed the provisions of the 1934 Act. The 1950 Act provided pregnant women with the following measures: a period of rest, for a term of 6 weeks before and 2 months after childbirth; a further period of rest for industrial and agricultural women workers or for individual workers, if deemed necessary by the Inspectorate of Labour; the prohibition of dismissal during pregnancy and for 1 year after childbirth; an allowance equivalent to 80% of normal remuneration, sustained by the social security system. The 1950 Act partially applied to outworkers, domestic, and family workers. As for other protective standards and job restrictions, the Act of 1934 remained in force.

Finally, the Act of January 1963 prohibited employers from dismissing women because of marriage. This single-sex protective measure aimed to remove one of the most widespread sex discriminations against women. In fact, it was a protective measure which dealt with women's equality.

In 1971 workers' motherhood was once again an object of the legislators' attention. The Act of December 1971, now in force, reformed the 1950 Act. New protective standards can be summarized as follows.

During pregnancy and in the 7 months after childbirth women cannot be assigned to heavy, dangerous, or unhealthy work; they are moved to other jobs. A list of prohibited jobs is laid down in the executive regulation of the 1971 Act. The length of maternity leave is now fixed as 2 months prior to the presumed data of delivery and 3 months afterwards. The Inspectorate of Labour can impose a further period of rest for the health of the woman. The prohibition of dismissal covers the whole period of pregnancy and confinement, until the child has reached 1 year of age. The woman worker unfairly dismissed is entitled to obtain reinstatement. The maternity allowance is equivalent to 80% of normal remuneration.

With special regard to child care, the 1971 Act entitles women workers to protract maternity leave for a maximum term of 6 months. The benefit is equivalent to 30% of normal remuneration. Working mothers also have the right to absent themselves from work during illnesses of their children up to 3 years of age. These leaves are not remunerated. Finally, the working mother may take advantage of two daily rest periods, until the child reaches the age of 1 year.

The overview in this section shows that protection of workers' motherhood has reached a good level of efficiency. Nevertheless, the lack of public services, especially creches, makes child care an exclusive and private concern of the mother. She is protected from the strains of work, but she is unprotected from the strains of motherhood and household duties. Workers' motherhood, even if protected, still remains a relevant factor of discrimination against women. Dual responsibility of employment and children damages women's professional growth.

In summary, one can tentatively conclude that protective standards have reached their aim of guaranteeing job security to women, in spite of mother-hood. However, these standards have not established equal conditions in employment, to which motherhood is prejudicial. In my opinion, legal protection of workers' motherhood is not a factor of discrimination. Discrimination depends on the responsibility of motherhood itself.

Some different remarks need to be made with respect to the preservation (until 1977) of protective/restrictive legislation.

During the economic and industrial reconstruction, and up until 1962, the female occupation rate rose. Economic development offered employment opportunities to women too. In that period, discrimination against women substantially consisted of low pay, inferior positions, and dismissals because of marriage and motherhood. Beginning in 1963, the year in which the progressive reduction of employment started, women were turned out of the official labour market. The labour market analysis has shown that the low rate of official female occupation depended on economic policies. The unofficial female occupation rate was high. Women, turned out of the factories, were engaged in unofficial and unlawful outwork, with no labour contracts and guarantees. Preferentially turning out women also depended on 'rigidity' of female work. But 'rigidity' essentially depended on social structure and women's role in society.

It is undeniable that legal job restrictions and protective standards made the use of female labour more rigid. Nevertheless, this additional factor of rigidity was no additional disability for the female labour force. It became a disability only when the demand for 'flexibility' in working increased. To eliminate discrimination against women, the repeal of protective standards was not necessary. On the contrary, the repeal was necessary in order to eliminate the legal rigidity of female work. I dare say that legal protection had not been a factor of discrimination in itself. Obviously, the preceding remarks do not exhaust the evaluation of the impact that legislative protection had on women's working condition. On the one hand, within protective legislation (namely the 1934 Act) there were still absurd and out-of-date standards; e.g. the prohibition of morally dangerous work. On the other hand, legal discrimination against women workers really existed in Italian law.

It seems timely to recall that the post-war Italian governments did not implement the Constitutional provision of equality in employment. In spite of even more efficient legal protection of working mothers, many differential treatments based on sex were retained. I pointed out above the differences in wages. Moreover, social security legislation, drafted on the assumption that primary breadwinners are always male, established: a lower retirement age for women than for men; unfavourable standards relating to women's old age pension, survivors' pension, and family allowances.

THE ACT OF DECEMBER 1977: EQUAL TREATMENT BETWEEN MALE AND FEMALE WORKERS

During the seventies the large growth of the feminist movement in Italy drew general attention to women's conditions. With special attention to working conditions, the debate focused on 'discrimination' in employment. In spite of the common awareness that women's inferior positions are grounded on social and factual discrimination, the debate concentrated on legal equality; progressively women's requests for real equality focused on differential treatments.

Originally, from a juristic point of view, differential treatment itself is no discrimination. Discrimination means a treatment which is unfavourable and unjustified, not merely differential. It is only today that one identifies legal equality with no discrimination, and discrimination with 'differential' treatment.

The political answer to women's asking for equality is the Act of December 1977: the Equal Treatment between Male and Female Workers Act.

A large political consensus supported the enactment of the Equal Treatment Act (ETA). A wide sector of political opinion expected (or seemed to expect) that the ETA would be able to change the realities of female labour and to increase women's employment, by means of new, equal opportunities. In the long run the consensus declined, and during recent years the ETA has not yielded relevant results.

As I shall try to show later on in this chapter, it could be foreseen that the ETA would be largely ineffective. Indeed, ineffectiveness was expected by the few annotators of the ETA. Thus it is not a surprise. Nevertheless, ascertaining the scarce practical success achieved by the ETA should not conclude the debate about equality. On the contrary, the analysis of the reasons why anti-discriminatory regulations are scarcely implemented could be the starting point for a serious discussion about equality and sex-based discrimination in Italy. I mean that the analysis of the experience in practice allows us to single out what limits and deficiences of the ETA are susceptible to remedy, and what problems are unsusceptible to being solved by anti-discriminatory regulations, however efficient.

Therefore, let me proceed with the analysis of the ETA, the contents of which can be summarized with regard to the regulated matters.

ACCESS TO EMPLOYMENT

With respect to access to employment, the ETA entitles women to the general right to compete on the job market with no restrictions. Any discrimination on the basis of sex is prohibited, whatever the sector or branch of activity and the level of professional hierarchy. The prohibition embraces direct discrimination (even when carried out by reference to pregnancy or marital and family status) and indirect discrimination. As for this last type of discrimination, which is very hard to prove, the ETA mentions discrimination carried out by means of advertisements or pre-selection procedures. The provision expressly refers only to these cases. However, jurists think that indirect discrimination also embraces superficially neutral criteria (including height and weight requirements, or experience and education prerequisites), which tend to reserve jobs for men.

The express reference to sex is allowed only in sectors of activities (like fashions, the arts, or showbusiness) where a particular sex is required. Any discrimination on the basis of sex dealing with access and contents is prohibited in vocational guidance and professional training.

Since the time of their enactment these provisions have hardly been enforced. The number of judicial decisions is minimal. But there are also well-grounded suspicions that the ETA has not had any spontaneous compliance. The small number of judicial decisions does not really allow one to conclude that discriminatory practices against women workers have ceased. On the contrary, it is common knowledge that women are still discriminated against in employment.

In my opinion there are two main reasons why the judicial enforcement of equality in access to employment is so poor.

First of all, many women workers are completely unacquainted with their legal rights. It seems very important that women become more aware of their rights and of the machinery available to them to guarantee their rights; but up to now no public institution has provided women workers with information, nor supported them in claiming equality. Until now the supporting of women workers' equality has been left to trade unions, but they still appear unprepared to deal with it.

Second, the reasons why judicial enforcements of the ETA has been unsatisfactory can be found in the ETA itself; i.e. that the sanctions and judicial redresses provided by the Act lack efficiency.

As for sanctions, any discriminatory acts relating to access to employment (but also promotion, dismissal, etc) are legally null and void. This refers to 'legal acts', however, not to material behaviour, of which the widespread discriminatory practices and omissions consist.

Intent to discriminate need not be proven. Nevertheless, some judges have stated that the burden of proving that the act was not based on any factor other than sex falls on the plaintiff. Other judges have stated that the plaintiff meets his burden by proving the discriminatory consequences of the act (*Cassazione*, 3 November 1982). The latter opinion, drawn from the legal experience of other countries, does not actually make the proof easier. Anyway, the plaintiff carries the burden of proving either that someone else gains an unlawful advantage from the act, or that her/his disadvantage is grounded on sex discrimination. Sometimes the plaintiff carries the burden of proving both.

As a general rule, nullity and voidness deprive the legal act of its effects, but it does not produce positive effects (as the reinstating of equal conditions). Thus, if the discriminatory act consists of giving an advantage to a worker of the opposite sex (hiring, promotion, economic benefits etc), the discriminated worker cannot derive any advantage in her/his turn from nullity and voidness of the act.

But I have to point out that, in two recent cases, the Civil Supreme Court stated that the advantages awarded by the employer to a group of workers solely because of sex discrimination should be extended to the less favourably treated workers of the opposite sex.

In the decision of 28 March 1980 the Supreme Court stated that the promotion awarded by the employer to male workers ought to be extended only to females performing substantially equal jobs. The Supreme Court argued that the discriminatory act (promotion) was null and void only in the part in which it excluded women from the benefit.

In the decision on 3 November 1982 the Supreme Court stated that the economic benefits granted to the male workers ought to be extended to women workers. In that case the employer had promoted both men and women, but male workers' promotion was dated back to the hiring, whereas females' promotion became operative as from the future. This way, only the males had been awarded back pay.

With regard to the discriminatory practices (active behaviour and omissions), the ETA provides a special complaints procedure. The provision does not apply to the employment in the public sector. It only concerns discrimination related to access to employment and to prohibition of nightwork in the private sector.

In these cases the judge, having received summary information, has the power to decree the cessation of the unlawful behaviour and the removal of its effects. The judicial redress seems to be very efficient and, in certain cases, it is.

As for the access to employment there are two possibilities. If no hiring took place because of sex discrimination, the judge will decree the hiring of the subject discriminated against. On the contrary, if an applicant was not hired by reasons of sex discrimination, but another applicant of the opposite sex was, then the removal of the effects is highly problematic. Should the judge decree a second hiring, or should he also decree the nullity and voidness of the previous hiring? In no judicial case has this question yet been answered.

The most significant cases are related to the indirect discrimination against women workers carried out by means of preselection procedures (in private and public sectors). For example, the requirement of a minimum height (higher than women's standard height) was deemed by judges in 1978 unnecessary for employment as a traffic policeman, but necessary for employment as a police officer in 1979. However, in the same year the requirement of having belonged to a military corps (to be employed as a watchman) was deemed to be directly discriminatory, for in Italy women are excluded from every military corps. In the same way the refusal to hire a woman because of pregnancy was deemed a discriminatory act. It should be mentioned, though, that in this particular case it was a matter of one of those heavy job activities prohibited to pregnant workers.

As pointed out above, in the legal cases mentioned the judge has the power to reinstate equality in employment by removing sex discrimination. This power effectively depends on the circumstance that the conflict between male and female workers is only potential.

Things run differently if the conflict is actual; that is if a man and a woman are actually considered for the same job. Discrimination consists of giving an advantage to one of the applicants by reasons of sex, and in denying the advantage to the applicant of the opposite sex. The removal of sex discrimination grants an immediate advantage to the sex-discriminated applicant, but deprives (or could deprive) the previously advantaged applicant of the unlawful advantage.

In a sense the efficiency of judicial redress is the cause of its scarce implementation, because the petition is a sort of declaration of war between male and female workers.

THE DEROGATION OF EQUALITY: HEAVY JOB ACTIVITIES AND NIGHTWORK

Collective agreements can derogate women's unlimited access to employment: but only if particular job activities are concerned. The latter provision implicitly repeals previous single-sex protective rules, which prohibited the employment of women under the age of 21 (18 from 1975) in dangerous, unhealthy, and heavy work and in underground work. The latter provision also repeals legal restrictions relating to hours and shifts, now equal for men and women workers.

The ETA retains the prohibition of nightwork in manufacturing industries. Nevertheless the prohibition, narrower than it was in the 1934 Act, can be derogated by collective agreements, with special regard to production requirements. With regard to heavy job activities and nightwork, Italian legislators' choice has not been clear enough.

As a general rule, single-sex protection is deemed to be incompatible with equality. The contradiction between equality and protection is considered to be a theoretical necessity. The few exceptions probably do not change the sense that equality has in the ETA. But the rules about heavy job activities and nightwork are very ambiguous. The legislators imposed equality, but retained the prohibition of nightwork. Then they ascribed to the trade unions the power to remove this job restriction and the power to reinstate the restrictions just removed (heavy job activities). These ascriptions are highly problematic, because they entitle trade unions to derogate the ETA (hence statutory law) or to issue compulsory single-sex protective standards. Legislators set trade unions a very arduous task. In my opinion, the difficult responsibility of deciding whether and/or when the ETA has to be derogated (or protective standards have to be issued) fully explains why trade unions have been so prudent.

The provisions concerning nightwork and heavy job activities have in fact been scarcely enforced by collective bargaining. Since the enactment no more than a 100 collective agreements at company level have been made, and most of them have concerned the removal of nightwork prohibition.

An example, drawn from judicial cases, can help in understanding the role trade unions are called to play, and how fine the balance is between protection and equality.

In some cases the employer refused to hire women workers, because under the ETA the employment of women at night is banned. The employer assumed that in his factory the employment of female labour was impossible by reasons of a necessarily continuous shift. The Courts compelled the employer to hire the women workers. The judges' opinion was as follows. Under the ETA the employment of women during the night is banned, but collective agreements at company level can derogate the ban: hence the ban is not absolute. For this reason the employer cannot refuse to hire a woman with the argument that he is prohibited from employing women for nightwork. He actually can employ them on the ground of collective agreements. This means that the trade unions will be compelled to draw up such agreements, and women will be able to work the night shifts.

Up to now, the provision ascribing to the trade unions the power to restrict the employment of women in heavy job activities has seldom been enforced. Sometimes collective agreements at company level include a 'statement of intentions' (*dichiarazione di intenti*). The two bargaining partners (management and trade unions) engage to provide new standards in working organization, aiming to improve conditions and to reduce strains for all workers, whatever their sex. But such an engagement is too great and too indefinite to be fulfilled in a short time.

Very few collective agreements have expressly banned women from heavy job activities. The main example of negotiated job restrictions (Accordo Pirelli, 7 October, 1981) presents a new pattern of trade union intervention. A set of job activities prohibited to women is specified: e.g. work involving the lifting of heavy weights, or work including a regular night shift. At the same time, the collective agreement provides for fostering the employment of women in traditionally male jobs. It seems to be a good way to counter job restrictions with new opportunities, and to conciliate protection and equality. However, to date, trade unions have adopted this approach too infrequently.

The lack of collective agreement means that women can be employed in jobs which were previously deemed to be too heavy to be performed by a women; and they actually are. This situation could give rise to some problems. If female workers are employed in work they are not in the position to deal with, the consequence could be women's autoexpulsion.

On the other hand, some problems emerge when a collective agreement banning women from heavy job activities has been drawn up. I recall the recent case of a young woman seeking to be hired in a mine. The employer denied her the hiring by reasons of sex; and, in spite of legal equality between male and female workers, the employer was not wrong. A collective agreement at company level provided that women would be excluded from some job activities (e.g. underground work) defined as 'heavy'. The only type of job available in the mine was heavy. Thus trade unions and the employer both complied with the ETA. But what of the Constitutional provision of equality?

EQUALITY OF REMUNERATION

The Constitutional provision of 'equal pay for equal work' has been reformulated by Article 2 of the ETA. The new formulation entitles women workers to equal pay for 'equal jobs or jobs of equal value'. The reference to equal value focuses on the evaluation which collective agreements settle on female job activities.

According to this Article, the system of professional classification should adopt common criteria for men and women. Differential classifications between male and female jobs are now prohibited.

The provision of equal pay does not solve the problem of the inferior earnings position of women. It essentially depends on the channelling of women into low-paid and/or marginal jobs; but it also depends on the inferior value that collective agreements systematically attribute to the attitudes and responsibilities which are embodied in job activities generally performed by women workers. Thus the provision of 'equal pay for jobs of equal value' has the goal of reforming the whole system of professional classification; but it is a long and hard road.

Nationally negotiated grading scales and professional classifications do not present substantially new patterns. Collective agreements at company level sometimes include interesting clauses, aiming to maintain women's employment rate.

In spite of the relevant political significance, the enforcement of these clauses could prove arduous; especially if the company is passing through a crisis. Considering the goal of maintaining the rate of hiring women by a company, the bargaining partners engage to foster women's employment in traditionally male jobs. Thus women are compelled to submit to a period of professional retraining.

The provision of equality also refers to promotion and professional growth (Article 3). Any discrimination on the grounds of sex is prohibited. Of course, factual equality is the prerequisite to enforce the provision.

In order to reinstate factual equality, the ETA provides positive discrimination in favour of women workers. As a general rule (but exceptions could be provided by collective agreements), periods when the employee has been absent from work because of pregnancy, confinement, or child care, count professionally as periods of work.

But collective agreements do not generally enforce this provision. To be promoted to a higher position, workers are generally required to have attended a course of professional training. Thus the opposite rule (provided by some collective agreements), according to which the promotion of female workers who are in the lowest position is automatic (which means that women are not required to submit professional training), is an exception.

Once again, I have to point out that, since the enactment, the provisions dealing with equal pay and equality in promotions and professional growth have had very little judicial enforcement. In my research I have found no more that two relevant decisions.

EQUALITY AND WOMEN'S FAMILY ROLE

The ETA introduced new special measures aimed at reducing the negative consequences arising from the dual responsibility of family and employment. The most significant measure extends to the father, as an alternative to the working mother, the right to be absent from work for child care and assistance. But the father can exercise the right only if the mother has expressly waived hers. Furthermore, the right to be absent from work does not apply to the father when the mother is a self-employed worker or a housewife.

This standard aims to equalize women in employment, promoting a more equal distribution of household duties between men and women. In spite of its promotional sense, the provision is scarcely enforced for several reasons.

First of all, child care is still a concern of women. Secondly, the scarce enforcement of the provision is due to the legal instrument itself, which has turned out to be an excessively complex machine. Anyway, whenever the father's earnings position is better than the mother's, it will be the mother who will exercise the right to be absent from work.

A BALANCE OF ENFORCEMENT OF THE EQUAL TREATMENT ACT

It is timely to outline a summary of the changes in Italy since the ETA was enacted. The balance of the enforcement is certainly positive for all the provisions with which compliance can be automatic. These provisions modified previous unfavourable standards relating to women's old age pensions, survivors' pensions, and family allowances.

The balance is also positive as regards the provision of a lower retirement age for women workers. The ETA entitles women workers to choose whether to retire on a pension at 55 or at 60, whereas men ought to retire at 60. This initially led to some conflicts in construction and difficulties in judicial enforcement. However, the rule is important, because it has laid down a positive discrimination in favour of women workers. As a consequence of this legal inequality, actual equality between male and female workers is closer.

A positive judgment can be given on the relevant innovating significance of other provisions laid down by the ETA (namely: the prohibition of any discrimination in access to employment, pay, promotion, professional growth, dismissal; the extensions of maternity leaves to the father). But I am bound to say that these provisions essentially have the value of a principle. As mentioned above, their enforcement is still unsatisfactory.

The lack of efficiency of legal sanctions and judicial redresses partially explains why the judicial enforcement of the most important provisions of the ETA has been so poor.

Of course, the women workers' lack of information about sex discrimination and awareness of their rights partially explains why women so often submit to discriminatory practices without complaining. In my opinion, however, the inadequate implementation of anti-discriminatory standards is fully explained by two further elements. First: the restrictive sense that equality (hence discrimination) has within the ETA. Second: the non-establishment of an administrative institution devoted to implementing equality between male and female workers.

About the latter element something, has changed recently. A decree of the Minister of Labour, enacted in October 1982, provided the establishment of an 'Equal Opportunities Committee'. In fact, the Committee still does not exist. However, the decree requires further discussion.

*The Equal Opportunities Committee

The aim of the National Committee was to promote equal opportunities for women workers and the fulfilment of equality between male and female

* Since the completion of this chapter, this Committee has been set up and its functions and powers are greater than described here.

workers. Under the 1982 decree the Committee:
(1) is based at the Ministry of Labour;
(2) is composed of representatives: (a) of the Prime Minister, of the Minister
    of Labour, and of other involved Ministers; (b) of workers' and
    employers' trade unions; (c) of political parties, women's associations,
    and feminist movements. Experts could be called to attend sessions of
    the Committee.

The Committee has the following powers:
(1) to issue 'Codes of Practice' aiming to specify fair and unfair behaviour,
    direct and indirect discrimination against women workers;
(2) to draw up proposals intended to implement equality and remove sex
    discrimination;
(3) to express opinions about complaints presented by women workers invol-
    ving a point of principle;
(4) to express opinions about sex discrimination regulations;
(5) to express opinions about governmental initiatives at international level
    in order to implement equality between male and female workers;
(6) to ascertain events related with sex discrimination.

As can be seen, the Committee is essentially an advisory organ. It lacks any
power of autonomous intervention, except for the power of investigating. It
cannot ask a court whether there has been a contravention of sex discrimination regulations. It cannot give assistance to individuals in cases of
complexity, or involving a point of principle.

The Committee is never directly involved in cases of sex discrimination.
That is, if the Committee is involved, it has no power to solve them. In my
opinion this could be a serious handicap for the efficiency of the Committee.
However, a one-legged committee is better than no committee at all.

EQUALITY AND POSITIVE DISCRIMINATION: NEW PERSPECTIVES

The preceding analysis shows that the ETA (even as regards its enforced
rules) has little impact upon the situation of real discrimination against female
workers in Italy.

I have already pointed out that the inadequate implementation of the ETA
depends on several elements. I have lingered over technical deficiencies and
practical limits of anti-discriminatory regulations. Let me now come to the
main question involved, *viz.* the concept of equality adopted by the ETA.
The sense in which the legislators use the word 'equality' (hence 'discrimination') is fully explained by the provisions related to access to employment,
.pay, and career. I have already emphasized that in the ETA the word
'equality' is used in a sense which is formal and absolute. The concept of
formal equality is grounded on the opinion that there is a contradiction

between equality and protection, and it is justified by the general feeling that discrimination against women stems from single-sex protective standards. But this opinion is too strict and often misleading. In Italy, as well as in other countries, experience shows that the derogation of the most ancient protective standards (that is sex-based restrictive legislation) does not exhaust the equalizing of women. In order to get actual equality, anti-discriminatory measures must be negative and positive at the same time.

On one hand, if women are equal subjects, every prohibition or job restriction must be eliminated. Generally speaking, women should be free to make their own choice of occupation. Physiological differences between men and women justify differential treatment only in limited cases, where the problem is to ensure the physical protection of women. Therefore, banning women from jobs potentially injurious to their different physiological state (such as work involving the lifting of heavy weights, or underground work) could be justified. Last, it seems important to prevent women, compelled by necessity, from accepting jobs prejudicial to their health.

On the other hand, legal equality does not imply matter-of-fact equality. We all know that social and political structures make the position of women on the labour market unequal.

Finally, there is a conflict between single-sex protection and legal equality of women workers. But there is no contradiction: as long as women are really unequal, separate and differential treatments would be required to implement legal equality itself. In other words, women's legal equality is a prerequisite for the promotion of factual equality, but does not mean 'equality' *tout court.*

Anti-discriminatory rules alone, without any other social and legal measures, cannot really work, and women cannot derive from them anything but modest advantages. The equalizing of women must include a set of positive discriminations aiming to guarantee factual equality. Equal employment opportunities must not just prohibit discrimination on grounds of sex. They require complex policies and special sex-based measures supporting women's employment.

This statement requires little substantiation. It is enough to compare the implementation of anti-discriminatory regulations with the present problems of female employment in Italy. During the past few years two positive changes have been recorded: the increase of the female participation rate; the increase of female employment in public and private services and public administration (see Table 5.1). These two positive data have been countered by the increase of female unemployment (see Table 5.2).

The positive data did not efface the traditional problems of female employment. On the contrary, new problems stem from the present occupational trend. First of all, the female unemployment rate among young people (age groups from 15 to 29) is high. Second, the return to the labour force of married women (having family responsibilities) and of elderly women is still difficult (see Table 5.3). The labour market does not supply them with enough opportunities.

Conditions of inequality persist, which prejudice employed women: differential wages and inferior earnings positions, depending on professional classifications and/or the channelling of women into low-paid and marginal jobs; inferior career opportunities, depending on the inferior mobility of female labour and/or the segregation of female labour in sectors which supply them with scarce opportunities for professional growth.

The present political and economic perspective is not favourable to the solution of these problems. Economists foresee a further increase in the unemployment rate (of both male and female workers) for the next 10 years. They also foresee that the sector of public and private services and public administration, in which an increase of women's employment has been recorded in the years 1977–81, will not be able to absorb the growth of the

Table 5.1   *Activity and unemployment rates by sex (percentages), Italy, 1959–81*

	Activity rates*			Unemployment rates		
	Men	Women	Men and Women	Men	Women	Men and women
1959	62.9	28.0	45.0	6.1	8.8	7.0
1960	62.5	26.4	44.0	4.8	7.4	5.6
1961	62.1	26.5	43.8	4.2	7.3	5.1
1962	61.2	25.7	43.0	3.5	6.8	4.5
1963	60.2	24.3	41.8	3.1	5.7	3.9
1964	60.2	23.5	41.4	3.3	6.8	4.3
1965	59.3	22.8	40.5	4.3	8.1	5.4
1966	58.5	22.0	39.8	4.7	8.9	5.9
1967	58.5	21.9	39.7	4.1	8.7	5.4
1968	57.8	22.1	39.5	4.2	9.5	5.7
1969	56.8	21.9	38.9	4.0	9.9	5.7
1970	56.6	21.8	38.7	3.7	9.6	5.4
1971	56.0	21.7	38.4	3.8	9.5	5.4
1972	55.4	21.3	37.9	4.6	10.9	6.4
1973	54.9	21.8	38.0	4.2	11.6	6.4
1974	54.8	22.0	38.0	3.6	9.6	5.4
1975	54.6	22.4	38.1	3.8	10.7	5.9
1976	54.5	23.2	38.5	4.2	12.2	6.7
1977	54.1	24.4	38.9	4.6	12.5	7.2
1978	54.1	24.5	38.9	4.7	12.6	7.2
1979	54.2	25.3	39.4	4.9	13.3	7.7
1980	54.4	26.0	39.9	4.8	13.1	7.6
1981	54.7	26.5	40.3	5.4	14.4	8.4

* Percentage of the total population in the labour force.
Source: ISTAT, *Annuario di statistiche del lavoro*, 1981.

female labour supply. The threat to women's employment arises from the reorganization of sectors (namely the private ones), new technology, and the reduction of public spending.

If these forecasts are correct, the policy-makers should deal with the following problems: the increase of the female labour supply, because of the

Table 5.2 *Labour force by Sex (in thousands), Italy, April 1981–April 1982*

	Men			Women			Men and women		
	April 1981	April 1982	Diff.	April 1981	April 1982	Diff.	April 1981	April 1982	Diff.
Labour force	14,918	15,029	+111	7,527	7,605	+78	22,445	22,643	+189
Employed	14,163	14,173	+10	6,456	6,506	+50	20,619	20,680	+61
—agriculture	1,819	1,657	−162	988	863	−125	2,807	2,520	−287
—industry	5,919	5,863	−56	1,829	1,792	−37	7,748	7,655	−93
—others	6,425	6,653	+228	3,639	3,852	+213	10,064	10,505	+441
•energy	187	209	+22	16	18	+2	202	226	+24
•industrial transformation	3,720	3,583	−137	1,738	1,701	−37	5,458	5,284	−174
•building	2,012	2,072	+60	75	73	−2	2,088	2,145	+57
•commerce	2,562	2,683	+121	1,273	1,340	+67	3,834	4,023	+189
•transport	1,014	1,008	−6	137	126	−11	1,151	1,134	−17
•credit and insurance	414	424	+10	166	188	+22	580	613	+33
•public administration and services	2,435	2,538	+103	2,063	2,198	+135	4,498	4,736	+238
Persons seeking employment	755	856	+101	1,071	1,098	+27	1,827	1,954	+127
—unemployed formerly employed	111	151	+40	95	120	+25	205	271	+66
—seeking first employment	418	521	+103	490	569	+79	908	1,090	+182
—others seeking employment (14/29 years)	226	184	−42	486	410	−76	713	594	−119
Non-labour force	12,526	12,480	−46	21,296	21,285	−11	33,822	33,765	−57
—of working age (14/70 years)	5,165	5,262	+97	13,336	13,451	+115	18,501	18,713	+212
—interested in working	167	173	+6	526	500	−26	693	673	−20
—of non working age	7,361	7,218	−143	7,960	7,834	−126	15,321	15,052	−269
Population	27,445	27,509	+64	28,823	28,890	+67	56,268	56,399	+131
Activity rates (1)	54.4	54.6	—	26.1	26.3	—	39.9	40.1	—
Unemployment rates (2)	5.1	5.7	—	14.2	14.4	—	8.1	8.6	—

(1) Percentage of the total population in the labour force.
(2) Percentage of persons seeking employment in the total labour force.
Source: ISTAT, *Supplemento al Bollettino Mensile di Statistica.*

Table 5.3 Women in the labour force by marital status and age (in thousands), Italy, 1980

Age categories	Single			Married			Others*			Women total			Men total		
	Labour force	Non-labour force	Total	Labour force	Non-labour force	Total	Labour force	Non-labour force	Total	Labour force	Non-labour force	Total	Labour force	Non-labour force	Total
0–13 years	—	5,652	5,652	—	—	—	—	—	—	—	5,652	5,652	—	5,828	5,828
14–19 years	743	1,842	2,584	26	46	72	1	3	4	770	1,891	2,661	913	1,829	2,742
20–24 years	765	413	1,178	362	409	771	5	2	7	1,132	824	1,956	1,380	523	1,904
25–29 years	324	101	425	674	737	1,412	15	3	18	1,013	841	1,854	1,663	126	1,789
30–39 years	275	82	357	1,446	1,978	3,444	70	18	88	1,810	2,078	3,889	3,667	51	3,718
40–49 years	188	89	277	1,179	2,203	3,382	127	74	201	1,494	2,366	3,860	3,591	109	3,700
50–59 years	156	166	322	688	2,209	2,898	139	321	460	983	2,696	3,679	2,868	584	3,452
60–64 years	17	95	113	84	703	787	29	253	282	130	1,050	1,181	415	633	1,048
65–70 years	13	152	165	52	898	949	27	560	587	92	1,610	1,701	287	1,229	1,516
71 years and over	7	248	255	16	664	680	25	1,363	1,388	48	2,275	2,323	115	1,555	1,671
Total 14–29 years	1,832	2,356	4,188	1,062	1,192	2,254	21	8	30	2,916	3,556	6,472	3,956	2,478	6,434
Total 14–70 years	2,480	2,940	5,420	4,531	9,182	13,713	414	1,234	1,647	7,425	13,356	20,781	14,784	5,084	19,868
Total	2,487	8,839	11,326	4,547	9,846	14,393	438	2,597	3,035	7,473	21,282	28,775	14,899	12,467	27,366

* Widowed, divorced, separated.
Source: ISTAT, Supplemento al Bollettino Mensile di Statistica, Anno 1981, 3.

ever-growing female interest in finding a job; and the increase of female unemployment, namely within young and elderly women, because of labour-saving policies in the sectors of production and services.

Thus, a policy dealing with women's employment should answer the following questions: how to expand female employment in sectors where male employment is prevailing; and how to retain the female employment rate in sectors of traditionally female employment.

According to a widespread opinion, the answer to all these complex questions could be found in an affirmative action programme, which includes single-sex protective measures (positive discrimination) aiming to guarantee women genuine equal opportunities.

In order to move towards the goal of equal opportunity for women, positive discrimination could consist of:

(1) supporting special education, training, and retraining programmes for women (e.g. vocational guidance, professional training, and qualification in non-traditional jobs);
(2) guaranteeing periods of absence from work for working women with family responsibilities; flexible hours; other working conditions aimed at encouraging female labour to remain in the labour market;
(3) fostering the access to employment of young women, and the return to work of middle-aged women, by means of special economic treatment, e.g. part-time, temporary employment, "education contracts" (mix of work and professional training). (June 1983).

SELECTED BIBLIOGRAPHY

Assanti, C. (1978). 'La disciplina giuridica del lavoro femminile', in *La disciplina giuridica del lavoro femminile. Atti delle giornate di studio di Abano Terme 16–17 aprile 1977*. Giuffrè, Milano.

Ballestrero, M. V. (1979). *Dalla tutela alla parità, La legislazione italiana sul lavoro delle donne*. Il Mulino, Bologna.

Ballestrero, M. V. (1982). 'I giudici e la parità. Osservazioni sull'applicazione giudiziaria della legge n. 903/1977', in *Politica del diritto*, pp. 463–482.

Ballestrero, M. V., Frey, L., Livraghi, R., and Mariani, G. C. (1983). *Lavoro femminile, formazione e parità*. F. Angeli, Milano.

Canosa, R. (1978). *Il giudice e la donna. Cento anni di sentenze sulla condizione femminile in Italia*. Mazzotta, Milano.

De Angelis, L. (1980). 'La legge di parità uomo-donna nella prassi giurisprudenziale', in *Il diritto del lavoro*, I, 331–345.

De Cristofaro, M. L., (1979). *Tutela e/o parità. Le leggi sul lavoro femminile tra protezione e uguaglianza*. Cacucci, Bari.

Frey, L., Livraghi, R., Mottura, G., and Salvati, M. (1976). *Occupazione e sottoccupazione femminile in Italia*. F. Angeli, Milano.

Frey, L., Livraghi, R., and Olivares, F. (1978). *Nuovi sviluppi delle ricerche sul lavoro femminile*. F. Angeli, Milano.

Galoppini, A. M. (1980). *Il lungo viaggio verso la parità. I diritti civili e politici delle donna dall'unità a oggi.* Zanichelli, Bologna.

Padoa Schioppa, F. (1977). *La forza lavoro femminile.* Il Mulino, Bologna.

Paolini, R. (1981). 'Considerazioni generali sulla legge 9 dicembre 1977, n. 903: in particolare sul procedimento speciale ex art. 15' in *Il diritto del lavoro*, I, 365–488.

Smuraglia, C. (ed.) (1980). *Problemi del lavoro femminile.* Materiali Universitari, Unicopli, Milano.

Treu, T. (1977). *Lavoro femminile e uguaglianza.* De Donato, Bari.

Treu, T. (ed.) (1978). 'Legge 9 dicembre 1977, n. 903. Parità di trattamento tra uomini e donne in materia di lavoro', in *Le nuove leggi civili commentate*, pp. 786–848.

Various authors (1982). *Atti del Seminario Internazionale di studi su: la parità tra lavoratori e lavoratrici e la tutela della salute.* Istituto Italiano di Medicina Sociale, Roma.

Various authors (1979). *Il costo del lavoro femminile.* Special issue of *Economia del lavoro*, p. 2.

Various authors (1979). *Il lavoro delle donne e la legge di parità.* Edizioni Lavoro, Roma.

Various authors (1980). *La forza lavoro femminile. Analisi e prospettive,* Special issue of *Economia, istruzione e formazione professionale*, p. 11.

Various authors (1978). *Parità tra uomini e donne in materia di lavoro: analisi e attuazione della legge.* Documenti del Comune, Bologna.

Ventura, L. (1979). 'La legge sulla parità fra uomo e donna nel rapportto di lavoro', in De Luca Tamajo, R. and Ventura, L. (eds), *Il diritto del lavoro nell'emergenza.* Jovene, Napoli.

Women at Work
Edited by M.J. Davidson and C.L. Cooper
© 1984 John Wiley & Sons Ltd

Chapter 6
Women at Work in Greece:
The Sociological and Legal Perspectives

Loukia M Moussourou
Sociologist, Athens, Greece
and
Sophia Spiliotopoulos
Attorney of Law, Athens, Greece

INTRODUCTION

In order to present a comprehensive picture of the position of women at work in Greece we have organized this chapter into two main parts. The first part puts forward a sociological viewpoint concerning the situation of Greek women at work, while the second section concentrates on the relevant legal issues.

THE SOCIOLOGICAL PERSPECTIVE

Introductory remarks

During the last 30 years Greece has been noted for the efforts put into socioeconomic development—by the process of changing an agricultural, rural, traditional society into an industrial, urban, modern one. The process itself, and the problems related to it, are, of course, outside the scope of this chapter. However, certain matters should be briefly stated, as they can be considered as crucial for the understanding of the topic in hand.

The points to keep in mind could be summarized as follows:

(1) The foremost demographic phenomenon of the last 30 years (1951–81) is the *ageing* of the Greek population: the proportion of persons over 65 has increased from 6.7% (1951 census) to 13.1% (1980 mid-year estimates) while in the female population the increase is more spectacular (from 7.3% to 14.3%).

(2) The above phenomenon is related to another three, also characteristic of the period under consideration: the falling natality rate, the falling average household size, and external migration.

More specifically the *natality rate* (i.e. live births per 1000 inhabitants) has decreased from 20.31 in 1951 to 17.94 in 1961, to 15.98 in 1971, and to 15.36 in 1980. It is to be noted that, since the 1970s, the natality rate tends to have stabilized at 15.00–16.00.

(3) The falling natality rate is related to the decreasing average *household size*: from 4.11 persons per household in 1951, to 3.78 in 1961, and 3.39 in 1971. One should note, however, that household size is determined both by the number of children and by the form of the family. It is thus maintained that urbanization has somewhat increased the number of nuclear families, while further decreasing the number of extended families—a minority in Greece since 1900 (Bialor 1968).

(4) Both natality and household size should be appraised in the light of *external migration* which, by its massivity and far-reaching effects, can be considered as the dominant socio-economic phenomenon of this period: from 1955 to 1977, 1,236,280 Greeks have emigrated (Kassimati; 1981)—of these 89.85% were 15–44 years old and 41.31% were women (Kassimati, 1981b).

(5) Geographic mobility did not take the form of external migration alone: the rapid *urbanization* of the Greek population is one of the most characteristic phenomena of the period under consideration. Thus, in 1951, 47.5% of the population were living in rural areas and this percentage, gradually decreasing, has come down to 30.3% according to the provisory data of the 1981 census.

(6) Economic development is apparent in the evolution of the *per capita gross national income*. This (at 1970 constant market prices), has increased from US$379 in 1951 to US$631 in 1981. In spite of the fact that the per capita income does not give an accurate picture either of the changes in the level and ways of life nor of the income differences between the socioeconomic categories which form modern Greek society, it has to be considered as an unmistakable pointer to the socioeconomic development of the country.

(7) Socioeconomic development and urbanization explain the general increase of the level of *education*. This increase is far more important that the overall statistical data tend to show. One has to consider the distribution of the population by age in order to grasp the importance of this development. For instance, in 1971, 14% of the total population (21.3% of the female population) were illiterate—but so were 3.7% (5% of the female population) of Greeks aged 25–29, and 41.2% (59.6% of the female population) of Greeks over 65. On the other hand, 11% of

the total population (9.9% of the female population) had had a secondary level education—but 20% (19.2% of the female population) aged 25–29 and only 4.6% (2.9% of the female population) over 65 had reached this education level.

The female stereotype

The model of the Greek woman has been determined by two main considerations: (a) that the normal 'place' of women is in the home, and (b) that the normal 'lot' for women is motherhood. These considerations explain the stereotype which obstinately keeps women outside the labour market (or in rigidly defined areas when in it), in spite of the drastic legislative measures taken and, indeed, in spite of social change.

According to the above stereotype the social status of women, and even their femininity itself, is liked with, and depends on, their role as housewives. The foremost importance of this role remains unchanged for those women who are in the labour market. Thus, on the one hand, the employment of a married woman is 'justified' by reference to household and family needs and, on the other hand, her priorities are unquestionably determined by her role as wife and mother and not by her identity as an employed or even a career woman (Moussourou 1984). Moreover, until very recently the image that school books presented about the working mother was one of a deplorable anomaly, due to the economic impasse usually created by the death of the husband–father–provider (Frangoudakes 1978). Therefore, the 'anomaly' of female employment does not reflect only on the employed woman herself but on her husband as well. The latter is expected to provide for his family; the employment of his wife proves that he is unable to live up to his role as provider: the employment of his wife is an affront to his masculinity (Avdes-Kalkanes, 1978).

In a recent research study, the majority of unmarried women workers questioned in one factory, stated that they meant to stop work once they got married—while some of them stated that they would decide according to the wishes of their future husband and the needs of their family (Nikolaïdou; 1978). Moreover, according to the findings of another research study, 18% of factory workers of both sexes do not even consider the employment of their daughters, and their only wish is to see them 'married well' (Collaros and Moussourou, 1982). Finally, a research study among returnee migrant workers (of both sexes) has somewhat clarified the attitudes towards the work of women according to their family status: 91% of the respondents stated that single women must work; 60% that married but childless women must work, and another 25% that these women should be able to work if the family needs the income; finally, only 7% maintained that married women with children must work and another 44% that they may work if the family needs the income (Collaros and Moussourou 1978). It has to be noted that, by definition, the subjects of the above research study (i.e. migrant workers having returned from Germany) had the experience of female workers in an industrial society—and, though this experience may have been traumatic for many of them (women as well as men), one is justified to suppose that sex-defined stereotypes have been somewhat affected.

Education

Greek sociologists have noted that, in Greece, the education of girls has a largely symbolic meaning while the education of boys has a mainly economic function (Tsoukalas; 1977). Thus it is not surprising that in many rural communities more girls than boys end up with a High School Diploma, since the latter often quit school in order to get on-the-job training or enroll at a technical school (Damianakos *et al.*, 1978).

It is, however, undeniable that the higher a woman's educational level the more the probabilities of her being in the labour market (Moussourou 1976). More specifically, in 1971, 22% of the illiterate women were economically active, 25% of the women having finished primary school, 31% of the women having finished secondary school, and 68% of the women with higher and university education (Moussourou 1983). In consequence, although the education of women may be considered to a great extent as 'symbolic', it turns out to have an economic function as well—not, perhaps, as absolute as the education of men but surprisingly clear. The 'symbolic' meaning of the education of women, combined with sexually determined stereotypes of educational aptitudes, lead to 'women's studies'. Thus, on the one hand (and up to very recently), certain branches of education were closed to men (e.g. home economics, nursing, nursery-school teachers) and certain others either did not receive women at all (e.g. military schools) or set a quota (e.g. the university schools of theology). On the other hand it is undeniable that women tend to monopolize certain branches (e.g. Arts), to have an imposing presence in certain others (e.g. Law) and to be still practically absent from many (e.g. the prestigious Athens Polytechnic, only 16% of the students of which are women).

A last point to be made on the matter of education is that, although sex differentiation is manifest in the kind of education received, there tends to be an equal participation of the two sexes at the different levels of education. Thus, between the school years 1967–8 and 1978–9, the percentage of women in the (non-obligatory) secondary level has increased from 45.8 to 49% of the students while in higher education (universities, academies etc.) it has increased from 32% to 39.2% between the years 1972–3 and 1978–9.

Occupation

The differentiation between 'male' and 'female' education reflects and enhances the differentiation between 'male' and 'female' occupations: both occupation and education are supposed to have to be suitable for women and are acceptable to the extent to which they are considered as 'becoming' to them. Thus, these differentiations express in fact the rigid division of labour in the traditional societies as well as the 'naturally' (i.e. sexually) determined roles in them.

However, reality may not be as simple, and its explanation may not be as 'mechanistic'. In Greece the occupation of women is considered in relation to the concept of the traditional economic function of the family (Moussourou, 1984). In this concept all family members contribute according to their (naturally and socially determined) abilities to support the family group and to achieve a better socioeconomic status. In Greek statistical data this attitude is reflected in the number of economically active women classified as 'unpaid family members': in 1981, 36.2% of all economically active women did belong to this category. Most of these women (80%) were active in the primary sector—and, in this sector, 70% of the economically active women belong to this category. As far as we know, the same attitude is reflected in cottage industry: although statistical and empirical data are either lacking or obsolete, we know that at least 50% of these industries have to do with weaving, embroidery and knitting, and that they involve women only—mostly middle-aged women and of very low educational level (Zervas et al., 1973).

Thus the discrimination against women is not only a matter of sexually determined occupations; it is foremost a matter of the sexually determined approach to the concept of economic activity itself: the basis for the decisions pertaining to economic activity is different between the sexes. The fact that these differences are socially induced does not alter the end result or diminish its importance—although it is, of course, crucial for its understanding and interpretation. Recent theoretical approaches (e.g. Moussourou, 1983) and research studies (e.g. Kassimati, 1981a) take into serious consideration the sexually differentiated approaches to economic activity.

The decision to work

To the extent to which Greek women enter the labour market and remain in it for reasons which are different from those of Greek men, this difference may explain much of the subsequent differentiation between male and female work and of the (direct or indirect) discrimination against the latter.

Why are the decisions pertaining to economic activity different between the sexes? Because each is socialized in a different world: the women in a world the axis of which is the family; the men in a world the axis of which is the economy. Therefore, the decision of the woman to enter the labour market is taken more in relation to the family and less in relation to the labour market itself. If every decision were roughly considered as the result of the appraisal of implied 'gains' and 'losses', the gains and the losses of the female worker are considered as such by reference to the family. It is at the level of this appraisal that the fight against discrimination should start—and that is why the recent changes in Greek Family Law are so important.

What do we know about the decision of the Greek married woman to enter the labour market or to remain in it? The main factors for the above decisions fall under three categories:

(1) the phase of the woman's family cycle as defined by the age of her children: Greek women tend to leave the labour market at least for as long as their children are of pre-school age;
(2) The level of and the kind of education that the particular woman has received; and
(3) The conditions prevailing in the labour market and the opportunities offered to women.

Concerning the work of mothers of pre-school-aged children, we should note that an important factor in their decision to be in the labour market may be the availability of a substitute for their mother role. In fact, research findings show that working married women belong more often to an extended family than non-working women do: 25% and 18% respectively among families of factory workers (Moussourou 1983). On the other hand, in 1978, only 5% of children less than 3 years old were attending a public nursery school—44% of children 3–6 years old were attending kindergarten (Moussourou 1983).

One should keep in mind that the importance of the above factors is relative to the (economic) necessity to work. Necessity brings and keeps in the labour market women with young children (and with inadequate care for them during their absence), with little education and no training—women who get the harder, dirtier and lower-paid jobs and who can hope for no improvement in their work status. For many working women the only meaning an improvement could have is for them to be able to stop working.

Discrimination has a different meaning altogether for those who can take into consideration its implication when deciding whether to work or not, than for those who cannot afford the luxury of such a decision.

Direct and indirect discrimination in employment

For the purposes of this part of our chapter, we consider as 'direct' the discrimination which is either explicit in the Law and judicial decisions, in training opportunities and jobs offered or proved by labour statistics (which may show discrepancies in actual pay, for instance).

We consider as 'indirect' the discrimination resulting from the socially determined conditions under which women decide to work—conditions which include the social role to which they have been socialized. Indirect discrimination cannot be abolished by direct measures (a change in the law, for instance); it can be fought through the long process of becoming aware of the implications of the different levels of deep-rooted convictions on which social practice rests. Indirect discrimination is at the basis of the composition of the female workforce (especially in terms of age, marital status, and education) as well as of its concentration in specific economic activities and in specific jobs. This concentration can be considered as a result of discrimination as far as it concerns depreciated activities and jobs.

We will briefly consider discrimination in the employment of women as concerns five different (though interrelated) matters:

(1) the concentration of women in specific jobs;
(2) the concentration of women in specific branches of economic activity;
(3) the differences in remuneration between men and women;
(4) the differences in actual promotion of men and women; and
(5) the differences of the effects of the economic crisis and unemployment on men and women.

'Female' branches of economic activity

According to the findings of the 1981 sample survey, women constitute 31.4% of the Greek work force. The main facts about the changes concerning this work force between 1951 and 1981 are the following:

(1) That women leave the primary sector slower than men do, which means that agricultural production rests to a very large extent on women: in 1981, 42.6% of the economically active in the primary sector were women. These women are, on the average, older than those active in the secondary and far less educated than those active in the tertiary sector (Moussourou, 1983).
(2) that women do not seem to favour the secondary sector; and
(3) that women favour particularly the tertiary, into which presumably enters the greater part of the increasing number of women possessing secondary and higher education (according to the results of the 1981 sample survey, 60% of the women employed in the tertiary did belong to this educational category). In fact women working in the tertiary have on the average a better education than their male colleagues.

We consider as indirect discrimination the concentration of women both in the declining primary sector and in branches of the secondary and the tertiary which are either in decline or developing very slowly. For instance, in 1971, 67% of the women active in the secondary sector were working in three industries in decline (namely: tobacco, textiles, and clothing)—which have collectively lost 16% of their manpower between 1951 and 1971.

'Female' jobs

In 1981, if for some reason women had suddenly stopped being economically active, the primary sector would have lost 4 in every 10 workers, the secondary 2 and the tertiary 3 in every 10. Moreover, some jobs would lose more than 5 in every 10 workers. These 'female' jobs were, in 1971: doctors and dentists (of which women were 5.5 out of every 10); schoolteachers (5 out of 10—but 10 out of 10 at nursery school and kindergarten); stenographers, typists, etc. (9.5 out of 10); telephone and telegraph operators (6 out of 10); building attendants, charwomen, etc. (8 out of 10); people occupied in washing, dry-cleaning, ironing, etc. (5 out of 10); barbers, hairdressers, beauticians (5 out of 10); spinners, weavers, etc. (7 out of 10); tobacco processors (6 out of 10); manufacturers of men's, women's, and children's clothes (6 out of 10).

The concentration of women in certain jobs may not be, in itself, a result or a factor of discrimination. The crucial fact in determining discrimination would be the discrepancy between: (1) the average pay in the sector and the average pay of the 'female' job and (2) the average pay of men and the average pay of women having the job.

Wages

Actual wages are determined on the basis of three categories of factors: (1) education, training, the skills acquired; (2) the working hours and overtime; and (2) experience and seniority. All three categories of factors operate against Greek working women. They are on the average less trained than men are, they have shorter average working hours (in industry, for instance, in 1980 the annual average of weekly working hours paid to workers was 41.9 for the men and 39.1 for the women), and they are younger than men—which means that they have fewer years in service, less seniority.

Since discrimination presupposes that the above factors are equal between the sexes, it would be imperative to consider the differentiation of wages in the light of this equality (or inequality). This is unfortunately impossible with the existing Greek data. It would therefore be inadvisable to maintain that the (manifest) inequality of average wages, e.g. in industry (where, in 1980, the ratio of men's and women's wages was 100:57 for the employees and

100:64 for the workers), in the 'female' textiles industry (100:59 for the employees and 100:72 for the workers), or in retail trade (100:70), is due to direct discrimination against women. It certainly is, however, due to indirect discrimination.

The above considerations should be kept in mind while evaluating certain interesting facts. The first of these facts is the discrepancy between men's and women's actual wages. It should be noted that, in industry, this discrepancy is greater between employees than it is between workers. The second fact to be noted is that the discrepancy between men's and women's wages seems to be greater in industry, in the secondary sector (in which, as we have seen, women hold a less favourable position). Finally, a third factor to be noted is that the discrepancy between men's and women's actual wages does not seem to be decreasing (though it may be doing so in 'female' industries, such as textiles).

In analysing the 1971 census data, Moussourou (1976) has pointed out that the factors which seem to be positively operating for men's wages (their age, training and seniority), seem also to be operating for the increase of the discrepancy between men's and women's wages—while women have higher actual average wages than men only when they both are very young.

Promotion

A research study made recently in industry has considerably helped to clarify the implications of the inequalities in promotion, by pointing out the differentiation of attitudes towards a career between the sexes (Kassimati, 1981b). This differentiation is, of course, the direct consequence of the different attitudes towards economic activity, already mentioned in this chapter.

Moreover, 'women enter the secondary labour market which has the lower wages, the less security, the less opportunities for promotion and advancement, the less specialized jobs' (Petriniotes-Konstas, 1981, p. 140). The worse conditions of work that women face (the matter of promotion included), are clearly the result of the indirect discrimination against them.

However, promotion is a matter of direct discrimination as well; women having the same qualifications men have, do not get promoted as much (and as far) as men do. This is clear in the case of civil servants (32.2% of which were women on 31 December 1977—36.1% on 31 December 1980): women were only 2.6% of Directors General (the highest rank in the civil service hierarchy) in 1977, only 1.9% in 1980. On the other hand, the ratio of women to men in the second highest rank in the hierarchy who were promoted in 1980 was 1 : 28—while the ratio of women having the qualifications required for promotion was 1 : 15 (Ministry of the Presidency, 1981).

In the light of the above one must be very careful when evaluating the meaning of the increase both of women employers and self-employed women between 1951 and 1971: the former by 255% and the latter by 176% (Moussourou, 1983). The increase, by itself an important indication of women's changing socioeconomic role, should be considered in reference to the reasons for this development as well as to the work conditions of the women concerned. So far, no empirical data permitting such a consideration are available.

Unemployment

In recent years the proportion of unemployed women is higher than the proportion of unemployed men (in 1981, 5.7% and 3.3% respectively). Also, the number of unemployed women is increasing more rapidly than that of unemployed men (between 1971 and 1981, by 92% and 22% respectively). This,

in spite of the fact that a growing number of women hold traditionally male jobs (in security, the merchant marine, transport) and that many young women now serve in the Armed Forces. The increase of the unemployment of young women is mainly due to the increase of their participation in the labour market and to the traditional preference of employers to employ men during periods of increased unemployment (Fakiolas, 1981, p. 58).

Of course, it is the second reason for the increase of female unemployment which answers to the definition of (direct) discrimination, already given in this review. This is, however, a reason assumed; i.e. no data exist permitting the appreciation of the role of this factor in the total increase of female unemployment.

On the other hand, one has to be extremely careful with data on unemployment—especially concerning the unemployment of women. Because

while the man who is not employed is considered and declares himself as unemployed (thus being included in the economically active population), the woman who is not employed is usually considered and declares herself as a housewife (thus not being included in the economically active population)—even when she is in fact unemployed (Collaros and Moussourou, 1980, p. 68).

SUMMARY

In this review, we have sketched the conditions under which the minority (so far) of Greek women are at work. It should be stressed, however, that both these conditions and the labour market are rapidly changing, and that the changes are to a large extent unpredictable, and due to two main reasons. The first reason has to do with the extensive legislative measures which are practically transforming the legal institutions and which are presented in the second part of this chapter. To date no indication exists as to the actual effects of new concepts and arrangements introduced on the rhythm and the content of the changes in the social institutions. The second reason for the unpredictability of relevant developments has to do with the Greek economy and its future. The rapidity with which the Greek economy will be able to overcome the crisis; the direction to which it will further develop; the effects of development on social, political, and cultural realities as well as the general effects of the interplay of these realities with socioeconomic development are all unknown factors. These are the factors on which depends the future of the country—and of its women. Let us now turn our attention to the important legal issues.

THE LEGAL PERSPECTIVE

Introductory remarks

Women's employment is regulated, in principle, by the provisions of Greek law concerning all workers, as well as by special provisions. The regulation of women's employment is governed by two fundamental principles: the *principle of protection* and the *principle of equality* with men. Explicit constitutional guarantee of these two principles is provided by the 1975 Greek Constitution.

The relevant constitutional provisions are specified and completed by ratified international treaties and/or by European Community Law.

Terms and conditions of employment are fixed

(1) as regards civil servants and employees of public agencies and local government authorities, by statutes and administrative acts of general applicability enacted on the basis of enabling statutes;

(2) as regards persons employed under a private law labour contract, in principle, by collective agreements at national, professional, or local level and, in some cases, at enterprise level, and, where collective bargaining fails, by 'arbitration decisions' (administrative acts of general applicability issued by special administrative organs of tripartite composition, presided by a judge and called 'arbitration tribunals') which are assimilated to collective agreements. Neither such instrument can diminish protection granted to workers by labour legislation. They provide for a minimum of obligatory remuneration and protection which can be surpassed by individual contracts. There are also employees of the State, public agencies, and local government authorities who are employed under a private law contract. The personnel of public corporations is also employed under such a contract.

The legal situation before 1975

In Greece, as in most other countries, the *principle of protection* preceded the principle of equality, as a reaction to the exploitation of female labour, which seems to have taken alarming dimensions—particularly in newborn industry and in commerce—towards the end of the nineteenth and the beginning of the twentieth century. The protective regulation of women's employment was aimed at the protection of their health (for reasons of eugenics too) and morals; it was also a means to combat competition with male labour. Protective legislation concerning women followed initially a parallel course to the protective legislation concerning minors.

Of course, more restrictions for minors, as regards access to and conditions of employment were enacted. However, protection of minors was unequal, on grounds of sex—boys being less protected than girls. Thus, while the general minimum age for access to employment (12 years since 1912) was fixed without discrimination, special minimum ages for dangerous work, mainly in industry, were fixed higher for girls (18) than for boys (16) (Spiliotopoulos, 1982).

Such protective provisions, along with the first measures for the protection of maternity, were included in the first important Greek legislative act regulating labour matters, No 4029/1912 'on the employment of women and minors', which has been completed by decrees issued for its application.

The protective legislation of women's employment was gradually completed with the ratification of several international labour conventions. On the other hand, some restrictions in women's employment introduced by the early legislation, such as the prohibition of work on Sundays and holidays, were subsequently abolished.

The *principle of the equality of sexes* was developed later and was initially applied in the public sector, mainly on the basis of UN convention 'on the political rights of women', ratitifed in 1953 and the statute enacted for the application of this convention. The latter allowed some exceptions for access to corps of ecclesiastical, police and military nature.

However, case law, based on the traditional interpretation of the general constitutional principle of the equality of the citizens although accepting that this principle was also applicable in cases of discrimination between men and women, allowed some more exceptions from the principle of equal access to public posts. Moreover, it was considered as being justified that some of the posts be accessible to persons of one sex only, for the 'interest of the service' or for the interest of the women themselves, or because some posts were considered more suitable for persons of a certain sex (Kallivokas, 1979).

On the other hand, since 1950 the basic salaries of civil servants and employees of public legal entities, as well as most additional allowances, were legally fixed on the basis of hierarchical grades, without discrimination on grounds of sex.

As regards persons employed on the basis of a private law labour contract, there were no provisions ensuring equal access, promotion, and terms and conditions of employment for men and women. Wage-fixing instruments provided lower minimum daily wages for women manual workers than for men; however, they provided equal minimum basic monthly salaries for non-manual workers.

The general national collective agreement of 26 February 1975 provided for the gradual equalization of minimum daily wages of non-specialized women manual workers with those of non-specialized men manual workers within a 3-year period, i.e. by March 1978.

Thus, from 1950 on there has been a trend towards the abolishing of sex-based direct discriminatory provisions as regards employment. On the eve of the entry into force of the 1975 Constitution such discriminatory provisions persisted primarily with regard to persons employed on the basis of a private law contract.

The legal status of women in the field of employment has been reflecting their legal status in the family. *Family law* as provided by the 1946 Civil Code, was based on the principle of the legal predominance of the husband. He was the 'head of the family', the decision-maker in all family matters, the principal breadwinner and children were under paternal authority. Women, as spouses and mothers, had limited rights and obligations under the law. Legally speaking, their role in family life was mostly indirect; according to case law developments the husband should ask for his wife's opinion before he made any decisions; however, his opinion prevailed. She could challenge his decisions in court as constituting an abuse of rights; and she could claim that the custody or other rights concerning her children be transferred to her by judicial decision, in cases where the father exercised his authority in a way contrary to the child's interest. Wives were not obliged to contribute to the maintenance of the family unless their husband was unable to do so, even if they had income from work or other sources. Parents (primarily the fathers) were obliged by law to provide a dowry to their daughter. As a rule, the property of the real estate constituting a dowry belonged to the woman, while her husband had control over its administration. The income from the dowry belonged to the husband but constituted the wife's contribution to the maintenance of the family.

However, contrary to what was provided not very long ago, in other European legal systems, married Greek women have always had full legal capacity; they did not need their husband's permission in order to enter into an employment contract and they freely administered their personal property and earnings.

The 1946 Civil Code (the first civil code to be enacted after the modern Greek State was created in 1830) has been considered retrograde as regards family law, because it reflected more the Roman law principles, as interpreted and elaborated by German scholars of the nineteenth century, than deeply rooted Greek customs and ignored the real role of women as wives and mothers and their contribution to social life. The 1930 draft Civil Code was granting more rights to married women. (Gazis, 1979; Papantoniou, 1980).

Constitutional and other guarantees for the equality of men and women

The 1975 Greek Constitution guarantees by special explicit provisions the equality of men and women. The constitutional guarantee of the equality of men and women is of particular importance, due to the hierarchical structure of the Greek legal order and to the judicial review of the constitutionality of legislation by all Greek courts.

The Greek Constitution is written and rigid; thus, it prevails over any other provision of Greek legislation. All State organs (legislative, administrative, judiciary) have the duty, imposed by the Constitution itself, to observe the constitutional provisions. Judicial review of the constitutionality of statutes, practised by all Greek courts since the middle of the last century, as a logical consequence of the supremacy and rigidity of the Greek Constitution and subsequent non-application of unconstitutional statutes, is formally required by the 1975 Constitution.

According to the 1975 Constitution, international treaties which have been introduced into the Greek legal order by statute, have been ratified and have come into force prevail over any prior or subsequent statute.

From the date on which Greece became a member of the European Communities (1 January 1981), community law has become not only a source of obligations for the Greek State towards the Communities but also part of the internal legal order. According to both the Constitution and the Treaty of Accession to the European Communities, community law prevails over all other provisions of the Greek legislation.

All Greek courts have the duty to examine whether statutes conform to the provisions of ratified international treaties and the community law, and not to apply statutes conflicting with these provisions.

Greek courts also have the duty to examine whether administrative acts of general applicability (decrees, ministerial decisions, etc.) conform to the statute provisions on the basis of which they have been issued, as well as to the Constitution, ratified international treaties and community law, and not to apply those which conflict with the above-mentioned provisions.

The conformity of collective agreements to the Constitution, ratified international treaties, and community law, as well as to legislation enacted in application thereof, is also judicially reviewed.

The Supreme Administrative Court ('Council of State') may annul, in whole or in part, on petition, unlawful, unconstitutional or contrary to ratified international treaties or community law administrative acts of general applicability including arbitration decisions, as well as ministerial decisions by which collective agreements are published; the latter amounts to annulment of the collective agreement itself. The petition can be filed either by the interested worker or by a trade union when the interests of all or part of its members are affected.

Trade unions can also pursue by judicial process claims of their members arising out of collective agreements or arbitration decisions. In the cases where provisions of the legislation, of any kind, or collective agreements are considered inapplicable or are annulled, self-executing provisions of the Constitution, ratified treaties, or community law are directly applicable by the courts, whether they have been invoked by the interested party or not.

Collective agreements and arbitration decisions are controlled as to their legality by the Ministry of Labour, before they enter into force. Infringements of labour legislation are punishable by penal and administrative sanctions.

Equal treatment

Article 4§2 of the Constitution provides that 'Greek men and women have equal rights and obligations'. This provision constitutes a concretization of the more general principle instituting the equality of citizens, which has been included in all Greek Constitutions ('Greeks are equal before the law', Article 4§1 of the 1975 Constitution, on the application of this principle see Manessis, 1980a).

The constitutional principle of Article 4§2 has a very wide scope. According to the doctrine expressed by the Council of State (Nos 3217/1977, 422/1983) this principle (a) forbids that unequal situations be created and the contents of citizens' rights and obligations be differentiated as regards both their mutual relations and their relations to the State, on the basis of the difference of sex and (b) requires that equal opportunities be granted to individuals of both sexes for the development of their personality, the freedom of their movement or individual activities, or their participation in social life. Thus we should consider as prohibited both direct and indirect discrimination.

In the field of employment, in particular, the scope of Article 4§2 comprises all the matters dealt with by the more specific provisions of EEC Directive 76/207 on equal treatment as regards access to employment, vocational training and promotion, and working conditions. This Directive, which has been in force in Greece since 1 January 1981, but has not yet been implemented by Greek legislation, should be taken into consideration as a source providing elements for the concretization of the constitutional principle of Article 4§2 and should thus facilitate the application of this principle, both as concerns identification of unequal treatment and its elimination, in the field of employment. However, as results clearly from the wording of Article 4§2, as well as from the above-mentioned case law, the scope of this constitutional provision is much larger. All civil and social rights consecrated by the Constitution are conditioned by the principle of Article 4§2; they belong both to men and women without discrimination.

According to Article 116§2 of the Constitution, divergences from Article 4§2 are allowed only for sufficiently justified reasons, in cases expressly provided by statute. As results from the parliamentary debates on this constitutional provision and according to the Council of State case law previously mentioned, and the opinion of authors (Gazis, 1976), this provision should be very strictly and narrowly interpreted and applied.

'Divergences should be allowed only in exceptional and limited cases, specifically and expressly provided by special provisions of statutes and justified either by the need to grant women greater protection (maternity protection, protection of health, family and childhood required by Article 21§1 of the Constitution) or on purely biological grounds which require the taking of particular measures or a particular treatment in view of a concrete case' (Council of State Nos 3217/1977, 422/1983).

We think that, in the field of employment, as allowed on 'purely biological grounds' divergences should be considered only those allowed by community law (Article 2§2 of EEC Directive 76/207), i.e. 'occupational activities (and, where appropriate, the training leading thereto) for which, by reason of their nature or the context in which they are carried out, the sex of the worker constitutes a determining factor'. This community law provision should also be interpreted strictly and restrictively and should cover only divergences justified by objective elements pertaining to the nature of the job and not determined in any way, directly or indirectly, by the sex of the worker (Commission, 1981).

The constitutional principle of Article 4§2 guarantees *equality of access* to posts provided and governed by statutes or administrative acts of general applicability, as well as *equality of treatment* during employment in such posts and of protection in case of dismissal. Discriminatory provisions of such statutes or administrative acts of general applicability are inapplicable, as previously mentioned.

Application of Article 4§2 for the annulment of individual administrative acts either based on a discriminatory administrative act of general applicability or interpreting such an act according to sex-based criteria, has already been made by administrative courts and thus *equality of access* and assignment to public posts has been secured in each particular case. In the first case the exclusion of women from posts of civil aviation air traffic controllers has been considered as a non-justified divergence from the equal treatment constitutional principle; in the second case the assignment of women civil servants exclusively to posts of typists, on the basis that these posts are traditionally held by women and the job is best suited to them, has also been considered as a non-justified divergence from the same constitutional principle. (Council of State judgments here above).

Thus, at least when it comes to civil servants, as well as employees of public agencies and local government authorities whose legal status is the same as that of civil servants, the concepts of 'male' and 'female' jobs or posts have been rejected, in principle, as unacceptable by constitutional standards. It has been considered that selection and appointments for access and transfer to posts during employment should be made according to personal merit, in view of the duties to be fulfilled, regardless of sex.

As a result of this case law, calls for candidacies for the filling of posts of typists in civil service, issued this year, were not addressed only to women, as was the case before. However, until quite recently some calls for candidacies for posts in public corporations and banks were addressed to candidates of one sex only, or fixed sex-based quotas for recruitment.

We must remind ourselves that direct discrimination, as to conditions of access, promotion, conditions of service, and dismissal, as regards civil servants, employees of public agencies, and local government authorities, had already been in principle eliminated on the basis of UN Convention on political rights of women, and subsequently by the law enacted in application of this convention, the Code for civil servants and the Code for local government authorities servants. The divergencies allowed by case law before the 1975 Constitution cannot be allowed any more. All above employees are protected against dismissal, until pension age, by the Constitutional guarantee of permanence.

However, there are still some provisions in the Code for civil servants which discriminate against men. Thus, although the general minimum age for access to the civil service is 21, this age is 18 for women, in the case of posts of typists and stenographers, while it is permitted to fix a lower than 21 age limit for the appointment of women nursery school teachers or nurses. Men are required to have terminated their military service or to have been discharged therefrom, but, even in the second case, they are not allowed access to the civil service before age 21.

Until 1982 special legislation provided for the training and appointment only of women as nursery school teachers, and fixed sex-based quotas for the training and appointment of primary school teachers. These discriminatory provisions were abolished in 1982. The new law contains a general provision, according to which the number of students to be admitted in all schools of post-secondary education (universities and higher schools) from the academic year 1983–4, shall be determined irrespective of sex. We do not know yet how this provision will be applied, particularly concerning schools for nurses and midwives which were, until now, accessible only to women.

As regards *promotion*, although there are no discriminatory provisions, official data (supra p. 131) show that there is in practice discrimination against women. Such discrimination is either indirect by legal standards or constitutes non-observance of the law. Case law has not yet identified such discrimination cases as being sex-based.

As concerns posts or employment not provided or governed by statutes or administrative acts of general applicability, but by individual agreements, equal access, and equal treatment during employment or in case of dismissal, is not provided by specific legislation. In such cases equality of treatment during employment for workers in general, has been secured for a long time by virtue of a judge-made general principle of law: the principle of 'equality of treatment', based on Article 288 of the Civil Code which requires that 'obligations be fulfilled according to good faith, fair usages being also taken into consideration' [Deliyannis and Koukiades, 1978; Karakatsanis, 1976b). However, as far as we know, this general principle has not yet been applied by the courts for the elimination of sex-based discrimination.

It is now considered by some authors (e.g. Karakatsanis, 1976b) that this general principle is based on Article 4§1 of the Constitution. We think that, in relation to sex discrimination, this principle should be interpreted and applied according both to Article 4§2 of the Constitution and EEC Directive 76/207, at least until legislation implementing this EEC Directive is enacted.

According to Article 116§1 of the Constitution, existing provisions contrary to Article 4§2 were to remain in force, until abolished, but no later than 31 December 1982. This covered only prior to 1975 Constitution provisions.

Although the transition period has come to an end there are still several discriminatory provisions, in several branches of law, which have not been formally amended. Such provisions are non-applicable and thus the rights or obligations provided by the legislation for persons of one sex belong, under the same conditions, to persons of the other sex. Any individual discriminated against by virtue of such provisions can claim his/her rights on the basis of Article 4§2 of the Constitution and the provisions relating to persons of the other sex. The courts must disregard the unconstitutional limitations or exemptions and satisfy the claim.

Typical examples of unconstitutional discriminatory provisions which have not been formally amended are those concerning the employment of char-women by services of the State or public agencies (employment is on the basis of a private labour law relation) as well as access to certain civil service branches (supra p. 134).

Unconstitutional *family law provisions* were amended in 1983. The concept of 'head of the family' has been abolished. All family matters relate to the joint decision-making of both spouses, who contribute to the maintenance of the family according to their capacities, by personal work and/or financial means. The dowry has also been abolished. Paternal authority has been replaced by parental authority which belongs to both parents and is jointly exercised by them (it can be exceptionally exercised by one of them, without discrimination) (Koumantos and Papachristou, 1983).

Equal pay

According to Article 22§1b of the Constitution 'all workers, irrespective of sex or any other distinction, are entitled to equal remuneration for work of equal value'. This constitutional provision does not only forbid discrimination on grounds of sex as regards remuneration; it has a wider scope. However, as regards equal remuneration of men and women, the above constitutional principle is identical to the equal pay principle of international labour convention No. 100, which has been ratified by Greece and prevails over all other legislation since it came into force (6 July, 1976).

Consequently, in Greece, a uniform principle is in force which requires equal remuneration for men and women. This principle has three sources: the Constitution, Convention No. 100, and Article 119 of the EEC Treaty. This principle is directly enforceable by the Greek courts;it renders inapplicable any contrary provision of the legislation or of collective agreements, and renders null and void any contrary private agreement. Thus, this principle covers not only legal rates but also effectively paid remuneration. Any worker whose remuneration is fixed at a lower rate than the remuneration of a worker of the opposite sex doing the same work or work of equal value, has a right to, and may claim, the higher remuneration on the basis of this principle (Karakatsanis, 1976a; Council of State No. 520/1983).

Another constitutional provision is also related to equal remuneration: pargraph 3 of Article 116, according to which provisions of ministerial decisions of general applicability, collective agreements, or arbitration decisions concerning remuneration, which are contrary to Article 22§1b, remain in force until they are replaced, but not for more than 3 years after the Constitution has entered in force (i.e. until 11 June 1978, at the latest). This transitory constitutional provision had the same meaning and purpose as the transitory provision of paragraph 1 of the same Article.

The term 'remuneration' used in Article 22§1b is specified by the more detailed provisions of Convention No. 100 and Article 119 of the EEC Treaty. Thus, remuneration includes not only minimum or basic wages or salaries, but also any other consideration, whether in cash or kind, which the worker receives directly or indirectly from his/her employer, in respect of his/her employment. All these elements of remuneration should be paid to all workers according to the same conditions and criteria, without any direct or indirect discrimination based on sex.

On the other hand, criteria for the concretization of the notion of 'work of equal value' and the comparison of jobs are also provided by Convention No. 100 and Article 119 of the EEC Treaty. However, criteria or systems of objective scientific evaluation have not been elaborated in Greece; in the absence of such criteria or systems, workers who consider themselves wronged have to prove in court, by any available means, that they perform the same work or work of the same value as workers of the opposite sex who receive a higher remuneration; the first is, naturally, relatively easier to prove than the latter.

As previously mentioned, minimum monthly salaries of men and women non-manual workers were equalized before 1975, and daily minimum wages of men and women non-specialized manual workers have been equalized since 1 March 1978.

However, until quite recently, direct discrimination in pay persisted in several professional collective agreements and arbitration decisions, different categories and different wages being provided for men and women. Such direct discrimination has been gradually abolished in most cases. Today, there are still some professional collective agreements and arbitration decisions which contain such direct discrimination. Separate categories according to sex are mostly being eliminated, but discrimination against former 'female' categories is thus simply disguised, since these are still exclusively or predominantly composed of women and are still classified in the lower scales as regards remuneration (Spiliotopoulos, 1983). A typical example is the national collective agreement for textile workers of 1982 as compared to the one of 1981.

There is also still discrimination in most collective agreements and arbitration decisions as concerns the conditions under which the so-called 'marriage' or 'family' allowances (a percentage of the basic remuneration paid directly by the employer to married workers) is to be paid. Usually, such allowances are provided for men, regardless of whether the wife is working or receiving a pension, while they are provided for women only if the husband does not work, or does not receive any pension. It should, however, be pointed out that there have recently been an increasing number of wage-fixing instruments (most of them concerning bank and public corporation personnel, as well as some national professional ones) that provide for the payment of said allowances to women too, without any restriction (Spiliotopoulos, 1983). The above-mentioned allowances undoubtedly constitute an element of remuneration, according to both Convention No. 100 and Article 119 of the EEC Treaty.

This issue has created quite a controversy in Greek case law. Until now, three judgments of supreme courts have been rendered on the matter: one by the Supreme Civil Court and two by the Council of State. All three judgments were based solely on the Constitution, although Convention No.

100 was applicable in all the cases and, in the third case, Article 119 of EEC Treaty was applicable too.

The first case mentioned above concerned a claim of a woman bank employee who received no marriage allowance from the bank which employed her, because of a discriminatory provision of the bank's internal rules.

The Supreme Civil Court judgment was based on the more general provision of Article 4§2 and not on the special equal pay provision of Article 22§1b. Although it accepted that, in principle, the same marriage allowance should be paid both to men and women, it considered that discrimination as to the conditions and/or the sum of this allowance in favour of married men was justified, as long as they were, according to the family law, then still in force, responsible for the maintenance of the family. This judgment has thus subjected the payment of above allowance to the modification of the unconstitutional family law provisions. (Judgment No 1465/1980).

The first Council of State judgment dealt with a petition for the annulment of an arbitration decision clause which provided for the payment of a family allowance by the employer to all married men and to married women only in cases where the husband did not work or receive a pension (typical collective agreement and arbitration decision clause). (Judgment No 4256/1979).

The Council of State based its judgment on Article 22§1b of the Constitution, and held that the arbitration decision challenged was not covered by the transition period of Article 116§3. Nevertheless, on the same grounds, it reached the same conclusion as the Supreme Civil Court in its above-mentioned judgment, and did not annul the challenged arbitration clause.

The second Council of State judgment dealt with a petition for the annulment of an arbitration decision clause which provided for the payment of a family allowance by the employer (Public Power Corporation) to all married men and women, except women whose husbands were employed by the same corporation or by the State. The Council of State judged that this allowance is a supplement of the salary of married men and women employees; consequently, the exemption of certain categories of married women from the payment of this allowance constitutes a discrimination between these categories and all other married men and women employed by the Public Power Corporation and the State, which is contrary to the equality of pay principle of Article 22§1b of the Constitution. Thus the Council of State applied the principle of equal pay in the wider sense provided by the Greek Constitution. One of the Justices, in a dissenting opinion, accepted that discrimination in general, as regards remuneration, is prohibited by Article 22§1b of the Constitution, and that the arbitration decision clause challenged was contrary to this constitutional provision. He considered, however, that the more particular issue of sex-based discrimination in pay is governed by

Article 119 of EEC Treaty and that, consequently, the clause challenged, inasmuch as it contained such a sex-based discrimination, should be annulled on the basis of above EEC Treaty provision and not on the basis of the Constitution. This last judgment constitutes an important step forward as regards the application of the equal pay principle, and particularly the elaboration of the concept of remuneration. (Judgment No 520/1983).

The aforementioned judgments are the only Supreme Courts judgments rendered until now, on equal pay of men and women issues. (See comments on these judgments: *Labour Law Review*, 1981, 1983; Spiliotopoulos, 1983).

It is to be noted that these judgments have not been concerned with the concept of work of 'equal value', as such an issue has not been raised in any of the cases. Thus, the above concept has not yet been elaborated by Greek case law.

Protection of working women by Constitution and legislation

The 1975 Constitution consecrates several *social rights*, among which are those concerning the protection of the family, marriage, childhood, and youth, as well as the protection of citizens' health. These rights belong to persons of both sexes without discrimination. As regards employment, these rights are implemented by special measures in favour of workers who are married and have a family (e.g. special benefits in cash or kind of conditions of employment allowing the fulfilment of their family duties), as well as health and safety measures for all workers and, more particularly, for potential parents. Restrictions of the employment of young people are also a means for their protection.

The Constitution also consecrates the social rights to work and to education and professional training. Women workers, in particular, and their children (both before and after birth and particularly during the period they are exclusively dependent on their mother for their survival, good health, and development), as well as their families are covered by the *protection of motherhood*, also required by Article 21 of the Constitution. Special measures should also be taken for the protection of potential mothers from conditions of work which involve pre- and post-natal hazards. However, men should also enjoy similar protection, as required by social rights provisions aforementioned.

Legislation implementing social rights should provide equal treatment for subjects of the same right, exemptions being non-applicable. According to some authors the constitutional provisions consecrating social rights guarantee the legal status of the subjects of these rights against any regression of the protective legislation; any legislative provision lowering the level of protection should be non-applicable as unconstitutional (Pararas, 1979; Spiliotopoulos, 1979, cf. Manessis, 1981).

Protective legislation

Until very recently, *maternity protection* was mainly based on the provisions of law No. 4029/1912 and international Convention No. 3 on maternity protection in industry and commerce. Thus, protection was unequal, according to the kind of labour relation, the sector or branch of employment, and the social security agency where the women was insured, and left several categories of working women uncovered. By virtue of Law No. 1302/1982, the international convention No. 103 on the protection of motherhood has been introduced in the Greek legal order. The scope of this convention comprises all women employed in industrial, non-industrial, and agricultural occupations, as well as women homeworkers, both in the private and the public sector.

According to the provisions of the convention and those of Law No. 1302/1982, *maternity leave* is 12 weeks, of which 6 comprise compulsory pre-natal leave. Dismissal during this leave is prohibited. For a period of 1 year after childbirth the mother has the right either to interrupt her work for 1 hour, or to start work 1 hour later, or to leave work 1 hour earlier, with no pay reduction. Several non-self executing provisions of the above convention need to be implemented by legislation. Such provisions are those concerning pre-natal, confinement, and post-natal medical care and hospitalization, as well as cash benefits to be paid during the leave; relevant Greek legislation now in force does not cover all categories of women workers affected by the convention (Valticos, 1958, 1983.)

More favourable provisions of national legislation are not affected by the above convention. Such provisions are those concerning maternity protection of women civil servants and employees of public agencies. Their maternity leave is 2 months pre-natal and 2 months post-natal, with full pay and confinement allowance; daily hours of work are limited by 2 hours if they have children up to 2 years, and by 1 hour if they have children up to 4 years of age; and they are fully protected from dismissal until pension age by the constitutional guarantee of permanence concerning all civil servants. Law No 1082/1980 prohibits termination of contracts of indefinite duration since employer knew of the pregnancy.

Leave without pay, for child-rearing or illness is provided for mothers by some collective agreements which cover a limited number of workers. Such leave should be provided to both parents, both on the basis of Article 21 as combined with Article 4§2 of the Constitution and EEC Directive 76/297. Some collective agreements grant paternity leave of 2–3 days, with full pay, to male workers.

It is prohibited to employ women who are pregnant or breast-feeding in some dangerous occupations. A general prohibition is provided by international labour convention No 136 introduced in the Greek legal order in 1976 (e.g. occupations involving exposure to benzene). Some collective agreements provide other prohibitions.

There are some special restrictions on all women's employment, irrespective of their age, for protective reasons. Some of them are provided by ratified international labour conventions (e.g. prohibition of employment which involves exposure to lead, of underground work in mines and quarries, of night work in industry). Others are provided by Greek legislation, as for example prohibition of night work in commerce; prohibitions of handling certain machines, such as wood-working machines; to be employed on certain engines, or to clean or lubricate engines in motion.

Prohibitions related only to dexterity or appropriate training or specialization are undoubtedly contrary to the Constitution and EEC Directive. As regards prohibitions which have been introduced for the prevention of physical or mental health or reproduction hazards, the balance between protection and equality should be envisaged in the light of scientific research on the hazards threatening both men and women, working conditions prevailing in each particular country being also taken into consideration (Valticos, 1970).

As already mentioned, several hazardous industrial occupations are prohibited to girls under 18 and to boys under 16. Most of these discriminatory prohibitions are provided by the 1912 Law and a decree enacted for its application in 1913. There must be no doubt that unequal protection of young workers constitutes discrimination prohibited by Article 4§2 of the Constitution and EEC Directive 76/207, while their equal protection is required by Art 21 of the Constitution and should be secured on the basis of international convention No. 138 (minimum age for access to employment), which has been introduced in the Greek legal order by Law No. 1182/1981. Consequently the present minimum employment age for boys working in hazardous jobs should be raised to 18; but even before this discrimination is formally abolished lower ages should not apply, as unconstitutional and contrary to convention No. 138 (Spiliotopoulos, 1982).

Control of provisions relating to employment

The application of provisions relating to terms and conditions of employment, as well as to the protection of workers' health and safety, as regards employment under a private law contract, is in principle controlled by labour inspectors, who are civil servants of the Ministry of Labour. There are some undertakings or occupations which are not controlled (e.g. purely agricultural occupations, work at home, family undertakings); these are not covered by provisions relating to terms and conditions of employment and workers' protection, nor by legal minimum wages. Labour inspectors have powers which can contribute decisively to the protection of workers and to the implementation and enforcement of the principle of equality (e.g. the power to mediate between employers and workers for the peaceful solution of their litigations, to lodge complaints for infringement of the legislation, etc.). However, their tasks are very difficult to fulfil, for several reasons, among which is the insufficiency of their number, as related to the number and the distance from labour inspectorate centres of the undertakings to be controlled; and their overburdening with many time-consuming duties in addition to those already mentioned. Besides, complaints of wronged women workers seem to be very scarce.

Final remarks

In the second part of this chapter, we have tried to follow the main lines of the evolution of Greek legislation and case law concerning the equality of men and women, as well as the protection of women in the field of employment. As regards equality, the evolution has been a slow but steady one within the last three decades. It has been accelerated since 1975, due to the relevant explicit provisions of the new Constitution. The explicit consecration of the equality of men and women at constitutional level, combined with the judicial review of the constitutionality of the legislation, has had a gradual but decisive effect on case law. Case law is not so rich, and has not yet dealt with all the issues and concepts related to equality of the sexes, nor has it been concerned with indirect discrimination. On the other hand, it has not been until now obviously affected either by community law or international labour convention No. 100. Most of the cases judged concern the tertiary sector and the most notable evolutions affect civil servants and public corporation employees.

Specific legislation implementing the equal treatment and equal pay principles has not yet been enacted, but is expected in the near future. This legislation, provided it implements these principles correctly and adequately, covers all sectors and branches of economic activity, provides effective sanctions, and improves legal remedies (particularly as regards the burden of proof which now belongs to the wronged worker) and contains all the supplementary measures required by EEC Directives 75/117 and 76/207, will contribute substantially to the more extensive and correct information of workers as to their rights and to the effective enforcement of these rights.

Legislation implementing international labour convention No. 103 is also necessary, in order that equal and effective maternity protection for all women workers be secured. Supplementary measures (such as parental leave) should also be enacted, in order to enable both parents to fulfil their family obligations. Other protective restrictions of women's employment should be very carefully studied, in view also of the fact that the workers in a considerable number of small-scale and cottage industries are predominantly or exclusively women and of the more general phenomenon of job segregation by sex, and educational and training level of women workers, and their working conditions, as well as the inadequacies of control.

The modifications of family law will most certainly promote the effective application of the equality principles, as it will help to eliminate any doubts or excuses based on concepts and principles which, although legally irrelevant in the employment field, have until quite recently prevented the evolution of case law in some matters. These modifications are also expected to promote a better understanding and regulation of the protection of Greek workers of both sexes, and of their families.

SELECTED BIBLIOGRAPHY

ATHENS YWCA (1982), The Greek woman.

AVDES-KALKANES, (1978), *He epaggelmatika ergazomene Hellenida* (The Employed Greek Woman). Papazeses, Athens.

BIALOR P., (1968). 'Tensions leading to conflict and the resolution and avoidance of conflict in a Greek farming community', in PERISTIANY, J.-G. (ed.) *Contributions to Mediterranean Sociology*. EKKE (National Center for Social Research), Athens.

COLLAROS, T. A. and MOUSSOUROU, L. M. (1978). *The Return Home*, Reintegration Center for Migrant Workers, Athens.

COLLAROS, T. A. and MOUSSOUROU, L. M., (1980). *Palinnostese. Stoicheia kai symperasmata apo mia empeirike ereuna* (The Return Home, Facts and Conclusions from an Empirical Research). Social Sciences Educational Centre, Athens.

COLLAROS, T. A. and MOUSSOUROU, L. M., (1982). 'Viomechanike apascholese, astikopoiese kai katoikia' (Factory Work, Urbanization and Housing), in Ethnike Ktematike, *Oikistike monada Thevas* (Thebes Ekistic Unit), Study 40a.

Commision des Communautés Européennes (1981). Rapport au Conseil sur l'état d'application du principe de l'égalité de traitement entre hommes et femmes, COM(80) 832 final, Bruxelles.

DAMIANAKOS, D. *et al.*, (1978). 'Vergina: eksygchronismos tes georgias kai koinonikos metaschematismos s'ena chorio tes kentrikes Makedonias' (Vergina: modernization of agriculture and social change in a village of Central Macedonia). *The Greek Review of Social Research, Athens,* issue 33–34, pp. 432–478.

DELIYANNIS, I. (1980). *Oikogeneiako Dikaio* (Family Law), vol. 1. Thessaloniki.

DELIYANNIS, I. and KOUKIADES, I. (1976). *Ergatiko Dikaio* (Labour Law), vol. A. Thessaloniki.

DELIYANNIS, I. and KOUKIADES I., (1978) *Ergatiko Dikaio* (Labour Law), vol. B. Thessaloniki.

FAKIOLAS, R. (1981). 'He anergia sten Hellada' (Unemployment in Greece), in Greek Chamber of Commerce, *Synedrio gia ten anaptyxe tes Halladas* (Conference on the Development of Greece). t. I, pp. 48–56.

FRANGOS, D. (1980). *Ho oikonomika energos plethysmos tes Hellados*. (The Economically Active Population of Greece), EKKE, Athens.

FRANGOUDAKES, A. (1978). *Ta anagnostika vivlia tou demotikou scholeiou* (Primary-School Reading Books), Themelio, Athens.

GAZIS, A. (1976). 'He epidrasis tou Syntagmatos epi tou Astikou Dikaiou' (The influence of the Constitution on Civil Law), in *He epidrasis tou Syntagmatos 1975* (The influence of the 1975 Constitution). Publications of the Greek Institute of International and Foreign Law, No. 9, Athens.

GAZIS, A. (1979). *Eisagogi isotitos dikaiomaton kai ypochreoseon ellinon kai ellinidon eis to astikon dikaion*. Ministry of Justice, Athens.

KALLIVOKAS, D. (1979). He archi tis isotitas ton dyo filon sti nomologia tou S.t.E. (The principle of the equality of sexes in the Council of State case law, in *Jubilee volume for the Council of State*, Athens–Komotini, Athens.

KARAKATSANIS, A. (1976a). 'To Syntagma kai to ergatiko dikaio', in *He epidrasis tou Syntagmatos 1975* (The influence of the 1975 Constitution). Publications of the Greek Institute of International and Foreign Law, No. 9, Athens.

KARAKATSANIS, A. (1976b.) *Ergatiko Dikaio* (Labour Law), vol. A. Athens.

KARAKATSANIS, A. (1980). *Ergatiko Dikaio* (Labour Law), vol. B/II, Athens.

KASSIMATI, (1981). *Taseis kinetikotetas ergasias sten Hellenike viomechania* (Trends of Occupational Mobility in Greek Industry). EKKE, Athens.

KASSIMATI, K. (1981b). 'Taseis tes endoeuropaïkes metanasteuses metapolemika', (Trends of Post-War Inter-European Migration), *Revue des Communautés Européennes*, 2–3, Athens.

KOUMANTOS, G. (1977). *Paradoseis Oikogeneiakou Dikaiou* (Lessons of family law), vol. A. Athens.

KOUMANTOS G. (1978). *Paradoseis Oikogeneiakou Dikaiou* (Lessons of family law), vol. B, Athens.

KOUMANTOS, G. and PAPACHRISTOU, Th. (1983). *Enas odegos sto neo oikogeneiako dikaio* (A guide to the new family law). Athens.

Labour Law Review (Epitheorisi Ergatikou Dikaiou), (1981), Editor's Comments on case law, Athens.

Labour Law Review (Epitheorisi Ergatikou Dikaiou), (1983). Editor's Comments on case law, Athens.

MANESSIS, A. (1980a). *Syntagmatiki theori kai praxi* (Constitutional theory and practice). Thessaloniki.

MANESSIS, A. (1980b). *Syntagmatiko Dikaio* (Constitutional law). I. Athens.

MANESSIS, A. (1981). *Syntagmatika dikaiomata; (a); atomikes eleftheries* (Constitutional rights; (a); individual freedoms), 3rd edn. Thessaloniki.

MARKOPOULOS, K. (1983). He prostasia tes mitrotetas meta ten kyrosi tes diethnous symvaseos 103' (The protection of motherhood after the sanctioning of international convention 103), in *Review I.K.A. for Security and Laboour Law*, pp. 145–152.

MICHAELIDES-NOUAROS, G. (1972) *Oikogeneiakon Dikaion, Paradoseis* (Family law, lessons), Athens.

MITSOU, T. (1982). *Les sources du droit du travail en Gréce* (monographie rédigée pour la CEE). Athens (xerox).

MOUSSOUROU, L. M. (1976). *He sygchrone Hellenida* (The Contemporary Greek Woman), Athens.

MOUSSOUROU, L. M. (1983) *Kyklos tes oikogeneiakes zoes kai gynaikeia apascholese*, (Family Cycle and Female Employment), PhD dissertation, Athens (xerox).

MOUSSOUROU, L. M. (1984). *He hellenike oikogeneia*, (The Greek Family), The Goulandris-Horn Foundation, Athens.

NIKOLAIDOU, M. (1978). *He gynaika sten Hellada* (The woman in Greece), Kastaniotes, Athens.

PAPANTONIOU, N. (1980). O eksynchronismos tou oikogeneiakou dikaiou kai he archi tes isonomias andron kai gynaikon (The modernization of family law and the principle of equality of men and women), in *O Polites*, March-April 1980.

PAPANTONIOU, N. (1957). *He kali pistis eis to astikon dikaion* (Good faith in the civil law). Athens.

PARARAS, P. (1979). 'He eleftheria tes ergasias kai to dikaioma pros ergasian tou arthrou 22§1 tou Syntagmatos (The freedom to work and the right to work according to article 22§1 of the Constitution), in *The Constitution*, vol. 5, pp. 259–280.

PETRINIOTES-KONSTAS, X. (1981). *Hoi prosdioristikoi paragontes tes gynaikeias symmetoches sto ergatiko dynamiko sten Hellada, 1961–1971*, (The Factors determining the Participation of Women in the Manpower in Greece, 1961–1971). PhD dissertation, Athens (xerox).

PETROGLOU, A. and SPILIOTOPOULOS, S. (1979). La protection de l'enfant en droit social, *Travaux de l'Association H. Capitant*, XXX, Paris, 1981.

Ministry of the Presidency (1978, 1981). *Statistical Bulletin for the Personnel of the Public Sector*. (In Greek).

SPILIOTOPOULOS-KOUKOULIS, S. (1980a). 'He rythmisi tes ergasias ton anelikon' (The regulation of minors' employment), in *Eklogi Thematon Koinonikis Pronoias*, issue No. 52, 53.

SPILIOTOPOULOS-KOUKOULIS, S., AGALLOPOULOS-ZERVOYANNIS, A. and PETROGLOU A. (1982). La position des femmes dans le droit du travail et la sécurité sociale, National report to the Xth Congress of the International Society for Labour Law and Social Security, Washington. (In press).

SPILIOTOPOULOS, S. (1982). La protection des jeunes au travail en Grèce (étude rédigée pour la Commission CEE). Athens (xerox).

SPILIOTOPOULOS-KOUKOULIS, S. (1980b, 1981, 1983). 'Oi‹›hypochreoseis ton kraton-melon tes Diethnous Organosis Ergasias kai e symvasi 100 gia ten isotita amoivon' (The obligations of the States-members of the ILO and convention 100 on equal remuneration), in *The Constitution*, vols 6, 7, 9. Athens.

TSOUKALAS, K. (1977). *Exartese kai anaparogoge. Ho koinonikos rolos ton ekpaideutikon mechanismon sten Hellada, (1830–1922)*. (Dependence and Reproduction. The Social Role of Educational Mechanisms in Greece, 1830–1922). Themelio, Athens.

VALTICOS, N. (1958). 'Monisme ou dualisme? Les rapports des traités et de la loi en Grèce (spécialement à propos des conventions internationales du travail)' in *Revue Hellènique de Droit International*, pp. 203–235. Athens.

VALTICOS, N. (1970). *Droit international du travail*. Paris.

VALTICOS N., (1983). *International Labour Law*, Holland.

ZERVAS, G. et. al., (1973). *Melete apographes drasterioteton cheirotechnias, oikotechnias kai kallitechnikes viotechnias* (Study of the Survey on Handicrafts, Cottage Industries and Art crafts). Athens.

Publications from the National Statistical Service of Greece (in Greek):
   National accounts of Greece, for the years 1948–75 and 1981.
   Results of the 1961 Census, 6 volumes.
   Results of the 1971 Census, 3 volumes.
   1981 unemployment sample survey.
   Statistical Yearbook (latest issue: for the year 1981).
   Yearly demographic statistics (latest issue: for the year 1979).
   Yearly statistics on education (last issue: for the academic year 1978–9).
   Yearly Survey on Employment in Urban and Semi-Urban Areas (latest issue: for the year 1980).

Note: This chapter has been completed in June 1984. Among subsequent developments is Law No 1414/1984 on sex equality in labour relations, which covers private law employment relations and liberal professions only. See comments thereon *S. Spiliotopoulos* and *A. Vayias* in Nomiko Vima, 1984.

Part II

Women at Work in Three European Countries

Women at Work
Edited by M.J. Davidson and C.L. Cooper
© 1984 John Wiley & Sons Ltd

Chapter 7
Women at Work in Sweden

Jeannie Scriven
University of East Anglia, Norwich, UK

INTRODUCTION

'We are clever in this country. There is discrimination, but they manage to cover it up'.

If one were writing about men at work (anywhere), the assumption would be that their dependants were all safely taken care of. In writing about women at work one is writing not only about their working lives, but about *all* aspects of their lives.

This chapter describes the position of women at work in Sweden. It has been written from an outsider's viewpoint, although hopefully many readers, both Swedish and non-Swedish, will find it interesting. It assesses the progress which women have so far achieved, and describes some of the concerns of Swedish women. Sweden is an important example for others seeking equality, since it is at the forefront of western countries in providing equality legislation. Equality for men and women is official government policy.

The findings of the chapter are based on official reports, on recent research, and on interviews with women in Sweden. It looks at legislation affecting women, training opportunities, working life, the visibility of women in Swedish life, and finally at the position of women in the 1980s. It ends with a consideration of the current debate concerning a proposal that a 'parent should stay at home to look after children', and future prospects for equality.

BACKGROUND INFORMATION

Sweden is the fourth-largest country in Europe, slightly larger than California, with a climate which ranges from very cold winters to warm summers, but milder than countries of corresponding latitudes such as Alaska and southern Greenland. Average temperatures in Stockholm are −3°C in

February and +17°C in July. Northern Sweden is famous for its midnight sun in summer, and the northern lights in winter. Sweden comprises thousands of lakes; half its surface is covered with forests. There is abundant hydroelectricity. A third of the population live in Gothenburg, Malmö, and Stockholm. Only 12% live in the five most northerly counties.

There are close links with other Scandinavian countries; Sweden is a member of the Nordic Council, and all members have reciprocal rights to move freely to jobs, obtain old age pensions, unemployment benefit, and other social services in any of the member countries.

Until industrialization Sweden was a poor peasant country. This instilled a spirit of self-sufficiency, particularly amongst women, since it was they who carried out all the household tasks whilst the men were away hunting or raiding. Sweden was not involved in either of the world wars; whilst other countries were suffering the trauma and upheaval of war, Sweden was developing peacefully into one of the world's leading industrialized nations.

In the nineteenth century women were allowed to go to university, and they had the same rights to inherit as men. In 1920 the Marriage Code put man and wife on an equal legal and economic footing. In 1921 women obtained the vote. Social reform in the thirties plus legislation prohibiting dismissal of women on grounds of engagement, marriage, pregnancy, or childbirth, were important steps forward. In the forties and fifties, whilst the rest of Europe was at war or trying to recover from its devastating effects, legislation made it easier for women to have a job and a family. Maternity leave was expanded, part-time work became available, and training for housewives wanting to work was initiated.

POPULATION

In the nineteenth century social unrest and poor harvests resulted in some 11.5% of the population emigrating between 1880 and 1893. In 1910 the population was 5.5 million, in 1955, 7.4 million, and by 1980, 8.3 million. Average life expectancy is high—78 for women and 72 for men; but there is a low birth rate—an average of 1.6 children per woman. Occupational activity is high; in the age group 16–64, 88% of men and 75% of women are economically active. Projections estimate that after 1986 there will be a decrease until the end of the century in the population.

Many men and women cohabit; they are regarded as being on a par with married couples both legally and socially. Also, 37% of all children born have unmarried parents. An 'average' Swedish household consists of fewer than three people; and 30% of all households consist of one person.

In the forties and fifties, Sweden developed rapidly. Extra manpower was needed to meet demand. This was met by encouraging women to go out to work, and to some extent by immigrant labour.

LABOUR MARKET POLICY

The overall aims of the government's economic policy are rapid growth, full employment, balace of payments, and equitable income distribution. The labour force is made up of about 2.3 million men and 1.8 million women. Women with children under 7 are the ones who have been joining the labour force in increasing numbers in the seventies.

In Swedish surveys no distinction is made between those who are 'employed' and those who are 'working' (that is, physically present at the time the survey was made). A large number of 'employed' people may be on leave from their jobs to study or to look after children. Every employee is legally entitled to take leave of absence from his or her job to study. It is relatively easy for people to move in and out of education for re-training, and also easier to re-enter the workforce.

SOCIAL LEGISLATION, EDUCATION, AND TRAINING

Social Insurance Schemes

Health insurance

All Swedish citizens and residents are insured under the national insurance act, which entitles them to allowances for medical expenses including dental, hospital, paramedical treatment, and visits to the doctor. There is no charge for advice on contraception. Some travel expenses will be refunded with respect to treatment, and also in order to visit dependants undergoing hospital treatment. Drugs prescribed are also subsidized.

Sickness benefit and parental insurance

Sickness benefit is normally 90% of earned income. Parental insurance provides benefit for 7 months in connection with childbirth, 1 month before the birth and 6 months after. These 6 months can be *divided between the two parents*. This encourages the shared responsibility for bringing up children. The payment is for 90% of earned income. It is also valid for adopting and foster-parents. In addition to the 6 months, a further 180 days benefit are payable at varying rates. These days may be taken at any time, beginning with delivery and ending with the *child's first year in school* (at the age of 7), and may be taken *by either parent*.

Paternity leave

Fathers are entitled to 10 days leave of absence with parental benefit at childbirth, even if the mother is receiving parental benefit for the same child at the same time.

Parental benefit

Parents who have to look after a child, and thus are not able to work, can receive parental benefit if:

(1) the child is ill;
(2) the childminder is ill;
(3) more children are born into the family (the father can receive parental benefit to stay at home and look after the children whilst the mother is in hospital);
(4) the child has to attend a child welfare clinic;
(5) The parent wants to visit the day care centre (1 whole day per year per parent).

Parental benefit entitlement is for 60 days a year for each child.

Pensions

The basic old age pension is currently payable at 95% of the base rate, approximately 16,000 Swedish kronor per year. (In addition to the basic pension, there are other benefits depending on the contributions made during the period of working life.) If both man and wife are pensioners, then it is 77% of the base rate, a combined pension of 26,000 Swedish kronor per year. It is also possible to obtain housing subsidy and the pension is usually exempt from tax. (These are the figures given for 1981.)

There are also schemes for disability pensions and allowances, widow's pension, children's pension, children's supplement (payable to any pensioner who has children under 16 living at home), and child care allowances (payable to parents nursing children under 16 at home). A wife's supplement may be paid to a woman married to a pensioner, provided she is 60 years old. This is the difference between the pension paid to two unmarried people and that paid to those who are married. There are schemes for pension supplements and earnings-related benefits.

Care of the aged

One factor affecting employment opportunities for women is the provision for the care of the elderly, since in most countries it is traditionally women who care for the aged. In Sweden local authorities organize social home help, which is free or costs very little. There is a special transport system for elderly or handicapped people who would otherwise find it difficult to move about unaided. The charge is the equivalent of the local bus fare. There is a huge welfare net for the elderly including sheltered housing and nursing homes. A summary of the social insurance schemes is presented in Table 7.1.

Family planning

Abortion

The main principle in the abortion act of 1975 is that the woman herself decides if an abortion is to be carried out. The act specifies:

(1) Abortion is free upon request up to the end of the eighteenth week of pregnancy.
(2) Before the twelfth week, the woman need only consult a doctor; thereafter she is required to discuss the matter with a social worker as well. The woman may be refused an abortion only if the operation involves a risk to her life or health.
(3) An abortion before the end of the eighteenth week may not be refused without review by the national Board of Health and Welfare.
(4) After the end of the eighteenth week of pregnancy the approval of the Board of Health and Welfare is necessary to obtain an abortion, and there must be special reasons. Such approval may not be granted if the foetus is judged to be viable.

In principle, contact with a social worker is compulsory after the twelfth week. Abortion counselling is also provided free. The effect of the act is that since 1970 there have been no illegal abortions in Sweden. The number of abortions carried out each year has remained constant (see Table 7.2).

It is unofficially estimated that abortions cost 30 million Swedish kronor per year, and it is also rumoured that privately some doctors are furious about this 'misuse' of medical expertise. But is is said that doctors do not dare to express this opinion publicly.

Table 7.1 *Summary of social insurance schemes*

HEALTH INSURANCE *Allowances for medical expenses*	*Sickness benefit*	BASIC PENSION *Main benefits*	*Special benefits*	SUPPLEMENTARY PENSION
Care by a doctor Dental care Care at a hospital Paramedical treatment Travel expenses Drugs	Sickness benefit Voluntary sickness benefit Parental benefit	Old-age pension Disability pension Widow's pension Children's pension	Children's supplement Disability allowance Child care allowance Wife's supplement Municipal housing subsidy Pension supplement Partial pension	Old-age pension Disability pension Widow's pension Children's pension
WORK INJURIES INSURANCE Allowances for medical expenses Sickness benefit Life annuity Death benefit			UNEMPLOYMENT INSURANCE Daily benefit Labour market support	

Table 7.2   *Number of abortions and abortion rates*

Year	Number of abortions	Abortion rate per 1000	
		Total population	Women 15–44 years
1975	32,500	4.0	20.2
1977	31,460	3.8	19.2
1979	34,700	4.1	20.2
1980	34,800	4.1	20.1
1981	33,090	3.8	19.3

Source: Central Bureau of Statistics (1982).

However, the statistics presented in Table 7.3 show that teenage abortions and teenage pregnancies have decreased.

Table 7.3   *Teenage pregnancies, per thousand—women aged 15–19*

Year	Pregnancy rate	Birth rate	Abortion rate
1973	54.3	31.1	23.2
1975	57.4	28.8	28.6
1977	47.1	22.1	25.0
1979	39.1	17.3	21.8
1980	37.0	15.7	21.3
1981	31.6	15.0	20.6

Source: Central Bureau of Statistics (1982).

Family planning services

The service aims to use preventive measures as the first resort, and abortion as an emergency; each individual has the right to decide on the number and spacing of children. Efforts are made on three fronts:

(1) family planning and advisory services;
(2) reduced-cost contraceptives;
(3) information.

Sterilization is available to men and women on request (see Table 7.4).

Equality legislation

The Act on Equality between Women and Men at Work came into force in

Table 7.4 *Number of sterilizations*

Year	Men	Women	Total
1976	2,122	2,311	4,433
1978	1,935	3,981	5,916
1980	3,345	6,857	10,202

Source: Central Bureau of Statistics (1982).

1980. It aims to promote equal rights as regards work, working conditions, and opportunities for self-fulfilment in employment. Both the public and private sectors are covered by the act, and it is aimed at employers. A government-appointed Equal Opportunities Ombudsman is responsible for ensuring compliance with the act, which has two main parts. One part contains rules on the prohibition of discrimination on grounds of sex, and the other deals with active measures to promote equality. Furthermore, there is provision for an Equal Opportunities Commission, as well as rules governing sanctions and procedures.

The ban on discrimination means that an employer may not disfavour an employee or job-seeker on the grounds of his or her sex. Exceptions are made for what is known as the favourable treatment of the under-represented sex, and also for the furtherance of ideological or other special interests.

An employer who contravenes the ban can, in certain cases, be sentenced to payment of compensation. Disputes on discrimination on grounds of sex will normally be tried by the Labour Court. The obligation of an employer to take active measures to promote equality implies that the employer shall make planned and goal-oriented efforts to further equality in the work-place in proportion to the resources available.

The Ombudsman intervenes firstly with persuasion; only if employers do not voluntarily comply with the rules is the case referred to the Labour Court. The Ombudsman is also responsible for informing the public and helping to mould public opinion. The law applies only to employment. It does not affect other areas of ordinary life. This gives rise to the suspicion that government commitment to equality is far from total.

All the political parties have some form of equality programme, and most unions have equality officers. There are also organizations such as the Fredrika Bremer Association which are active in equality work. Officially, women have the same civil rights as men.

Divorce

A divorce takes 3 weeks if both parties are agreed, and if there are no children under 16 involved. Otherwise there is a 6-month 'consideration' period, during which the parties may continue to live together. There is provision for shared custody. If a parent fails to maintain his/her child after divorce, then the state guarantees a minimum level of subsistence.

Child care provision

In 1973 Parliament ratified a law on pre-schooling, which came into force in 1975. The aim of pre-schooling is defined as being 'in close collaboration with the home, to foster an all-round character development and a favour-able physical and social development in children'. The act obliged local authorities to earmark places in nurseries and day care centres for all 6-year-olds, and for other pre-school children who have special need of stimulus and support. The act was changed in 1977 to cover children aged up to 12 years old. Local authorities must make sure that children of studying/working parents obtain child care places.

Table 7.5   *Provision of child care places in proportion to the number of children aged 0–12*

	Day nursery	Percentage of all children	Family day care home	Percentage of all children	After-school places	Percentage of all children
1975	76,100	10	50,800	7	24,500	4
1977	102,200	14	64,800	9	35,000	5
1982	179,300	26	81,900	12	76,600	12

Source: Central Bureau of Statistics (1982).

In 1976 an expansion programme was planned to provide an extra 100,000 new nursery places and 50,000 after-school places, and the government sharply increased its subsidies towards the costs of operating such centres. By 1982 26% of all pre-school children have a place in a child care centre, or are looked after by a community-employed childminder. (This is a third of all pre-school children whose parents are either studying or working.) Although by 1982, 12% of all 7–12-year-old children had places in after-school centres, this represents only 6% of all 7–12-year-olds whose parents are either studying or working (see Table 7.5).

Child care centres are financed by the local authority with the help of government subsidies and fees paid by parents. They are staffed by trained nurses and pre-school teachers. The ratio of adults to children is 1 to 4. The centres are usually open from 06.30 to 18.30 hours. Fees vary from area to area, depending on the policy in force. Payment may be on a sliding scale according to income. There are usually waiting lists for places.

Private child care centres are also available. However, the 'deal' can often be that not only do parents sometimes have to pay a large deposit on taking up a place, but they also have to work a few days a week at the centre, and perhaps take on administrative duties. This sort of arrangement penalizes the mother, since it is more likely to be her who does this unpaid work, therefore freeing the father for full-time work, or else overworking herself. Jonung (1978) argues that child care:

may in fact reinforce the division [in the workforce] because pressure on men to share the child care is reduced, making it possible for male career patterns to survive and delaying any restructuring of work life . . . Most women do not wish to leave their young children in day care centres the many hours that are required in full-time jobs and even more so in career positions. A one-sided push for day care centres with no change in working conditions will probably mean that women will remain in female occupations, in inferior positions, and in part-time jobs.'

Quality of child care

It has been argued—even by those in favour of child care—that the quality of child care provided by local authorities is not good enough. They maintain that there are too many employed in these centres who do not actually like children, and they point to the high rate of turnover of the staff involved. There are also very few men employed in these centres—since affection by men towards young children is still regarded with some suspicion by some members of the public. But these criticisms are only expressed by very few.

Equality-promoting projects

The government has earmarked a special fund of 1 million kronor to pay for equality-promoting measures in government departments and agencies. The national telecommunications administration has carried out a 2-year pilot project intended to persuade members of the under-represented sex to apply for jobs dominated by the opposite sex. Some non-commissioned careers in the armed forces have been opened up to women. The state-owned mining company in Kiruna in the north of Sweden has taken measures to get women into men's jobs. Currently some 5% of underground miners are women, although they do not necessarily do the 'heaviest' work. Some have argued that this scheme was introduced to keep good (male) miners in their jobs; with highly-paid jobs open to their wives, families would choose to stay in a remote part of the country (with severe weather conditions for a large part of the year), rather than moving to a different part of the country. And there does appear to have been some hostility by some men towards the scheme.

In 1977 the Volvo Motor company in central Sweden used positive discrimination to provide women with the chance to aspire to skilled positions. Although a quarter of the work force were women, few had skilled jobs. None of the 'foremen' were women. A programme of advanced training was formulated, and advertised to women already employed by the company. Consequently, 39 women out of a total of 500 applied, and eventually 17 were accepted. Those not accepted were approached individually about some alternative form of training.

The training project aimed to alter the labour situation for women, and to accommodate individual needs and aspirations. It was hoped that women selected would provide a good example for other women workers to follow in the future. Westlander (1983) found that supervisors, who had not been consulted in the formulation of the programme, were more sceptical of its success. The 17 women were given the opportunity to attain men's conditions (whether or not this was actually what the women perceived as being desirable). They took part in the project in order to obtain more stimulating work. Many (male) engineering workers thought that the scheme was unfair; but most of the women involved thought that management should make more training opportunities available to them. What the training course *did* achieve, however, was to make the women aware of their subordinate position within the firm. But that did not diminish their commitment to progressing with their careers.

There is also a government 'equality subsidy' available—an employer who provides training for women in typically male occupations (or vice-versa) can get a wage subsidy for each hour of training. However, internal recruitment is excluded, and there has to be a shortage of suitably skilled workers. If men are available for the job, then there is no subsidy available for training women.

Education and training

Comprehensive school

There is compulsory education between the ages of 7 and 16, which is carried out at a comprehensive school. The goals set for this period are 'to impart knowledge and train skills, to foster all-round personal development and to prepare for increasing involvement and social responsibility'. Classes may not exceed 25 between the ages of 7 and 10, and not more than 30 between the ages of 10 and 16. There is free transport to school, if required, and free school meals.

Secondary school

After comprehensive school, students may elect to study at an integrated upper secondary school. About 85% of comprehensive school-leavers do so. Education at secondary school is aimed to complement what students will be doing when they leave, and thus is vocationally orientated. There are no charges for fees, and books and meals are provided free.

Students may choose to study one of the following three 'lines':

(1) arts and social studies;
(2) economics and commercial subjects;
(3) scientific and technical subjects.

Each 'line' lasts for between 2 and 4 years. Availability of places in different 'lines' may be limited, and students' preferences are often linked to current employment prospects. Since temporary relief jobs and unemployment schemes are not available for those under 18, there has been an increase in the take-up of places at secondary school level.

Girls tend to pick shorter 'lines' than boys, and there is a marked difference

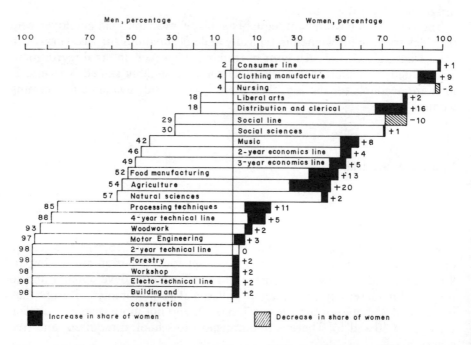

Figure 7.1 Choice of secondary school 'lines' in 1977, and change since 1971 (*Source*: SO report P1 1977:1; SCR Statistical Bulletins U 1978–9)

in the choice of subject; this is particularly true of those from non-professional backgrounds and is clearly illustrated in Figure 7.1. Most boys choose scientific , engineering, technical, and construction 'lines', whilst girls opt for the traditional 'female' lines such as nursing, consumer education, clerical work, liberal arts, and social studies.

University and tertiary education

Women make up almost half of all the students at university. In 1977 the rules for admission were changed, so that credit points for admission could be obtained for applicants over 25 years old, who have more than 5 years' work experience. Caring for one's children is regarded as work experience. This is obviously an encouragement for women to attend.

Choice of subject is, once again, largely determined by sex. Figure 7.2 shows that choices made in secondary school are perpetuated at tertiary level. The Figure shows that women are making inroads into typically male subjects, and men are encroaching into traditionally 'female' subjects. Another form of alternative vocational education is provided by tertiary schools. Women predominate here because most cater for training for such jobs as nursing and teaching. Credit points for admission can be gained for work with non-profit organizations such as parent–teacher associations.

Adult education

Women make up almost 70% of those enrolled in municipal adult education, such as evening classes, and they are also in the majority at the institution known as the Folk High School. The official manpower training programme for the unemployed is taken up both by men and women, but—as in secondary education—choice of subject is usually along 'traditional' lines. This is also reflected in study circles which are organized by local educational associations.

Staff training programmes

About a quarter of all employees, both in the private and public sectors, take part in staff-training programmes. Women are under-represented on them, as are immigrants. Women manage to be allocated places on shorter courses concerned with trade union activities, whilst on longer and more professional courses men predominate.

Grants and financial aid

Students who need financial help for university or college receive a non-

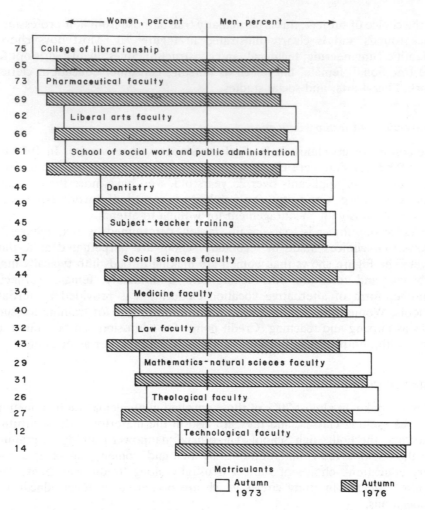

Figure 7.2 First-year enrolments at universities and colleges, 1973 and 1976
(*Source*: UKA report 1975:10; SMU 77:32)

repayable grant from the central government and a repayable local loan. For graduate students there are a number of special grants available.

WORKING LIFE

Taxation

In 1971 a system of taxation was introduced which taxed individuals rather than family units. This change encouraged women to work, since with a sharply progressive taxation system it is advantageous to have two wage-earners in a family. (Unearned income, for example from investments, is jointly taxed.) The disadvantage of individual taxation is that housing subsidies and child care charges are calculated against 'family' income, which includes both wage-earners. As a result it is often not worthwhile for a woman to work full-time, as the extra income after tax is offset by increased payments elsewhere. Opinion is divided as to whether individual taxation enhances equality.

Full-time and part-time work

Hours of work are defined as full-time (more than 35 hours per week), long part-time (20–34 hours per week) and short part-time (1–19 hours per week). Forty-five per cent of women work part-time compared with 5% of men. Part-time work is usual for women with young children; conversely, men with small children work longer hours than men the same age without children. Two factors lie behind these statistics—lack of child care facilities and the fact that women do most of the work in the home.

As can be seen from Figure 7.3, it is women who avail themselves of part-time work. Part-time work caters for short-term needs such as child care facilities; if a parent works part-time, then the children do not have to spend long hours at a child care centre. But as Figure 7.3 clearly shows, only 5% of men do *not* work full-time. Women work part-time in order to allow men to work full-time. In so doing they pay a price. When they retire they will receive a lower supplementary pension, they are less likely to be promoted, and they will have lower status. Opportunities to be influential at work also diminish, such as the chance to take part in union activities or discussion groups to alter conditions at work. By working part-time, women confine themselves to the lower-paid, more routine 'female' jobs.

If less than 22 hours per week are worked, inferior social benefits follow. It is also more difficult to assert one's right to staff training opportunities, and to be influential at work. A law has been passed which makes it possible for parents of children under 8 to work reduced hours with corresponding loss of pay; but it is the mothers who take this option. As has been mentioned before, fathers with young children work correspondingly longer hours than men without young children. There are grounds for assuming, therefore, that it is the division of labour in the home that makes it hard for women to progress at work; at the same time it allows employers to impose demands on men to work overtime, to go on business trips, and to attend other after-hours activities.

Women as Managers

As long as employers (usually men) have an image of the 'committed' execu-

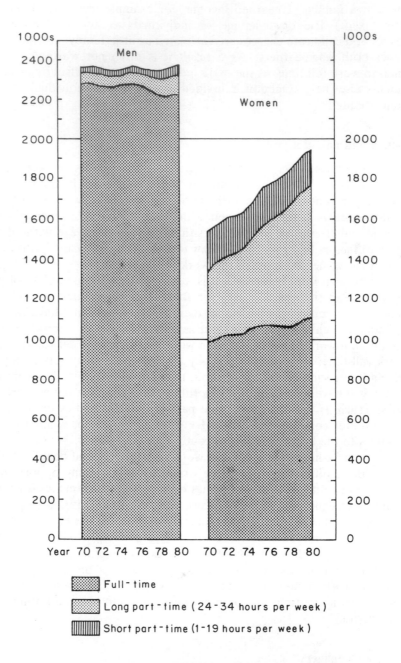

Figure 7.3 Men and women at work, 1970–80: full-time and part-time (*Source*: Central Bureau of Statistics, 1981)

tive who works long hours as the ideal company worker, then women will find it difficult to be accepted in a managerial position. And this is borne out by the fact that few women are managers, particularly in the private sector (see Table 7.6). This is at odds with recent research which suggests that women have a managerial style which suits the needs of business and society in the future (Wistrand, 1981).

Table 7.6 *Percentages of women as managers in private and municipal employment (women in selected positions)*

Private employment	
Routine tasks	61
Less independent work	27
Fairly independent work	9
Independent work	2
Executive position	0.2
Municipal employment	
Social services assistant	69
Social services inspector	22
Department head	20
Social services director	9

Source: Wistrand (1981).

At the very time when women are at last managing to break through into managerial positions there appears to be a move towards rejecting extra responsibility in the work-place amongst those who can choose to take up executive positions. Wistrand (1981) argues:

A particular problem for women who would like to advance in their organizations is that it is becoming increasingly common in Sweden to regard being a manager and taking on more qualified work assignments as somehow 'negative'. One often hears that it is getting harder and harder to find people who want to be leaders. It is even said that those women are smart who refrain from accepting high positions, since they involve a lot more work without correspondingly greater benefits in terms of money or job satisfaction. Ironically enough, now that the time finally seems ripe for accepting women as leaders, many no longer consider it a desirable goal!

Women are needed in managerial positions to 'open doors' for other women lower down in the organization. Could it be that this suggestion causes women to question their own motives, and may in fact deter some from success?

Segregation by Occupation

The choice of 'lines' right back at secondary school, and perpetuated at tertiary level, provides the key to the employment of women in the work

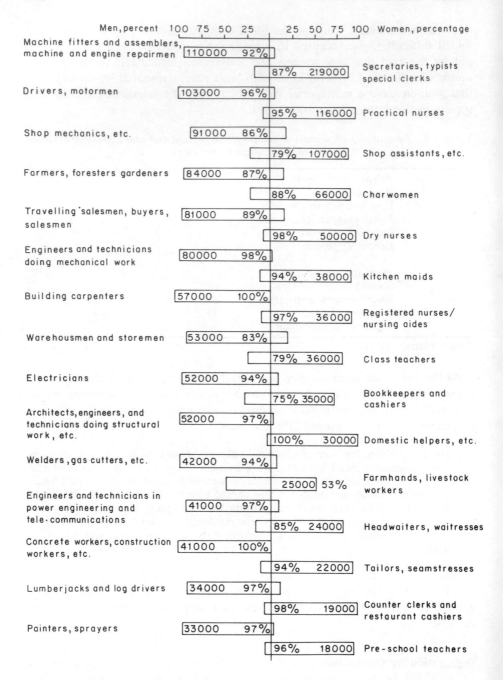

Figure 7.4 The most common occupation for men and women, 1975 (*Source*: Central Bureau of Statistics, 1976)

force. The increase in work participation which took place in the 1970s was in 'women's' work and also mostly in the public sector—in office work, health and medical care, and teaching. Figure 7.4 shows this segregation by occupation.

It is suggested that women have only come to play an important role in the Swedish labour force because there has been a shortage of labour; this implies that as soon as there is a surplus of labour, then the 'last in, first out' principle applies. Removing women from the work force is one way of reducing unemployment.

Not only are women segregated by occupation, but also by position and earnings in occupations where they compete on an equal footing. Teaching has long been regarded as a 'female' occupation. If we look at the different categories of teachers presented in Table 7.7 for example, we find that men dominate the higher positions.

Table 7.7   *Sex distribution in different categories of teachers, 1980*

	Women	Men
Class teachers, grades 1–3	98.8	1.2
Class teachers, grades 4–6	64.1	35.9
Subject teachers	50.1	49.9
Subject teachers with PhD	14.4	85.6
Study directors	24.6	75.4
Principals	8.7	91.3
Local superintendents of education	2.9	97.1

Source: Central Bureau of Statistics (1981).

Although there is equal pay, women still earn wages and salaries which are lower than men's (see Table 7.8).

Table 7.8   *Women's pay level in 1977—white-collar workers women's average pay, if men's = 100)*

Executive position	87
Independent work	88
Fairly independent work	90
Less independent work	93
Routine tasks	93
Other routine tasks	96

Source: Central Bureau of Statistics (1978).

Currently women are going into men's jobs because the traditional 'female' areas in the public sector are no longer recruiting. Jonung (1978) maintains that this entry is because no other jobs are available.

RESPONSIBILITY FOR THE HOME

In spite of equality legislation, it is still women who are *primarily* responsible for the home and for caring for the children. The shortage of child care facilities remains a barrier to women taking a more active part in working life. In a survey made in 1974, households where both worked full-time were asked about chores in the home. The results are illustrated in Table 7.9.

Table 7.9

Percentage of households	Task done by women
100	All laundry
70	All preparation of food
55	All cleaning
53	All shopping
50	All dishwashing

Source: National Board of Health and Welfare, Levnadsförhållander (1976).

An investigation of 100 families with children in Stockholm in 1977 showed that even when women worked fewer hours, their total hours of work inclusive of household chores were longer than men's (73 hours per week as against 66 for men). Most men undertake on average half the number of household duties when compared to women. It is not surprising that women have little spare time or energy to make career 'breaks'. Jonung (1978) argues:

changing the sexual division of the work force requires changing the sexual division of work in the home, such that it becomes as common for the man to bear the home responsibilities as for the woman to do it.

She continues:

Sexual equality requires changing the role of men as well as the role of women. As long as men do not assume their share of the duties at home, women will not be able to compete in the market on equal conditions with men. This requires changing working life and child care patterns so that children no longer are costless to father while costing mother most of their advancement opportunities. Equality in the labour market requires an equal participation by men in work in the home.

Jonung and Thordarsson (1980) maintain that 'women have, in fact, not left the home. They still bear the main home responsibilities and carry that burden with them out into the market.'

SWEDISH LIFE AND THE VISIBILITY OF WOMEN

To the casual visitor, Sweden seems very egalitarian. Women are visible as police officers, passport control officers, and bus drivers; women are also very active in the many sporting activities—skating and skiing in winter, for example, and tennis and swimming in summer. There is great emphasis on keeping fit, and about a quarter of the population belong to sporting associations.

Sweden also seems a very 'safe' country to the visitor. Speed restrictions on roads are strictly adhered to. The Swedish government is even considering introducing legislation to make the wearing of rear-seat belts in vehicles compulsory. Open-air skaters carry emergency equipment with them in case they or someone else falls through the ice. It is against this egalitarianism and 'safety' that great emphasis is placed both in the educational system and in society on the 'social responsibility' of each individual. Caring for others is part of this ethos. Women, therefore, find it easy to do jobs which reflect the value of society, such as nursing and teaching.

Women appear to take more part in public life than in other western countries. Many newsreaders and reporters on television are women; in provincial newspapers there are reports and pictures of women active in Swedish life, as well as pages specifically earmarked for features on women. Men can be seen pushing prams and in charge of children in supermarkets.

Political and Union Life

Politics is often conducted on terms dictated by 'unliberated' men. Those men who take their full share of family responsibilitiy have no time for politics. They are helping to care for the home and children (Wistrand, 1981).

Under the proportional representation system as practised in Sweden, women stand a far better chance of being elected than under the British 'first past the post' system. The number of seats in Parliament is calculated according to the number of votes each party receives. For the first time, women outnumbered men in exercising their right to vote in 1976 (see Table 7.10).

Table 7.10 *Voting behaviour in men and woman, 1970 and 1976 (percentages)*

Year	Men	Women	Difference
1970	90.4	89.0	1.4
1976	93.9	94.3	0.4

Source: Wistrand (1981)

At present approximately 25% of the seats in the Swedish Parliament are held by women. This proportion is one of the highest internationally. The spread is fairly evenly distributed between the parties, as can be seen by examining Table 7.11.

Table 7.11   *Women Members of Parliament (percentages) 1979*

Moderate Party (conservative)	21.9
Liberal Party (Fp)	23.7
Centre	31.3
Social Democrats	27.3
Left Party Communists	25.0

Source: B. Wistrand (1981)

In 1983 there were four women cabinet ministers out of a total of 20 ministries—those of Health, Employment, Higher Education, and Energy. For the first time a women held a post which is traditionally a 'male' area—that of energy. Although a quarter of the Members of Parliament are women, only 15–19% of the Members of the Standing Committees are women. These committees vet all proposals which are taken up in Parliament and only on three occasions have these been chaired by women.

Again the proportion of elected women Members of Parliament failed to be reflected in the membership of Cabinet-appointed commissions. Women's participation rates were 15% on average. Many members of commissions are nominated by interest groups, which are not covered by the Equality Act. Women make up approximately 7% of government agency membership and about 2% of directors of trading agencies and state-owned industries.

At local level the proportion of women in decision-making bodies varies between 14 and 31%. Women are generally better represented in the party executives than they are in Parliament, although they are not often elected as officials (see Figure 7.5). Women make up approximately 1% of the membership of the Swedish Employers Federation, and only rarely does a woman ever become one of the 62 deputy members. Few women are to be found at the top of business firms. They are very poorly represented in unions; they have crept into the lower positions but very rarely make it to the top. Whilst making up 30–46% of the members in 1976, less than 20% of members of union boards were women, and less than 10% made it to chairman level.

It is said that the home milieu teaches women to play a conciliatory role; they are not conditioned to make demands. Avoidance of conflict forms an integral part of the traditional female role. Women are often not prepared to violate the traditional role, and research indicates that they find it difficult to assert themselves in non-supportive company (Wistrand, 1981).

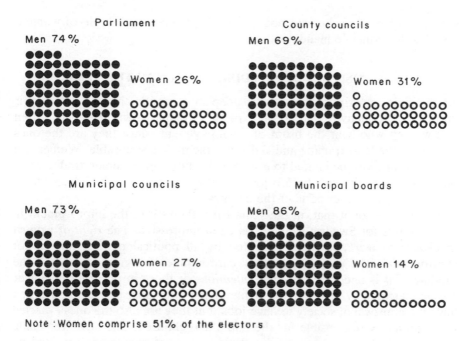

Note : Women comprise 51% of the electors

Figure 7.5 Distribution of women and men in decision-making bodies, 1979
(*Source*: Fredrika Bremer Association)

The Media

Currently legislation is being considered which would ban sexual discrimination in advertising. Job advertisements are no longer accepted by newspapers if they discriminate between men and women. In 1978, women made up 33% of the membership of the Swedish Journalists Union; but top positions were again filled by men, and nearly all news evaluators were men.

The National Committee on Equality (1979) reported that 'the mass media have a built-in conserving effect because they mirror the society we have and the role patterns which equality-promoting work seeks to change'. One of the charges which can be made against advertising is that it reflects an 'ideal' world (ideal for those making the advertisement) and projects images which are often not valid now. Appealing to consumers overrides all other considerations. Sex roles in advertising do not necessarily reflect sex roles in society.

In 1976 Swedish Radio, together with its union, arranged a project whereby women could train for technical jobs, and men could learn to type. Managers were trained in equality work. This project affected long-term personnel policy and programme policy. Legislation put forward in 1977 in the Radio Act included the general principle that the equal worth of all human beings should be protected, but did not specifically single out the role of women, nor was the principle mandatory.

THE POSITION OF SWEDISH WOMEN IN THE 1980s

At the time of writing, the west is deep in recession. New technology is improving productivity, but at the expense of employment prospects. Often it is women who bear the brunt of unemployment, since they are the ones who, with the least training and skills, are the most dispensable. Women are also more likely to be limited to a specific locality, since women traditionally put family commitments before jobs; they are unable to take advantage of new openings in other parts of the country.

There is no doubt that, in the years from 1960–1980, the improvement in formal rights for Swedish women has been impressive. The *right of women to choose to work* has been accepted by all political parties, and is not controversial. The provision of child care is taken for granted, even if the funding of it is under debate. The *intentions* of those in positions of power are unquestionably to foster the rights of the individual in society. Women have the approval of society to have jobs, but they are also the ones *expected* to be primarily responsible for the home and children. The advances made by women in formal rights and legislation have not been complemented by a shift in attitude and behaviour by men (and opinion-makers). It is very tough for women; they are expected to be as good as, if not better than, men at work, to take responsibility for the home and children, perhaps act as a supportive partner, and lead an active social life as well. Yet it is more likely that career women themselves need to be the recipients of support rather than the traditional providers of support. The 'intellectual' idea of the rights of women to play an active part in society has implications for men; it requires a change in behaviour from passive to active role *in the home*.

THE CURRENT DEBATE

In late 1982, and early 1983, there were suggestions from the opposition Moderate Party that parents might be paid to stay at home to look after children, since the cost of child care provision was so high. The 'parent' staying at home would receive 40 Swedish kronor per day for doing so. This suggestion resulted in rumours in other European countries that women in Sweden were 'choosing' to return to the home; but this rumour does not even begin to mirror the truth. The economic recession has made employment difficult both for men and women, but women have been particularly hard hit.

Politicians, usually men, cleverly try to mask unemployment; they declare that 'women are choosing to stay at home'. The truth is that politicians want to rid themselves of any guilt feelings about unemployment. Somehow it is 'all right' for women to be unemployed and to stay at home (since this is where they have traditionally been), but not all right for men to be unemployed and also stay at home. So female unemployment is explained away as a 'return to the home'. But if the *only* choice for women is unemployment and staying at home, then that is no 'return to the home'. It is simply window dressing to disguise the true unemployment position. It is a direct result of the economic recession that the suggestion is made that a 'parent' should stay at home to look after children. When there was a lack of labour in the fifties and sixties, women and immigrant labour were used to meet that shortage. Now that there is a surplus of labour, the 'suggestion' is made that a 'parent' should stay at home to look after the children.

The shallowness, and indeed the short-sightedness, of the suggestion does not fool many; women who have had to fight to obtain and keep jobs will not easily relinquish their rights.

The party currently in power, the Social Democrats under Olof Palme, are in favour of organized child care. It expands the public sector and therefore increases the Social Democrats' share of the vote. Those employed in child care centres can quite reasonably be expected to vote for the party that created their jobs and is committed to retaining them. The opposition party maintains that child care provision is expensive. They wish to find alternative ways to provide it. In so doing they will trim down the potential Social Democrat vote, and cut expenditure in the public sector.

But in making the suggestion that a 'parent' should stay at home to look after children, and be paid 40 Swedish kronor per day, the opposition party are clever enough not to mention that they are in fact *realistically* talking about women. It is normally women who would be 'expected' to stay at home; and as we have seen, it is women who earn the lowest wages and are more likely to lose jobs through the effects of the recession and updating machinery. But in avoiding making a distinction between men and women, the opposition party cleverly disguises the unspoken discrimination which their suggestion puts forward. When interviewed on television the leader of the Moderate Party was asked if he wanted to see a return to the system of au-pair girls and nannies again? He deviously replied—why not au-pair boys? It must be admitted that there is awareness by politicians of the equality issue; but this does not make this particular proposal less discriminatory.

In fact, the suggestion only goes to show how vulnerable the advances made by women in the recent past are. The equality act deals only with work. Other aspects of women's lives are subject to the vagaries of economics, public opinion, and traditional attitudes. In times of turbulence—and the eighties will surely be so—women's rights can easily be viewed by those in positions of power (mostly men) as expendable and a product of affluence. The *effects* of the equality act are difficult if not impossible to evaluate; and it is said that in Sweden reforms are evaluated in terms of money (men's values?). The benefits of equality are not easily visible. There is no *clear* difference in productivity between businesses or services with a large proportion of women, and those with few or none. This is because even where the majority of employees are women, those who hold the top positions are men. And if there *were* a marked difference it could be that it would be attributed to something other than the effect of the participation of women.

In times of turbulence it is far easier to adhere to traditional value systems, since they do not require time and energy to rethink and re-evaluate. The creation of new jobs requires immense effort, innovation, time, and energy. It is far easier for politicians to resort to traditional attitudes and suggest that the so-called second wage-earner/'parent' be released from the job market to stay at home and look after children than to radically innovate and respond to the needs of *all* the population and prepare for skilled manpower requirements in the future.

Yet a politician need only look at current statistics which show that a third of Swedish households/families are made up of one person to see that the old-fashioned idea of a second wage-earner is not necessarily valid. The rumour that 'in Sweden women are choosing to return to the home' is *factually incorrect*: it is true that unemployment has affected women more than men (as it has in the European Community) but there are no indications to support the suggestion that women are opting out of the labour market. On the contrary, once having entered the work force, women are very reluctant to give up their new-found power and careers. What women are discovering, however, is that there is *invisible* prejudice against women. It is men who are in control of promotion, of research grants, and it is men who are the 'gatekeepers' in working life. As a result, women are demanding a reassessment of working life, hours of work, child care provision and domestic duties.

The role of women

Swedish women are expected to perform three roles—those of career woman, mother, and partner. They have to juggle with the varying commitments of family, household and career. In comparison, the position of some career women in America (as outlined in Chapter 10) seems enviable. There they choose to concentrate on their careers until their 30s, by which time they are in a position at work to dictate working conditions to suit them. Once at the top of their profession, they then decide to have children, secure in their ability to continue with their career *on their terms*, and secure in their ability to buy in first-class child care.

It can be argued that, in Sweden, working life is dominated by men's values, whilst home and family commitments are based on women's value systems. This conflict can cause stress, added to which there is the notion of 'social responsibility', and a lifestyle which may involve the running of a small second home in the country.

CONCLUSIONS

The progress that Swedish women have made for their rights has reached a critical stage. The current economic recession has called into question previously accepted ideals and aims. What passed as desirable and indeed worthy may, in the harsh economic conditions of the 1980s, be considered a luxury and beyond the resources of a 'realistic' government. Thus the progress which women have made is likely to be increasingly under attack, especially in areas where it is seen to 'cost' money.

Although the *labour market policy* is that *everyone* should have the right to a job, the recession has nonetheless affected women more than men. *Pension* and *social insurance schemes* are geared to meet the requirements of the full-time, full-life worker, and not designed or flexible enough for those who take time out to have children or work part-time.

Lack of *child care provision* also affects women's ability to participate fully in the job market. The *choice of subject* to be studied at secondary school provides the key to the employment prospects of women. Until and unless this barrier is broken down, *before the vital choices are made*, then women will continue to be segregated by occupation, and will not make inroads into the male-dominated areas of employment. This requires a tremendous effort, since behaviour is determined by attitudes, which in turn are influenced both by rational and irrational feelings.

Equality-promoting projects, although laudable in breaking down barriers and providing examples for others to follow, come at *too late a stage*. Decisions are made early in life, and qualifications are difficult to achieve without a great deal of sacrifice later in life. It is often too late to alter career patterns, and therefore gain entry into professions where women are under-represented. Women make career decisions which are more likely to be short-term; they also choose to take shorter educational courses, preferring to earn money rather than spend longer studying. *Dissemination of the consequences of career choice* is one area where efforts should be made to alter the segregation which is found in Swedish working life.

Women have the same *legal* and *political* rights as men. They also play an important part in the cultural life of the country, and have initiated many activities which cut across traditional boundaries. They have also taken a practical stance in promoting the cause of equality. The Women's Centre in Stockholm, for instance, runs on the premise that 'there is no blueprint for liberation'. It is currently seeking finance for a project to demystify computers. The plan is for women computer technicians to dismantle a computer, so that women with no formal education or training can learn to use a computer as a tool, and not be intimidated by the technical jargon and mystiques which have grown up round it.

It is quite acceptable for women to play their part in society without having to rely on men, and discrimination in any overt form is not sanctioned by the government or its agencies. But what is needed is not only passive acceptance of the case for equality by those in positions of power, but *active commitment* to it, particularly by men. This would encourage others to behave more positively, without fearing that they were showing 'weakness', or acting in a way which was not accepted by society. For women to be able to play their part in society on the same terms as men requires a change in attitudes, in social stereotyping, and also in expectations. Men often fear that supporting equality will reveal themselves as vulnerable and imperfect—yet fail to realize that it is imperfections which make people interesting. Men who are unwilling to reassess both themselves and others and *accept this change*, can quite easily undermine efforts to promote equality. The 'intellectual' support of equality without attendant changes in attitude and behaviour can be very destructive and stress-inducing.

Men must also expect to sacrifice some of their career prospects in order to care for *their* children, and take responsibility for *their* homes. Only when women are relieved of half of this burden can they expect to compete at work on the same terms as men.

In spite of these reservations and criticisms, women in other western countries can only be envious of the facilities available, and the progress made by women in Sweden. However, Swedish women feel that the future does not promise much in the way of equality legislation to cover areas other than working life; they feel that progress already made will also come under attack. Different women's groups, such as political groups and anti-nuclear groups, are pulling in different directions. Yet now is the time for *consolidation*, for a gradual whittling away at the power areas where women are almost ignored, and a strengthening of areas where women have gained influence. Some women are angry and in a hurry, and feel that they have waited too long, whilst others are sympathetic to the difficult 'transitional' stage of men. It is easy for those seeking equality to become polarized and break up into small, ineffective groups.

But Sweden's achievement *is* an example to others. Provided that there is a change in the traditional choices made by girls at school, there is no doubt that, by the end of the century, the qualities and capabilities which women possess will no longer be a neglected asset in many areas of Swedish life.

ACKNOWLEDGEMENTS

I should like to acknowledge the help of Mona Eliasson, Christina Jonung,

Eva Rossell, and Gunella Westlander, and to thank the Principal and staff of the Henley Management College for their Women's Scholarship scheme.

REFERENCES

National Committee on Equality between Men and Women (1979). *Step by Step: National Plan of Action for Equality*. Stockholm.

Jonung, C. (1978). 'Sexual equality in the Swedish labour market', *Monthly Labour Review*, **101** (10).

Jonung, C., and Thordarsson, B. (1980). 'Women returning to work: Sweden', in Yohalem, A. M. (ed.), *Women Returning to Work*, pp. 107–159.

Westlander, G. (1978). *Conclusions of Some Empirical Studies on the Present Personnel Policy for More Equal Treatment of Men and Women in some Swedish Enterprises*. International Congress of Applied Psychology, Munich.

Westlander, G. (1983). *Equality of the Sexes in an Organizational Perspective*. Evaluation of a training project for women factory workers. National Board of Occupational Health and Safety, Stockholm.

Wistrand, B. (1981). *Swedish Women on the Move*. The Swedish Institute, Stockholm.

Statistical Sources
Fredrika Bremer Association, Stockholm.
National Board of Health and Welfare (1976), Levnadsförhållanden.
National Committee on Equality between Men and Women (1979), Stockholm.
The Central Bureau of Statistics (1977–1983), Stockholm.
The Swedish Consulate, Hamburg.
The Swedish Institute, Stockholm.

Women at Work
Edited by M.J. Davidson and C.L. Cooper
© 1984 John Wiley & Sons Ltd

Chapter 8
Women at Work in Finland

Kaisa Kauppinen-Toropainen,
Elina Haavio-Mannila, and
Irja Kandolin

Institute of Occupational Health,
University of Helsinki
Finland

INTRODUCTION

In 1980 women made up nearly half (47%) of the Finnish labour force. The participation of women in economic life in Finland is not a new phenomenon: in the countryside women traditionally took care of the cattle and worked in the fields in addition to raising large families. At the beginning of this century 37% of the agricultural and 36% of the non-agricultural labour force were women. Between 1920 and 1970 women formed about 40% of the total labour force. The most remarkable change in women's employment has been the great increase since 1960 in the proportion of gainfully employed married women in the non-agricultural sectors (Haavio-Mannila and Jallinoja 1980).

In 1981 only 10% of women of working age (15–64 years) were full-time homemakers (Labour Force Interview Survey, 1981). In fact, the full-time housewife was seldom found in Finland, owing to the late and very rapid industrialization and urbanization (in 1950, 42% of the population was on the land and in 1975 only 12%). The proportion of families economically provided for only by the husband is, and always has been, small in Finland, and most women work irrespective of their family situation.

The labour force participation of mothers with small children is very common in Finland. Of mothers with pre-school children, 77% were gainfully employed in 1980. Over the years the labour force participation of mothers has become less and less dependent on the number of their children; whereas in 1950 the number of children tended to decrease the attendance of work of urban mothers, in 1980 the birth of a second or even a third child did not reduce the participation. Only the fourth child tended to keep mothers at home (Jallinoja, 1980; Official Statistics of Finland, 1983). As a result there is no longer the pattern of interrupted employment for married women that existed in Finland up until the 1960s, and that still exists today in most western industrialized countries, where women aged 25–39 stay home because of family responsibilities (ILO, 1981).

Table 8.1 *Part-time employees (percentages) by reason for part-time work, less than 30 hours a week, in autumn 1981 (according to this definition of part-time work 12% of women and 3% of men were working part-time)*

	Females	Males
Difficult to get full-time employment	12	6
Shortage of work	7	15
Care for home or children	24	3
Health or age	8	12
Studies	9	30
Normal working hours of the branch less than 30 hours a week	18	12
Longer working hours not economically necessary	7	0
Other reason, unknown	14	21
Total (%)	99	99
N	(129 000)	(33 000)

Source: Labour Force Interview Survey (1981).

As is evident from the previous chapters in this book, women in Finland participate in the labour force more frequently than women in most other western countries. Only in eastern European countries is the proportion of women in the labour force at the same level as in Finland, or even somewhat higher (ranging from 44% in Hungary to 52% in the Soviet Union in 1978—see Chapter 11) (Biryukova, 1980; Gömöri, 1980). In the previous chapter we saw that in Sweden the proportion of women in the labour force is somewhat over 40% and the situation is similar in Denmark; in other words, high but clearly lower than in Finland. In most western European countries the labour force participation of women is about 30% (ILO, 1981).

The strong involvement of women in the labour force in Finland is also evident in the fact that most of them are in full-time employment. Only 16% of women were part-time employed in 1981, that is, worked less than 35 hours a week (Labour Force Interview Survey, 1981). This figure is very low compared with figures for the other Nordic countries: Sweden 43% and Denmark 49% in 1978 (ILO, 1981). Only a small proportion of men (5%) were working part-time in Finland, which is typical also of other countries.

The reasons for part-time employment rates being different for men and women are illustrated in Table 8.1. Women cite care of the home and children, as well as a tight job market. Among men the most common reasons cited for part-time work are studies and a tight job market.

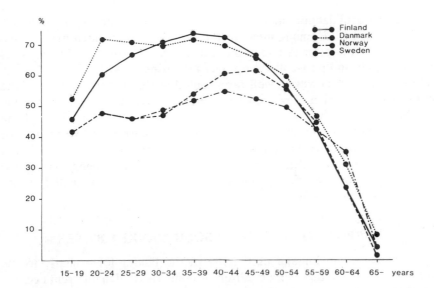

Figure 8.1   Proportion of married women who are economically active, according to age, in the Nordic countries in 1975. (Definitions of the economically active population differ: in Denmark the economically active are those who work either full-time or part-time; in Finland, those who work at least one-half of the normal working hours in that branch of industry; in Norway, those who work at least 1 hour a week; and in Sweden those who work at least 20 hours a week.) *Sources*: Official Statistics of Finland (1978); Official Statistics of Norway (1976); Official Statistics of Sweden (1976); Statistical News (1976)

In the autumn of 1981 about 20% of women in full-time employment wanted to move into part-time work. However, this desire was dependent on the woman's family situation: nearly one-third of women with children under 7 years of age wanted to do part-time work, but only temporarily. When the woman had two small children the percentage was as high as 41% (Labour Force Interview Survey, 1981).

Clearly, then, there are pressures among women for reorganization of working hours, especially daily working hours. There is no system in Finland like that in Sweden, which permits parents with small children to shorten their daily working hours from 8 to 6. To be adequate, reorganization would not have to mean just a move to part-time work but more flexibility and self-determination of employees in regard to work schedules.

Working women in Finland have organized themselves into trade unions more often than women in other western countries. This may be related both to the low proportion of part-time workers and the mushrooming of white- and pink-collar workers' unions in the seventies (Cook *et al.*, 1984). In 1978 the proportion of labour union membership among working women was 84%, as against 87% among men. In the past 10 years women have joined labour unions at a faster rate than men, and this is as true for blue-collar as for white-collar and pink-collar employees (Saarinen, 1979).

Women are not, however, well represented at the leadership level of the unions. The proportion of women members in SAK, the union representing blue-collar workers, was 43% in 1981, but only 8% of the members of the governing bodies of the union were women. The corresponding figures for TVK, the union representing mainly pink-collar employees, were 8% and 3%. Here, as in Howe's definition, pink-collar employees roughly correspond to lower white-collar employees and employees of female-dominated service occupations (Howe, 1978).

SEGREGATION OF THE LABOUR MARKET BY SEX

Although women in Finland participate in the labour force nearly to the same degree as men, they work in different industries and in different occupations than men. Jobs are clearly segregated by sex: there are men's jobs and there are women's jobs (Anttalainen, 1980).

In 1980 about half of the labour force was concentrated in occupations totally segregated by sex; that is, in occupations where 91–100% of the workers were of the same sex. Only 7% worked in occupations where the numbers of men and women were about the same, or where 41–60% were of the same sex (Figure 8.2). The segregation by sex has remained highly stable during the past 30 years. The quantitative increase of women in

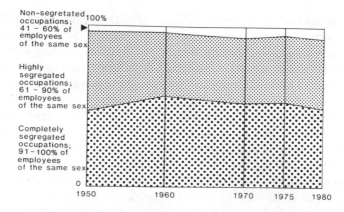

Figure 8.2   The distribution of employed men and women in non-segregated, highly segregated, and completely segregated occupations in 1950, 1960, 1970, 1975, and 1980 (*Source*: Kauppinen-Toropainen *et al.*, 1983a)

the labour force has not changed the qualitative aspects of women's work (Kauppinen-Toropainen *et al.*, 1983a).

The segregation of the labour market by sex is not unique to Finland but, as outlined in other chapters, is typical of all western countries. In eastern European countries the segregation is less obvious (ILO, 1981; Nikolayeva-Tereshkova, 1982). (See Chapter 11).

Figure 8.3 shows that the distribution of men's and women's occupations is a mirror-image, where most of the work force is clustered at the extremities in the segregated occupations and only a small part in the middle in the non-segregated occupations.

Women also work in a narrower range of occupations than men: in 1980, 50% of female wage-earners were engaged in only 13 occupations, whereas 50% of male wage-earners worked in 24 occupations (Kauppinen-Toropainen *et al.*, 1983a).

Among women the most common occupations were charworker, shop assistant, clerical worker, nurse, bank teller, social worker, nurse's aide, and secretary. Most of these occupations were almost totally segregated by sex. Thus 98% of charworkers, 94% of clerical workers, and 89% of social workers were women. Among men the most common occupations were transport worker, construction carpenter, forestry worker, electrician, machine mechanic, machine-tool setter, manager, shop assistant, warehouseman, and fitter–assembler. These occupations, too, were highly segregated

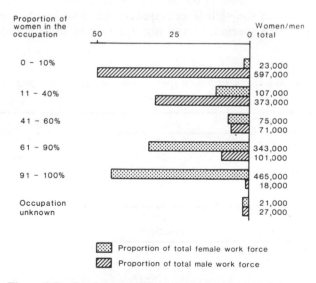

Figure 8.3   Sex segregation of the labour market in 1980
(*Source*: Official Statistics of Finland, 1983)

by sex. For example, 98% of transport workers, 92% of managers in private companies, and 99% of construction carpenters were men.

Nevertheless the difference in the width of the occupational spectrum for men and women is not as pronounced in Finland as in other western countries. Chapter 10 highlights that in the USA, for instance, half of the female labour force was concentrated in 17 occupations and half of men in 63 occupations in 1970 (Kanter, 1977). In Australia half of the women were concentrated in 9 occupations and one third in only 3 occupations; but half of men were in 41 occupations (Power, 1975). A similar situation is apparent in France, where 10 occupations employed about 60% of women in 1970 (ILO, 1981).

HIERARCHICAL POSITION OF WOMEN

The sex segregation of the occupational structure also means that men and women occupy different positions in the occupational hierarchy, with women mostly at the lower levels.

One indicator of the hierarchy is the socioeconomic position. Employees are divided into white-collar and blue-collar workers according to the traditional distinction between manual and non-manual work. White-collar employees are further divided into an upper and lower stratum (pink-collar workers; see Howe, 1978). Occupations in the white-collar stratum require a university degree, or are in leading positions in organizations of the public or private sector. The distinction between skilled and unskilled workers is roughly according to the skill level required, but also involves elements of the division between specialized and non-specialized work (Pöntinen et al., 1983).

Table 8.2 *Socioeconomic distribution (percentages) by sex in Finland in 1980 (wage-earners, aged 15–64)*

	Men	Women
White-collar employees	17	9
Pink-collar employees	24	48
Blue-collar workers		
Skilled	50	21
Unskilled	9	21
Total (%)	100	99
N	(1438)	(1273)

Source: Pöntinen *et al.* (1983).

Half of the male wage-earners are skilled workers, whereas about half of the females are pink-collar employees. There are more women than men in the unskilled occupations, and women also seem to have difficulty obtaining white-collar jobs (see Table 8.2).

The occupational hierarchy stands out prominently in the medical and nursing sector. The lower the position in the hierarchy, and the more the work involves daily contacts with patients, the more women there are in that occupation. At the same time the autonomy and prestige of the work, as well as the pay, are low. The occupational hierarchy in hospitals reflects the division of occupations into men's and women's work.

Men also occupy leading positions in the female-dominated sectors such as office work and banking. Only 3% of female but 42% of male bank clerks were section managers in 1980. By contrast, in sales work, where 75% of employees are women, about half of the department chiefs were women (Official Statistics of Finland, 1983).

WOMEN AS RE-PRODUCTION WORKERS

The various occupations can further be seen according to the closeness of human contact involved in the work. A job may involve very close and long-lasting contacts (a nurse or a medical doctor with a patient), it may involve only superficial and short-term contacts (salesperson in store), or the job itself may not require any closer personal contacts at all (painter).

Although this is a very rough division, it adds a new dimension to the discussion of the sex segregation of the labour market. Women's occupations are more often than men's occupations people-oriented, demanding close contacts with patients or clients. This can be seen in Table 8.3, which shows

Table 8.3 *Selected occupations (percentages) according to the intensity of human contact demanded, for men and women (wage-earners)*

	Women	Men
Caregiving work	9	1
Caring work	9	1
Custodial work	0.5	2
Teaching	4	3
Public service work	13	7
Invisible maintenance work	14.5	2
Office work: clerical and managerial work	23	8
Other, intellectual, professional, or artistic work	4	6
Transport and communication	3	10
Industrial and construction work	18	54
Agricultural	1	5
Other, not classified work	1	1
Total (%)	100	100
N	(881,151)	(967,713)

Source: Official Statistics of Finland. Population and Housing Census 1980; Helsinki (1983).

that women (17%) work more often than men (about 2%) in caregiving and caring sectors, as nurses, midwives, nurse's aide, and social workers. Women also engage in various types of service work, either in public or invisibly. Women are more often than men cooks or kitchen hands, charworkers, and cashiers in stores and restaurants.

As women concentrate in re-productive sectors such as caregiving, caring, and service, men (53%) more often than women (18%) work in productive sectors, in manufacturing, and in construction. These different sectors are visualized in Figure 8.4. The polarization of the labour market by sex means not only that men and women perform different jobs but that there are qualitative differences between men's and women's work.

WORK CONTACTS BETWEEN MEN AND WOMEN

Even where the division of occupations by sex is pronounced, daily contacts between men and women at work are usual. A case study on work contacts by Haavio-Mannila *et al.* (1983), based on 577 personal interviews with economically active urban men and women aged 25 to 64, showed that 60% of men and 72% of women were in daily contact with the opposite sex. Only 7% of the men and 5% of the women hardly met the opposite sex during the working day (Table 8.4). Work was classified as *segregated* if it was done only or mostly by members of one's own sex and the daily contacts were only or mostly with one's own sex group. Thirty-nine per cent of the men, and 27% of the women, were doing segregated work. Work was classified

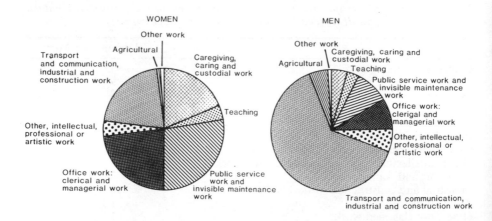

Figure 8.4   The distribution of men and women in various sectors (the figure is based on Table 8.3) (*Source*: Official Statistics of Finland. Population and Housing Census, 1980; Helsinki, 1983)

as *complementary* if men and women performed different sorts of work but had daily contacts with each other: a female secretary and a male manager in the same office, for example. Forty-four per cent of the men, and 54% of the women, reported complementary work. Work was classified as *integrated* if a person performed roughly the same sort of work as members of the opposite sex. Seventeen per cent of the men, and 19% of the women, performed integrated work.

Table 8.4   *Sex structure of job and workplace (percentages)*

	Persons doing the same sort of work		Daily contacts at work	
	Men	Women	Men	Women
Only women	1	40	—	5
Mostly women	1	31	6	21
Both men and women	15	13	54	65
Mostly men	32	5	33	6
Only men	42	1	7	1
No workmates or contacts	9	10	—	2
Total (%)	100	100	100	100
N	(281)	(296)		

Source: Haavio-Mannila *et al.* (1983).

Almost half of the men reporting segregated work were production workers (Table 8.5). Among women the picture was quite different, in that the segregated work was more evenly scattered over the various occupations. Complementary work for women mostly meant clerical work. Integrated work was often, particularly among women, professional.

There was a close connection between sex segregation and socioeconomic status. In segregated work the largest group of men were blue-collar workers, while women were very predominantly pink-collar or blue-collar workers. In complementary work the largest group of men were blue-collar workers, while two-thirds of women were pink-collar workers. In integrated work almost every second man and woman was a white-collar employee. Thus segregated work was more typically done by blue-collar workers, and integrated work by white-collar employees regardless of sex.

Work contacts and the quality of work

The quality of segregated, complementary and integrated work of men and women is shown in Table 8.6.

Table 8.5 *Occupations and socioeconomic status of men and women according to sex segregation of work (percentages)*

	Segregated		Comple-mentary		Integrated		Total	
	Men	Women	Men	Women	Men	Women	Men	Women
Occupation								
Professionals (technical, physical science, social science, humanistic and artistic work)	20	25	23	21	24	47	22	27
Administrative work	6	—	14	2	24	7	12	2
Clerical work	5	20	7	34	15	11	7	26
Sales work	6	4	6	13	4	13	5	10
Production work	46	21	30	6	24	8	35	10
Transport and communication	13	—	11	3	4	7	11	3
Service work	5	31	10	21	4	7	7	21
Total (%)	101	101	101	100	99	100	99	99
Socioeconomic status								
White-collar employee	21	11	26	11	47	50	28	18
Pink-collar employee	21	48	29	65	28	30	26	54
Blue-collar worker	58	41	45	24	25	20	46	28
Total (%)	100	100	100	100	100	100	100	100
N	(109)	(81)	(125)	(159)	(47)	(56)	(281)	(296)

Source: Haavio-Mannila *et al.* (1983).

Segregated work typically meant:
  mechanical, physically strenuous, and exhausting work;
  long and rigid working hours;
  solidarity among workers of one's own sex;
  instrumental attitude to work.

Complementary work typically meant:
  not many friends of the opposite sex among workmates;
  solidarity among workers of one's own sex;
  a sense of purpose in life derived from work.

As men and women have separate jobs in the complementary work, competition between them is avoided. But solidarity among workers of the same

Table 8.6 *Quality of men's and women's work according to sex segregation of work, proportion of yes-answers (percentages)*

	Segregated		Comple-mentary		Integrated		Total	
	Men	Women	Men	Women	Men	Women	Men	Women
Nature of work								
Makes one tired	64	75	54	62	49	66	57	66
Possibilities for promotion	39	20	50	37	45	30	45	31
Involves inde-pendent planning	78	44	78	60	72	88	77	61
Requires further training	84	59	80	74	87	82	83	71
Related to care and attendance	9	23	18	31	19	36	15	31
Long hours of work (40 hours/week or more)	80	57	67	54	62	43	71	53
Relations with workmates								
Solidarity among workers of one's own sex	64	48	52	52	28	30	53	47
Friends of the opposite sex among workmates	16	7	29	24	53	52	28	24
Immediate supervisor is man	95	40	89	55	77	82	89	56
Meaning and rewards of work								
Works mostly for the money	28	20	18	13	21	5	22	13
Work gives a sense of purpose	63	64	77	75	75	86	70	74
Emotional support from workmates	30	41	33	51	32	55	32	49
High salary	68	12	74	25	76	55	71	27
Relationship between family and work								
Job worries taken home	41	44	47	50	51	66	45	52
Family has to suffer because 'heart' is at work	45	25	39	32	65	49	45	33
N	(109)	(81)	(125)	(159)	(47)	(56)	(281)	(296)

Source: Haavio-Mannila *et al.*, (1983).

sex, and the scarcity of friendships with the opposite sex, suggest that there are conflicts between men and women. The traditional complementary pattern serves better the interests of men than those of women. Men more often (47%) than women (25%) were in leading positions, and their work involved more autonomy and was more challenging. The experiences of women in daily contacts with such men can be expected to reveal to them the inequalities in everyday working life and their own 'underdog' position and create a sense of 'sister solidarity'.

Integrated work typically meant:
  friendship and even love between men and women at work;
  a sense of purpose in life derived from work;
  job worries taken home;
  family suffers because the 'heart' is at work.

Workers in integrated work might be described as 'work-addicts'. They take job worries home, at the expense of their families. Similar work unites the sexes in integrated work, as shown in the lack of solidarity with members of the same sex.

Quality of women's work

According to the same study by Haavio-Mannila *et. al.* (1983), the following tend to characterize women's work regardless of their daily contacts with men:

  work is related to care and attendance;
  the job provides little autonomy;
  work is not challenging;
  work hours are short;
  salary is low;
  work makes one tired;
  emotional support is derived from workmates.

The social quality of women's work is expressed in two ways. On the one hand women give care and attendance, and on the other hand they receive emotional support from their workmates. Similar findings have been reported by Kanter (1977), and in another Finnish study by Riska and Raitasalo (1982).

Kauppinen-Toropainen *et. al.* (1983b) found that women's work did not involve decision-making or independent planning as much as men's. The industrial work, in particular, was regarded by women as monotonous and lacking in autonomy and self-determination. Table 8.7 shows that women enjoy their work when it is related to other people.

Caregiving is more autonomous and challenging than other work done by

women. It involves decision-making, requires further training, and demands
a wide spectrum of skills and knowledge.

Table 8.7 *Some characteristics of women's caregiving and other work; percentages
of yes-answers*

Characteristics of work	Caregiving work*	Other work
Work:		
Involves decision-making	75	57
Requires further training	83	66
Is interesting	96	83
Has high time pressure	64	56
Is mentally stressful	61	51
Is physically strenuous	48	31
Makes one tired	77	61
Pays well	30	34
Gains appreciation by others	65	52
Offers possibilities for promotion	29	32
Gives a sense of purpose to life	85	69
Total	(92)	(204)

*Women who replied in the study: 'My work is related to care and attendance.'
Source: Haavio-Mannila *et. al.* (1983).

Caregivers more often than other women have a female supervisor. Sixty
per cent of them had a woman as their immediate superior compared with
30% of women in other work.

Not unexpectedly there are also some negative features of caregiving and
caring work. It is mentally stressful and physically strenuous, it makes one
psychologically exhausted after the working day. This may be because the
number of clients easily exceeds one's psychological capacity to cope with
the situation: too many pupils *vs.* one teacher; too many patients *vs.* one
nurse; too many clients *vs.* one social worker. This new syndrome of psychological exhaustion is called 'burn-out' (Pines, 1980).

WOMEN IN MANAGERIAL POSITIONS

There are very few studies on women's managerial styles and skills. One of
the reasons for this is the small number of women in leading positions.
There is a hypothesis afloat, however, to the effect that women favour more
democratic and human-centred managerial styles than men.

A Finnish study supported this hypothesis. Women managers favoured a
more human and participatory approach than men, which was also effective.
The theoretical framework of this study was Reddin's 3D (Rantanen, 1981).
Women were also good listeners and preferred groupwork to authoritarian

style. The small number of women in top managerial positions in general is reflected in the small number of women in this study; of 900 managers only 6% were women. Nevertheless, the managerial style of women, as found here, gives us reason to believe that women are more flexible than men and prefer the kind of organizational climate (participatory, autonomous) that the new technology is demanding.

As shown in a study by Kauppinen-Toropainen *et. al.* (1983b), women managers seem to enjoy their work. Female managerial work was associated with a low rate of emotional exhaustion and stress, even lower than male managerial work.

The low rate of stress found here is in contrast to some other studies, which have shown that women managers work under high pressure and have a high rate of emotional problems (Welner *et. al.* 1979). The marital status, and the number of children, need to be taken into account in this connection, as Davidson and Cooper (1980) have reported that married executives with children were under greater stress than single or divorced executives. However, the small number of female managers in this representative study made controlling the marital status difficult.

Family responsibilities have been regarded as the main obstacle in the way of female career advancement. Managerial work is considered so demanding and time-consuming that it has been regarded as impossible for women to combine work and family responsibilities. In the USA most women in mid-managerial positions are either unmarried or, if they are married, have no children (Crawford, 1977). Davidson and Cooper (1980) found differences in the social background of male and female managers in England. Male managers were more often married than female managers, and among women managers there were more divorces than in the average female population. Moreover, women managers had fewer children than English women on the whole.

Corresponding conditions probably existed in Finland in the 1960s (Jalli-noja, 1980). Today, however, the situation is quite different, as can be seen in Table 8.8. Hardly any differences are seen between women in the various occupational groups. Women in top managerial positions are married as often as women in general. Only farmers constitute a slight exception in being married more often than other women.

This picture was supported by another Finnish survey, carried out by *Jaana* (1982), a popular women's magazine in Finland, and included structured interviews with 500 women. Table 8.9 shows that white-collar and blue-collar women do not differ from each other in the number of children they have. The white-collar women in this study included also pink-collar women, and the blue-collar women were either skilled or unskilled.

With the exception of farmers, women in the various occupational groups have about the same number of children. Farm women clearly have more children than other women.

A committee was recently set by the Finnish Ministry of Education to investigate the problems of women in academic life. Women become doctors 2 years later than men, for example, and they gain professorships when 4 years older than men. (In 1980 only 8% of the professors at Finnish universities were women.) Naturally part of this time lag is due to the woman's family responsibilities, but this is not the only reason. Single women were not found to progress in their academic careers faster than married women. In fact, women with one or two children were more productive and successful than other women. The committee concluded that neither family nor children were the real obstacles; it was more the hidden, non-visible discrimination in recruitment, informal communication, and even mentorship which hindered women's advancement in academic life (Committee Report, 1982).

Table 8.8 *Married women as percentages of all women working in different occupational groups, according to age in 1980*

	age				Total
	−24	25–29	30–49	50–64	
All women	26	61	76	65	65
Farmers	52	88	92	79	85
White-collar top managers	34	55	72	59	67
Pink-collar supervisors	28	58	72	60	64
Blue-collars	24	59	74	63	61

Source: Official Statistics of Finland (1982).

Table 8.9 *Number of children of women, in different occupational groups, (percentages)*

Number of children	White-and pink-collars	Blue-collars	Farmers
No children	20	19	14
One child	29	24	5
Two children	30	33	23
Three children	14	15	14
Four children or more	7	9	44
Total (%)	100	100	100
N	(192)	(194)	(22)

Source: Jaana Survey (1982).

Also subjectively, women do not think that their children restrict their careers (Table 8.10). Rather her sex as such seems to be the major obstacle to advancement.

Knowing how to combine work and family responsibilities is an important problem for economically active women in Finland regardless of their occupational or hierarchial position.

FEELINGS ABOUT WORK

As a rule women enjoy their work. As can be seen in Table 8.10, work outside the home gives them a feeling of independence and a sense of more

Table 8.10   *Feelings about work and family-life (percentages)*

	I feel exactly like this	I feel somewhat like this	I don't feel like this	Difficult to say
All economically active and married women (N=328)				
I enjoy my work	67	23	6	4
My work keeps me active	65	26	5	4
My household is a mess because of my work	16	30	50	4
I often find it difficult to concentrate on my work because of my family responsibilities	2	8	86	4
I am often so tired after work that I don't have the energy to begin at home	23	39	34	4
Work outside the home gives me a feeling of independence	57	26	13	4
My husband is jealous about my time at work	4	6	86	4
All economically active mothers with small children (N=162)				
I have a bad conscience because I don't have time enough for my children	18	29	33	20
My children restrict my career development	6	7	66	22
Because I am working outside the home I concentrate better on my children	21	30	29	20

Source: Jaana Survey (1982).

active participation in society. The main sources of job dissatisfaction were related to the following:

'my salary is too small' (64%);
'women are not equal to men at the work-place' (34%)
'women do not get the sort of work they desire' (34%); and
'women do not have the possibilities for advancement that men have' (31%).

(The percentages refer to the 328 economically active women from the *Jaana* survey.)

An indirect sympton of job dissatisfaction was the finding that about one-third of the women from this study would not recommend their work to their daughters, as can be seen from Table 8.11.

Table 8.11 *Would you recommend your own job to your daughter? (percentages)*

	White- and pink-collars	Blue-collars	Farmers
No	48	70	45
Yes	49	28	36
Difficult to say	3	2	9
N	(192)	(194)	(22)

Source: *Jaana* Survey (1982).

Blue-collar women would not, as often as white- or pink-collar women, recommend their work to their daughters. About half of the white- and pink-collar women would like to see their daughter doing the same type of work they are now doing.

There are some contradictory aspects about women and their job satisfaction. As a rule women report themselves happy with their work, but at the same time unhappy with the quality of the work and with the unequal treatment of women at the work-place.

Finnish women attach great importance to their work, according to other interview studies in 1979. Thirty-nine per cent of the economically active women claimed to get their main satisfaction in life from their work. Men emphasized the importance of work somewhat more (51%) than women. However, the Finnish women valued their work as the central life interest more often than Swedish women, and even more than Swedish men (Alkula, 1981).

HOUSEHOLD DUTIES AND WORK OUTSIDE THE HOME

The fact that women play a double role may be one of the sources of reported tiredness at work. Women still do about 70% of all housework in Finland

(Niemi *et. al.*, 1981). Relative to other national groups, Finnish men never-theless participate in housework to a high degree, as can be seen in Table 8.12.

Table 8.12   *Time used in gainful employment and domestic work by economically active men and women in selected countries in 1975–81.* Hours per week and sex ratio (women/men)*

Country and year of time budget study	Gainful employment			Domestic work		
	Men	Women	Sex ratio	Men	Women	Sex ratio
Finland, 1979	44	37	0.9	14	26	1.9
Norway, 1980/81	44	27	0.6	16	33	2.1
Poland, 1976	53	46	0.9	15	34	2.2
United States, 1975	48	35	0.7	11	25	2.3
Hungary, 1976/77	51	45	0.9	11	29	2.6
United Kingdom, 1974	46	31	0.7	9	25	2.8
Switzerland, 1979/80	47	37	0.8	5	19	3.8
Japan, 1976	54	47	0.9	4	21	5.5

* Journey to and from work included.
Source: Niemi (1983).

Finnish men contributed somewhat less time than Norwegian and Polish men to household duties but more than men in the United States, Hungary, the United Kingdom, Switzerland, and Japan (Niemi, 1983). Thus working women still devote almost twice as much time to domestic work as working men. Women use 16%, and men only 8%, of their time for domestic work (Figure 8.5).

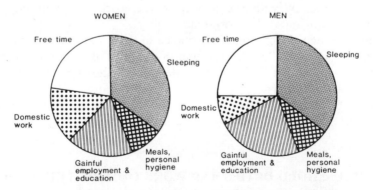

Figure 8.5   Use of time by employed persons (*Source*: Niemi *et al.*, 1981)

Blue-collar women are more satisfied with their husbands' participation in domestic work than white-collar and pink-collar women, even though the blue-collar men show less initiative. The symmetrical family, where wife and husband equally take care of the household work, seems to characterize better the Finnish middle-class than working-class families.

It is interesting to find that dissatisfaction among women with their husband's participation in domestic work has increased during the past few years, even though there is a clear tendency showing that men today are more active than some 20 years ago (Haavio-Mannila, 1980). Perhaps this is a sign of a more critical attitude among women who nowadays demand a more active participation from their husbands. Women are not satisfied with their husband merely 'helping' them with household duties, but expect a more independent and active participation. This increase of dissatisfaction can be seen in Table 8.13.

Table 8.13   *How satisfied or dissatisfied are you with the amount of domestic work done by your husband? (percentages)*

	Whole country in 1982*	Helsinki in 1966†
Very satisfied	32	48
Rather satisfied	46	41
Dissatisfied	20	11
Number of wives	(354)	(102)

* *Jaana* Survey (1982)
† Haavio-Mannila (1967).

The extent to which the husband participates in family life and domestic work has proved to be a good measure of the woman's happiness and life satisfaction in general. The *Jaana* Survey showed us that the more actively the husband takes part in family life the more satisfied his wife is with her work, her marriage, her hobbies, and her children.

Table 8.14 shows which household duties are done by wife alone, by husband alone, and which jointly by wife and husband. Husbands very seldom do domestic work alone, except for small repairs at home. Joint participation of husband and wife is mostly in child-rearing, weekly cleaning and shopping. The same study established that masculinity of men in the eyes of women is not diminished when they participate in household work.

THE CHANGES IN MEN'S ROLES

Men participate today more actively than before in child-rearing, which shows them wanting to enlarge their roles. Young men suffer from guilt

Table 8.14   *Which of the following things at home do you do alone or together with your husband (percentages)*

	Wife alone	Mostly wife	Husband and wife together	Mostly husband	Husband alone	Difficult to say
All economically active and married women (N=328)						
Making breakfast	50	12	24	5	5	4
Making dinner	58	17	17	2	1	5
Daily cleaning up	51	20	22	1	1	5
Weekly cleaning up	39	16	38	2	1	4
Washing dishes	39	16	33	3	2	7
Shopping	37	19	36	4	3	1
Small repairs at home	4	3	16	36	37	4
All economically active mothers with small children (N = 162)						
Putting the children to bed	22	16	56	3	—	3
Dressing the children	29	22	41	1	1	6
Helping the children at mealtime	30	16	39	1	1	13

Source: *Jaana* Survey (1982).

feelings when they neglect their children and families because of work responsibilities. This is a new phenomenon, evident not only in Finland but in other countries, too. Young men have started to ask whether success at work must be at such cost (Evans and Bartholomé, 1979).

Table 8.15 shows about half the men in Haavio-Mannila's *et al.* (1983) study to agree with the statement that they should have devoted more time to their children when the children were small. Women suffered from guilt feelings much less than men. Other studies, too, have shown that men as well as women regard the time when their children were small as the happiest time of their lives. It is an urgent question, then, for women and increasingly also for men, how to avoid the psychological burdens and guilt feelings generally associated with this period.

The problem is one of reorganizing and re-evaluating the different demands of work and family. The changes in female roles and expectations necessarily demand changes in male roles.

The change already taking place in male roles is reflected in the paternity leave system which was started in Finland in 1978. Fathers now have the right to 6–12 days' leave from work at the birth of their child. The paternity leave has already become quite popular, and in 1983 about 25% of fathers

Table 8.15 *When you think back on the time when your children were small, do you feel you should have devoted more time to them instead of doing other things?*

	Men	Women	Total
Yes, absolutely	23	15	19
Yes, but it would have been hard for me to find time	26	16	20
No, I feel I devoted enough time to the children	27	50	40
No, I feel the other things I did were more important	2	—	1
The children are still small	21	17	19
Don't know/not sure/won't answer	1	2	1
Total (%)	100	100	100
N	(253)	(316)	(569)

Source: Haavio-Mannila *et al.* (1983).

(altogether 15,360) utilized the benefits and stayed at home from 6 to 12 days. Maternity leave lasts 258 days, of which the father is entitled to use 25, 50, 75, or 100 days after the mother has used the first 100 days of it. Thus the maternity leave in Finland is more and more coming to resemble a parental leave.

The men who have taken paternity leave have mostly reacted very favourably towards the new system. They report close and warm relations with their baby as well as the mother. Fathers in full-time employment have otherwise very limited opportunity to be with their newborn children, which does not make a good start for a positive child–father relationships in the future. The shared maternity leave also has another effect of making it more difficult for employers to discriminate against women on the basis of long maternity leaves.

There is also a system in Finland allowing husbands to attend the child-birth. In the *Jaana* Survey, 50% of women agreed with the statement 'it is important that fathers attend the birth of their child', 29% disagreed with the statement, and 21% found it difficult to say. White-collar and pink-collar women were more positive about the statement than blue-collar women, though the differences were small.

Through the shared experiences of work, housework, child-rearing, and even birth itself, the traditional barriers between men's and women's roles are being broken down. The effects, which promise to be revolutionary, are not only felt within the family but are carried over into society in general.

CONCLUSIONS AND DISCUSSION

Finnish women participate in the labour force, on a full-time basis, more actively than women in any other western country. In 1980 nearly half of the entire labour force in Finland were women. As a rule, women enjoy their work outside the home. The work generates positive feelings such as, 'Work outside the home makes me feel independent', or 'I concentrate better on my children and on my family when I work outside the home'. Negative aspects relate to the unequal treatment of women at the work-places.

The labour market is almost totally segregated by sex. There are women's jobs on the one hand and men's jobs on the other. Women work more often than men in occupations requiring close human contact, in occupations such as nurse, midwife, nurse's aide, and social worker. As a rule, women enjoy their role as caregivers. Women also do various types of service work, either in public (cashier in shops or banks) or invisibly (kitchen hands, charwomen).

The segregation of the labour market by sex means not only that men and women perform different jobs but also shows qualitative differences between men's and women's work. Women's jobs are more monotonous and less challenging, and they are more often 'dead-end' jobs than men's jobs. The quantitative increase of women in the labour force has not changed the qualitative aspects of women's work.

Family duties have often been regarded as the main hindrance to female career development. Recent studies indicate, however, that the family situation does not tell the whole truth. There is non-visible discrimination in recruitment, in informal communication, and in the preconceived ideas of managers which also slows female advancement.

Today Finnish men participate in domestic work more actively than ever before, though women still do about 70% of all domestic work in Finland. Women are not satisfied with the situation. They want a more active and independent participation on the part of their husbands: mere 'helping' at home is no longer sufficient.

Many younger men are attempting to go beyond their traditional roles. Success in business life no longer compensates in the way it used to, for the sacrifices made to family life. This is a new phenomenon, found in other countries as well as Finland. Changes in women's roles must be met by changes in men's roles. Both need to be fully revised.

REFERENCES

Alkula, T. (1981). *Work Expectations of Finns*. University of Helsinki (in Finnish).
Anttalainen, M.-L. (1980). *Women's Work—Men's Work*. Publications of the Prime Minister's Office 1980:1, Helsinki (summary in English).
Biryukova, A. (1980). 'Special protective legislation and equality of opportunity for women workers in the USSR', *International Labour Review*, **119**, 51–65.
Committee Report (1982). The problems of women in academia. Report no. 33, Helsinki, 1982 (in Finnish).
Cook, A., Lorwin, V., and Daniels, A. (eds) (1984). *Women and Trade Unions: Studies of twelve industrialised countries*. Temple University Press, Philadelphia.
Crawford, J. (1977). *Women in Middle Management: selection, training, advancement, performance*. Forkner Publishing, New Jersey.

Davidson, M., and Cooper, C. (1980). 'The extra pressures on women executives', *Personnel Management*, June, pp. 48–51.

Evans, P., and Bartholomé, F. (1979). The relationship between professional life and private life. Stencil Paper, INSEAD. Fontainebleau.

Gömöri, E. (1980). Special protective legislation and equality of employment opportunity of women in Hungary. *International Labour Review*, **119**, 67–77.

Haavio-Mannila, E. (1967). 'Sex differentiation in role expectations and performance', *Journal of Marriage and the Family*, **29**, 568–578.

Haavio-Mannila, E. (1980). 'Division of domestic tasks in the family', *Sosiologia*, **17**, 186–194.

Haavio-Mannila, E., and Jallinoja, R. (1980). Changes in the life patterns of families in Finland. National report based on statistics and earlier studies. Working Papers 13, Department of Sociology, University of Helsinki.

Haavio-Mannila, E., Jallinoja, R., and Strandell, H. (1983). Changes in the life patterns of families in Europe, Finnish frequency distributions by sex. Publications 37, Department of Sociology, University of Helsinki.

Howe, L. K. (1978). *Pink Collar Workers: inside the world of women's work*. Putnam's Sons, New York.

International Labour Organization (1981). Advisory Committee on salaried employees and professional workers. Problems of women non-manual workers: work organization, vocational training, equality of treatment at the workplace, job opportunities. Report III, International Labour Office, Geneva.

Jallinoja, R. (1980). 'Men and women', in T. Valkonen, R. Alapuro, M. Alestalo, R. Jallinoja, and T. Sandlund (eds). *Finns: the structure of society during the period of industrialization*, pp. 222–250 WSOY, Porvoo-Helsinki-Juva (in Finnish).

Kanter, R. M. (1977). *Men and Women of the Corporation*. Basic Books, New York.

Kauppinen-Toropainen, K., Haavio-Mannila, E., Kandolin, I., and Simonsuuri-Sorsa, M. (1983a). *Women and Work*, Reviews 57. Institute of Occupational Health, Helsinki (in Finnish).

Kauppinen-Toropainen, K., Kandolin, I., and Mutanen, P. (1983b). Job dissatisfaction and work related exhaustion in male and female work. *Journal of Occupational Behaviour* **4**, 193–207.

Labour Force Interview Survey 1981 (1982). Statistical Report TY 21. Central Statistical Office of Finland, Helsinki.

Niemi, I. (1983). *The 1979 Time Use Study Method*. Central Statistical Office of Finland, Helsinki.

Niemi, I., Kiiski, S., and Liikkanen, M. (1981). *Use of Time in Finland*. Studies 65, Central Statistical Office of Finland, Helsinki.

Nikolayeva-Tereshkova, V. (1982). 'Women and socialism', *Proc. USSR Academy of Sciences*, **IX**, 142–155.

Official Statistics of Finland (1978). Population and Housing Census 1975, Volume IB: Occupation and Industry. Central Statistical Office of Finland, Helsinki.

Official Statistics of Finland (1982). Population and Housing Census 1980, Volume VII: Housing—dwelling units and families. Central Statistical Office of Finland, Helsinki.

Official Statistics of Finland (1983). Population and Housing Census 1980, Volume IB: Occupation and Industry. Central Statistical Office of Finland, Helsinki.

Official Statistics of Norway A 813 (1976). Labour market statistics 1975. Central Bureau of Statistics, Oslo.

Official Statistics of Sweden (1976). Population and Housing Census 1975, part 6:2. National Central Bureau of Statistics, Stockholm.

Pines, A. M. (1980). *Burnout: from tedium to personal growth*. Free Press, New York.

Power, M. (1975). Woman's work is never done—by men: a socioeconomic model of sex-typing in occupations. *Journal of Industrial Relations*, **17**, 225–239.

Pöntinen, S., Alestalo, M., and Uusitalo, H. (1983). The Finnish mobility survey 1980: data and first results. Suomen Gallup Oy Report no. 9, Helsinki.

Rantanen, E. (1981). The efficient Finn is an isolated bureaucrat. *Talouselämä* (Finnish Business Weekly), **19**, 24–32 (In Finnish).

Riska, E., and Raitasalo, R. (1982). Sex segregation of the Finnish occupational structure: its implications for the psychosocial aspects of women's work. *Economic and Industrial Democracy*, **3**, 431–444.

Saarinen, J. (1979). The presence of women at the decision-making level of labour unions, political parties, agricultural producer organizations and cooperatives at the end of 1978. Council of Equality, Prime Minister's Office, Helsinki.

Statistical News (1976). Danmarks Statistik A:21, Køhbenhavn.

Welner, A., Marten, S., Wochnick, E., Davis, M., Fishman, R., and Clayton, J. (1979). Psychiatric disorders among professional women. *Archives of General Psychiatry*, **36**, 163–173.

APPENDIX

Occupational distribution of women and men wage-earners

	Women	Men
Caregiving		
Physician, nurse, midwife, assistant nurse	71,614	9,702
Physiotherapist, masseur	3,536	639
Hygiene and beauty treatment	5,592	174
Caring		
Social worker	17,775	2,099
Child day care centre staff	13,361	183
Housekeeper in private service	6,068	66
Home help	9,340	57
Child care in families and at home	20,175	10
Director and nursing staff at child day care centres	4,967	195
Psychologist	1,146	322
Religious–social work	2,057	2,544
Custodial work		
Prison guard, policeman	1,487	21,438
Teaching		
Staff of universities and institutions of higher education	1,856	3,970
Primary school teacher	9,723	5,394
Secondary school teacher	23,015	15,089
Other occupations in teaching and training	4,346	5,601

	Women	Men
Public service work		
Public relations and employment service staff	2,462	2,906
Bank and post office cashiers; cashier in shop and restaurant	14,391	328
Shop personnel	65,065	24,185
Commercial salesman, agent	1,693	12,051
Buyer, salesman (office)	3,407	7,003
Shop supervisor, department chief	6,026	6,068
Restaurant service	19,949	2,649
Travel service work	2,008	7,886
Leisure time and hobby guidance	1,611	1,575
Invisible maintenance work		
Cook, kitchen hand	38,557	2,497
Housekeeping manager, hotel and restaurant matron	5,841	751
Laundering, dry cleaning and pressing work	3,929	321
Charworker	70,676	1,555
Building caretaker	8,167	17,078
Office work: clerical and managerial work		
Managers	10,198	52,421
Book-keeper	13,617	1,370
Secretary, typist	32,194	1,427
ADP operator	6,304	1,996
Clerical worker	137,711	24,971
Other, professional, intellectual or artistic work		
Engineer, architect	1,891	24,239
Chemical, physical and biological work	9,723	9,582
Juridical work	1,267	3,640
Economist, statistician and other engaged in research	4,365	8,716
Pharmacy work	5,870	175
Librarian, archivist	5,946	965
Artistic and literary work (journalist, editor)	6,137	8,541
Productive work in transport and communications, construction and manufacturing:		
Transport and communications	29,417	96,973
Construction work (painter, wood worker)	19,462	170,812
Manufacturing work	128,690	285,131
Mining and quarrying work	167	5,676
Supervision work in technical field	8,441	55,871

	Women	Men
Agriculture, forestry:		
Garden and park worker	6,436	3,816
Farm worker (also dairymaid)	4,261	5,625
Foresty work	1,740	36,575
Other, not classified work	7,474	14,855
N	(881,150)	(967,713)

Source: Official Statistics of Finland. Population and Housing Census 1980. Volume I B. Occupation and Industry. Central Statistical Office of Finland, Helsinki (1983.) The occupational classification is based on the International Standard Classification of Occupations (ISCO).

Women at Work
Edited by M.J. Davidson and C.L. Cooper
© 1984 John Wiley & Sons Ltd

Chapter 9
Women at Work in Portugal

Maria do Carmo Nunes
Department of Employment, Lisbon, Portugal

WOMEN IN THE LABOUR FORCE

Women's employment in the sixties*

In Portugal in the sixties, women entered into active working life at an ever increasing rate. Until then, successive falls in the female work rate had occurred, a fact to be attributed either to the pattern of economic development, or to the closely-knit family structure of society and the downgraded position of women in the ideology of Salazar†, which essentially reserved to women the role of mother and housewife.

Table 9.1 *Women in the labour force*

	Labour force (thousands)		Women's Activity rate (as percentage of female population)	Housewives (thousands)
	Women	Total		
1940	678	3050	16.9	2283
1950	737	3289	16.8	2525
1960	606	3423	13.1	2894
1970	857	3396	19.0	2310

Source: Instituto Nacional de Estatistica, Population Census (1940–1970).

However, in the beginning of that decade two events occurred which had a significant influence upon the entry of women into active working life. One was mass emigration, which between 1960 and 1973, covered around 1.4

* This chapter has been based on the author's unpublished study 'Women in the labour market', 1981.
† Salazar, Prime Minister (1932–68), principal leader of the dictatorship which was overthrown in April 1974.

million Portuguese people, especially men. Second was the army draft to the wars in the former colonies, which took away from the labour market a growing number of men (around 130,000 in 1973). This exodus of such an important volume of male active workers caused labour force shortages which continued throughout that decade.

It was from agriculture, particularly, that the largest emigration stream came, and it was also from there that an intense migration flux to the main urban and more industrialized centres took place, consequently it was agriculture which suffered the most. Here the role played by women in the rural areas increased, fully replacing men both in small private family plots, and in the proletariat of the areas of big-landownership. Women's rate of participation in agricultural employment rose sharply from 7.4% in 1960 to 17.8% by 1970.

Table 9.2   *Employment by major economic sectors*

Economic sectors	1970		Variation 1960–70(%)		Women as percentage of all employed	
	Men	Women	Men	Women	1960	1970
Primary	827,055	178,795	−38.4	+68.0	7.4	17.8
Secondary	756,660	264,660	−3.4	+50.7	18.3	25.9
Tertiary	753,635	386,020	+27.4	+20.4	35.2	33.9
Total	2,334,350	829,475	−14.0	+37.7	18.2	26.2

Source: Instituto Nacional de Estatistica, Population Census (1960, 1970).

In the secondary and tertiary sectors the replacement of the male labour force by the female's work was not as evident as in agriculture, and the increase of women's employment in these sectors can be explained by the type of economic growth which can be observed in the final lap of the 1960s and early 1970s, namely during the 1968–73 period. Monopolies started to take a firmer grip over the economic system, as can be seen with a largely open door to foreign capital, the imports of capital-intensive technologies, and the rise in exports; all these factors greatly influenced women's employment.

In industry, the traditional sectors such as textiles, clothing, and footwear were those that mostly contributed (with around 60%) to the positive variation of women's employment in the manufacturing industries. Nevertheless, the branches which were technologically more advanced, and which had large participation of foreign capital or that were directly controlled by national financial groups (non-electrical machinery, metal engineering, transport equipment, electrical goods, and other manufacturing industries) were much more dynamic in the creation of women's jobs. However, these jobs were mostly temporary and underpaid, with very high production rates, appealing to manual dexterity and attention, the type of work reserved for the female labour force.

In the tertiary sector three factors were determinant in the creation of female jobs: firstly, the growing monetarization of the economy with an expansion of the financial system and a growth in sepculation; secondly the rapid increase of tourism, where foreign investments had an important role; and thirdly the intensification of market relations which replaced personal and community relations, thus converting a great part of domestic work into labour controlled by capital. It is in fast-moving industries such as banks and insurance, trade, restaurants and hotels, and personal services (which include laundries, hairdressers, and cleaning), who during this period showed greater dynamism in the creation of jobs for women. On the contrary household services was the only branch of the tertiary section where women's employment dropped. Another aspect worth stressing was the steep rise in the number of women employed in the public administration services. This is a traditional sector, without prestige, and with lower wages than those in the private sectors of the services, which have shorter working hours allowing for an easier conciliation between office hours and domestic life.

Besides the already mentioned reasons for the entry of women into active working life, it is also relevant to refer to the cultural influence of the more developed European countries in the change of consumption habits and living patterns, and the following work of women outside the home.

However, and in spite of all this evolution, it is a fact that in 1970 women's activity rate is still at a very low level, 19%, thus allowing us to classify them as the country's first labour force reserve. This fact attributes to women a double dimension: whenever production requires a larger labour force, women are mobilized, as was the case of the period 1960–73, and on the other hand, it is women who first suffer the selective consequences of unemployment, as in the period after 1974.

Recent evolution: 1974-82

With the April Revolution and the European recession, the labour supply increased and the demand become strongly recessive, thus disturbing the relative equilibrium which existed in the labour market (until then unemployment rates had never gone past 3%).

After 25 April 1974, and the decolonization that followed, approximately 250,000 active people entered the country (soldiers and civilians from the African ex-colonies) while at the same time the crisis hitting principal countries in Europe which imported our labour force, led these countries to reduce their annual average acceptance of emigrants, from a previous figure of 140,000 between 1970 and 1973, down to 40,000 between 1974 and 1977, and down to only 20,000 after that; thus putting an extra pressure on the labour supply.

The recession in Europe had, on the other hand, other negative consequences for the Portuguese economy, by reducing Portuguese exports and the number of tourists visiting the country, and by raising the prices of imported raw materials.

To these recessive factors, which were due to external causes, one must surely add the reaction of many firms in Portugal to the political and social changes which occurred after the April Revolution. In fact, in 1974 and 1975 some national and multinational companies, namely in clothing and electronics, until then attracted by the cheapness of the female labour force, carried out a large number of dismissals, which above all affected women.

Other more traditional industries, with a majority of women employees, also reacted with many dismissals, as a consequence of wage rises in those years affecting their weak productive structure.

It is in this post-25 April 1974 framework that unemployment became more serious, and has become even more so since then. One can see that whatever year employment rises, its rate of growth is less than that of the active population, so economic activities can hardly absorb newcomers to the labour market, especially in areas where women are significantly represented.

Besides the trend which was expressed throughout the previous decade, for an ever-growing participation of women at work, it is fair to mention that some measures which were taken after 1974 had an encouraging effect on the access of women to the labour market. Some examples of this are the wage increases resulting from the setting of a national minimum wage, and the following reduction in the wage gap between men and women, unemployment benefits, a longer maternity leave, and the extension of social benefits to farm-workers and to private household workers.

As a final result of these dispositions, the female activity rate rose from 32.4% in 1974 to 36.1% in 1982, and this leads us to conclude that not even the recession nor the very high rates of women's unemployment (12.6% in 1982) dissuaded them from looking for a job, either those who became unemployed or those looking for a first job. It should be noted, however, that these figures are taken from the Household Employment Survey, and they are not totally comparable with those of the Census. As far as women at work are concerned, their activity rates are well above the 1970 Census because this survey includes as active workers many people who in the Census were given as inactive, as being the case of unpaid family women workers in agriculture.

Between 1974 and 1982, and in spite of the economic recession, women's employment as a whole rose by about 11%. Figure 9.1 verifies that until 1979, and in spite of the fall in the number of female salaries workers, women's employment at large did not fall very markedly. The main explanation for this is the existence of a very significant number of unpaid female family workers (around 26% in 1982), especially in agriculture. When jobs

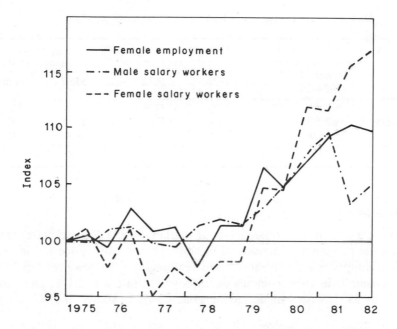

Figure 9.1   Evolution of employment (*Source*: Instituto Nacional
de Estatistica, Household Employment Survey, 1975–1982. *Note*:
1st semester 1975 = 100)

became more difficult this status became an alternative to unemployment or
to abandoning the labour market. To add to this, all non-organizaed sectors
of the economy gained importance during this period, notably through a
steep rise in clandestine labour, work at home, and occasional work. On the
other hand, female salaried employment in industry suffered the sharpest
fall (about −11% between 1974 and 1978, against +19% for men) as a result
of the dismissals and the compression of labour demand, especially in the
modern and dynamic sectors such as plastics products, basic metal industries,
and metal products, machinery and equipment.

Besides the facts already pointed out, female employment has tended to
be concentrated in the tertiary sector, which has been more protected from
the recession. In the past few years, it was this sector which contributed
to the absorption of the women's labour force, especially in the public
administration, education, health, and trade sectors, thus leading to a situation in the tertiary sector where women's participation rose from 40.5% in
1974 to 44.6% in 1982 (see Table 9.3).

Generally in the past four years the rise in women's employment has
continued to take place essentially in the already traditional feminine sectors.

214 WORKING WOMEN

Table 9.3 *Employment by major economic sectors*

Economic sectors	Variation of women's employ-ment(%) 1974–1982	Women as percentage of total employment		1982 (thousands)	
		1974	1982	Men	Women
Primary	−7.6	46.6	51.8	507	544
Secondary	+7.1	30.8	26.8	1073	392
Tertiary	+36.9	40.5	44.6	800	645
Total	+10.9	39.4	39.8	2387	1581

Source: Instituto Nacional de Estatistica, Household Employment Survey (1974, 1982).

The unemployed women

Tensions existing in the women's labour market, after 1974, are better translated by the progressive increase of unemployment rates, since the increase in labour supply is a much more vivid feature than the compression in the labour demand. In 1974 women's unemployment rate was 2.1%, and was at its peak by 1981, with 14.9%, having gone down to 12.6% in 1982. On the

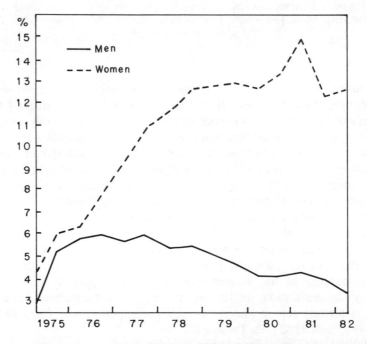

Figure 9.2 Unemployment rates (*Source*: Instituto Nacional de Estatistica, Household Employment Survey, 1975–1982)

contrary, with men, it went steadily up until 1976, when it reached 5.9%, but then it came down gradually, and by 1982 it was at 3.4%

The dominant feature of unemployment as a whole, and for women in particular, consists of the seriousness and specificity of juvenile unemployment. Out of the 310,000 unemployed in 1982, 187,000 were under 25, and of these 132,000 were women, this corresponding to a 22.8% unemployment rate. This difficulty of young women to secure their first job shows that, besides the already mentioned conjunctural reasons, there are other structural problems, such as the prejudice, and discrimination concerning the work of women, the very specific and limited type of jobs to which they have access, and above all their most insufficient vocational training (see Figures 9.2 and 9.3).

In the past four years the spreading of temporary hirings, especially in the sectors where women's work is predominant, substantially increased the insecurity of working women, and thus the number of the unemployed women looking for a new job is now above the number of those searching

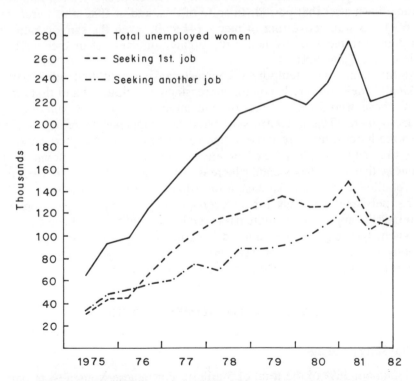

Figure 9.3 Unemployed women looking for first jobs or other jobs (*Source*: Instituto Nacional de Estatistica, Household Employment Survey, 1975–1982)

for a first job. This fact tends to create a situation of manpower rotation in the labour market, and has meant that the proportion of women unemployed for a long period has become smaller.

Table 9.4   *Percentage of unemployed women looking for another job by duration of unemployment*

Duration of unemployment	1974	1976	1978	1980	1982
<1 month	8.3	3.8	—	4.3	3.4
1–3 months	10.7	7.7	4.3	10.9	9.3
3–6 months	16.7	11.5	4.3	10.9	11.9
6–12 months	25.0	28.8	14.3	7.6	17.8
12+ months	33.0	48.1	77.1	66.3	57.6
Total	100.0	100.0	100.0	100.0	100.0

Source: Instituto Nacional de Estatistica, Household Employment Survey (1974–1982).

In effect, the share of women who are unemployed for 1 year or more, in the total number of unemployed women, increased between 1974 and 1978, coming down after that period. In spite of this, and in 1982, this percentage (57.6%) was well above that of men's (44.9%), given the same conditions, this demonstrated how women have greater difficulty than men in being rehired (See Table 9.4).

At the same time, temporary contracts have meant that adult women looking for new jobs are becoming increasingly unemployed and that among them, those who have an inferior education are especially vulnerable to unemployment. This is contrary to what has happened in previous years, when the hardest-hit were those women who had a secondary education.

As stressed before, in spite of the increase of women's unemployment, the female activity rate has steadily increased (a slight reduction in 1982 does not yet allow us to draw the conclusion of any possible setback).

This persistent tendency for an ever-growing participation of women in economic life appears to be quite irreversible. Not only are we in an economic recession, but some of the adopted laws preventing discrimination against working women have had no real impact as yet; nor were they reinforced by policies which facilitate women's access to employment.

PATTERNS OF WOMEN'S WORK

Marital status and age

In 1982 about 36% of the total of 5 million Portuguese women were part of the labour force, and a smaller proportion were housewives (22.5%). As can be seen in Table 9.5, the imports of men in the labour force was about 55%, since men continued to assume the primary responsibility of providing the income, and women that of looking after children and home.

Table 9.5 *Female and male population, 1982*

	Female		Male	
	Thousands	Percentage	Thousands	Percentage
Population	5008	100.0	4516	100.0
Civilian labour force	1808	36.1	2470	54.7
Employed	1581	87.4	2387	96.6
Unemployed	227	12.6	83	3.4
Armed Forces	1	—	73	1.6
Not in labour force	3199	63.9	1973	43.7
Keeping homes	1125	22.5	5	0.1
At school (10 years and over)	588	11.7	614	13.6
Under 10 years	779	15.6	852	18.9
Others	707	14.1	502	11.1

Source: Instituto Nacional de Estatistica, Household Employment Survey (1982).
Note: The islands of Madeira and Azores (representing about 5% of the total population) are not included in this survey.

However this pattern is beginning to change. Between 1974 and 1981 the proportion of married women in the female labour force increased from 51% up to 58%, while the number and percentage of single women had dropped as a result of growing school attendance (see Table 9.6)

Table 9.6 *Distribution of Women in labour force and unemployment by marital status*

	Labour force		Unemployment	
	1974	1981	1974	1981
Single	43.1	36.8	69.0	55.0
Married	51.0	58.1	31.0	43.2
Widowed	5.2	4.0	–	1.8
Divorced or separated	0.7	1.1	–	–
Total	100.0	100.0	100.0	100.0

Source: Instituto Nacional de Estatistica, Household Employment Survey (1974, 1981).
—Number too small for reliable estimate.

All this leads one to believe that this increase in the number of active married women may be contributing to narrowing the gap existing in the 1970 Census between the activity rates of single women of over 15 years of age (43.8%) and the married women (14%). By analysing the evolution of women's activity rates according to age groups in recent years, one is led to the same conclusion, as they increase for the 25–29 and 30–34 age groups.

In spite of this positive evolution, a great number of women still renounce their active life for good because of their family situation.

An examination of Figure 9.4 shows that the women's participation rate sharply rises to 24 years of age, reaching its peak in the 25–29-year age group. With the coming of marriage and the first children those rates initiate a decline which goes on with increasing age, even though children grow older and presumably make it easier for mothers to take up a job outside the home. Besides the lack of child care facilities, social prejudices against women's work, especially if they have children, and the lack of retraining and vocational programmes hardly encourage their re-entry into the labour market. It is also important to stress that part-time work has little relevance in Portugal (in 1982 only 7% of the total labour force, and 14% of employed women, were working less than 35 hours per week) and so does not play the

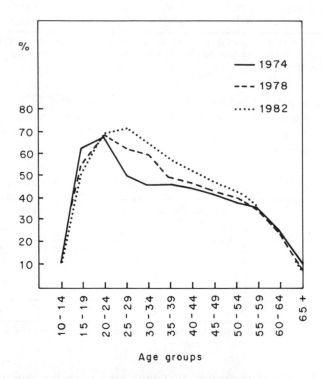

Figure 9.4   Women's labour force participation rates by age (*Source*: Instituto Nacional de Estatistica, Household Employment Survey, 1974, 1978, 1982)

role of conciliation, between the housework and the active life, that it does in some other countries.

The absence of more detailed data does not allow a wider analysis of women's participation in the labour force with relation to the family situation and the number of children.

Women's segregation by economic activity.

Statistics in Table 9.7 show an increase in the rate of women's participation in the work force in those sectors of activity which already had a significant rate of feminine participation: agriculture, trade, restaurants and hotels, public administration, education and health.

Table 9.7   *Women's employment by economic activities*

Economic activities	Percentage distribution	Share of women	
	1982	1974	1982
Agriculture and fishing	34.4	46.6	51.8
Mining	—	10.0	4.2
Manufacturing	23.9	40.7	37.5
Electricity, gas, and water	0.2	21.1	16.0
Construction	0.6	1.8	2.2
Trade, restaurants, and hotels	12.6	36.0	40.6
Transport and communication	1.4	13.8	13.5
Financing and insurance	1.8	34.3	31.8
Public administration	4.2	29.1	34.0
Educational services	7.5	77.9	80.3
Health services	3.9	66.7	70.9
Other services	9.5	54.5	54.7
Total	100.0	39.4	39.8

Source: Instituto Nacional de Estatistica, Household Employment Survey (1974, 1982).
— not significant.

In manufacturing, where the share of women has fallen since 1974, women's participation rate was greatest in the following branches shown in Table 9.8.

Table 9.8   *Women's share in manufacturing sector (1981)*

Clothing and footwear	71.1
Textiles	51.4
Food	42.9
Other manufacturing industries	36.5
Electrical machinery and goods	36.1
Chemical products	32.2

Source: Ministry of Labour, Statistics Department, Survey on Employment to Companies Employing Over 10 Workers (1981).

Women are still mostly concentrated either in the traditional industries of lower productivity (agriculture, clothing, textiles, food) or in those where work is intense and repetitive (electrical machinery and goods, other manufacturing industries), or still in those branches where, together with low wages, women perform similar tasks to those carried out in their families (health and education, personal and domestic services).

Occupational segregation of women

Table 9.9   *Women's employment by main occupational groups*

Occupational groups	Percentage distribution	Share of women	
	1982	1974	1982
Professional, technical, and related workers	8.7	52.2	56.8
Administrative and managerial workers	0.3	7.7	11.1
Clerical and related workers	11.9	40.0	43.9
Sales workers	8.2	35.9	41.3
Service workers	15.5	65.6	67.1
Agricultural workers	34.2	46.4	51.7
Production workers, transport equipment operators and labourers	21.2	26.4	22.0
Total	100.0	39.4	39.8

Source: Instituto Nacional de Estatistica, Household Employment Survey (1974, 1982).
Note: This unique up-to-date source of data on occupations does not give us figures for more detailed occupations.

According to the 1970 Census, around 60% of women were concentrated in the six following occupations: dressmakers, textiles workers, administrative clerks, shop clerks, and teachers, and of course agricultural workers. In spite of the fact that there is no available up-to-date data, one can assume that this situation still prevails.

In 1982 women were largely represented among service workers, agricultural workers (where they were mostly unpaid family workers), clerical, and sales workers; and were under-represented in administrative and managerial functions, and among production workers. Between 1974 and 1982 the share of women's participation increased in occupations usually considered to be female-dominated, and their increase among professional and technical staff is only due to the traditional recruitment of women in fields such as nursing and teaching.

Women's degree of qualification

The distribution of women employees in non-agricultural activities reveals their concentration in the lowest grades of the qualification's hierarchy, that is in jobs which require less training and less autonomy (see Table 9.10)

Table 9.10   *Distribution of employees in non-agricultural activities by degrees of qualification*

Degrees of qualification	Women		Men	
	1974	1981	1974	1981
Managers	0.1	0.2	1.0	1.2
Technicians	0.6	1.3	3.8	4.8
Administrative staff	13.0	17.7	9.5	8.8
Clerks	5.5	4.8	6.5	5.7
Foremen, team-leaders	0.9	1.1	5.3	6.0
Highly qualified	0.3	0.8	4.0	5.8
Qualified	20.4	20.2	27.7	33.8
Semi-qualified	23.3	34.2	14.0	15.4
Non-qualified	22.1	15.6	19.2	13.7
Apprentice	13.8	4.1	9.0	4.8
Total	100.0	100.0	100.0	100.0

Source: Ministry of Labour, Statistics Department, *Survey on Employment to Companies Employing Over 10 Workers* (1974, 1981).
Note: Agriculture, as well as public administration and other services' branches, are excluded from this survey.

Women in leading positions, such as managers, foremen and team-leaders, only represented, in 1981, 1.3% of the total number of women employees, while men's percentage was 7.2%; a situation which has hardly changed since 1974.

As far as production workers are concerned, the highest percentage is of semi-qualified women (34.2%), performing routine-type repetitive jobs, while for men the highest figure goes for the qualified personnel (33.8%), performing duties whose complexity requires vocational training or practice.

In addition, the percentage of women who are totally unqualified (15.6%) is still very large, and well above that of men's (13.7%). Between 1974 and 1981 there was a slight fall in this figure, due mainly to the increase in the semi-qualified group.

This situation, which clearly expresses the secondary function of working women, is mostly due to their limited vocational training, either before they enter working life, or due to very few possibilities for re-training during their professional life, which consequently limits their chances of promotion.

WOMEN'S EDUCATION AND TRAINING

Education

The few available data relating to the educational degrees gained by Portuguese men and women, will limit us to only a few references, much more qualitative than quantitative, in an attempt to explain the education–employment relationship between the sexes.

By 1979 the illiteracy rate for the population over 14 years of age was still far higher for women (26%) than for men (19%) in spite of the fact that it dropped throughout the past decade, due largely to the enlargement of compulsive school attendance from 4 to 6 years after 1975. Since then, basic education schools (compulsive) have been mixed and programmes for both sexes are alike. The most dominant feature of this level of education is the very high number of failures and repetition of school years, this leading to a high drop-out rate of students (Ministry of Education, 1979).

As far as secondary education is concerned (5 more years on top of compulsive basic education), access is without sex discrimination, and here one notices an ever-growing proportion of girls attending this level of education. However, the options (in the 10th and 11th years) which female students usually choose are areas which are traditionally feminine. This is clearly shown in the preference for humanistic and arts subjects (74%) against only 5% for scientific and technical options. This situation is to a certain extent parallel with the one prevailing before the education system was unified in 1978 (aimed at eradicating differences between high schools and technical schools), when girls normally picked the high school, essentially geared at entering higher education (universities). Yet the big majority of those girls did not go on, and obviously remained professionally unprepared. The labour market clearly reflects this situation: in 1978 unemployment among women with this grade reached 32.7%.

In higher education, too, discrimination comes more from the type of degrees chosen by women than from the percentage of their attendance, which is nevertheless smaller than that of boys (proportion of young women: 42% in 1977/78).

While in the arts and humanistics degrees women are around 70%, in traditionally masculine areas this figure quickly reduces (25% in law and 14% in engineering), although one can perceive in recent years a certain trend for girls to diversify their choice.

Nevertheless, the structure of employees, according to different education degrees (laid down in Table 9.11) in spite of being unfavourable to women, does not reflect such marked differences between the two sexes as does the structure of the degrees of qualification (Ministry of Labour, 1981).

Table 9.11   *Distribution of employees by education and qualification levels*

	Women	Men
Education levels		
Totally illiterate	4.7	4.5
Can read and write, without diploma	8.6	7.2
Basic school (4 years)	53.7	55.9
Complementary School (6 years)	10.3	10.8
Secondary education (9 and 11 years)	8.9	6.6
Technical schools	4.7	5.6
University	0.8	1.3
Others	8.3	8.1
Total	100.0	100.0
Qualification levels		
Technical staff	1.4	3.8
Foremen, team-leaders	1.3	4.8
Highly qualified	2.6	3.7
Qualified	32.1	40.7
Semi-qualified	33.4	15.7
Non-qualified	12.2	12.1
Apprentice	9.2	8.8
Others	7.9	10.4
Total	100.0	100.0

Source: Ministry of Labour, Statistics Department, *Employees Maps* (1981).
Note: This very new source of data annually collected from all companies covers all employees
    except those in public administration, temporary rural workers, and domestic servants.
    Data related to qualification levels are obviously different from those included in Table
    9.10, due to the different kind of sources.

One should therefore consider that women's discrimination at work is not
only a result of their low school grades, but also due to the very limited set
of options which they have, either when entering the labour market or
throughout their working lives, in terms of vocational training and promotion;
this being a decisive factor for the definition of socio-professional and wages
hierarchies.

Vocational guidance and training

Theoretically both sexes have indiscriminate access to the vocational guidance
and training services.

Either vocational guidance, as given by the Ministry of Education to
youngsters in secondary schools, or the one organized by the Employment
Department, mostly geared to the adult working population wanting to
attend vocational training courses, barely cover the population wanting to
join the labour market. These services are visited on average every year by

around 12,000 people, of which one third are women; the vast majority being composed of youngsters aged between 15 and 24, with a basic school qualification or a secondary school diploma.

It is a fact that in these contacts above everything else it is still the stereotypes relating to each occupation that play a large role, especially when one is faced with a real possibility of a job. Moreover the total lack of measures prevents any opening of predominantly male occupations to women.

Training courses (around 26) in skill centres managed by the Employment Department are mostly aimed at covering traditional male-dominated areas. Of around 1000 workers, formed by these centres, every year, 8% of them are women.

Most of these followed training as typists or clerk–typists and only a few were trained for male-dominated areas (in 1982: 8 budget calculators, 8 carpenters, 1 plumber, 1 turner, 3 painters for building).

Training of women in new areas is strongly conditioned by the fact that infrastructures and programmes contents are not adapted to women's attendance. This, together with the small capacity of the skill centres, does not cope with the training needs of around 40,000 unemployed women without any qualifications looking for jobs through the Employment Department. Vocational training is carried out in a most disorganized fashion (apart from the Ministry of Labour, other departments such as those of the Agriculture, Tourism, and Health Ministries organize some training courses in their own specific spheres).

This has raised a large number of problems for youngsters when going on from student life to work life, a situation which is worsened by the non-existence of a duly organized system of apprenticeship.

WOMEN'S EARNINGS

The earnings gap between men and women

Earnings differentials between the sexes have been reducing substantially since 1974. In the whole of the non-agricultural activities the earnings gap was near to 50% in 1973, but it came down to 36% in 1974, and was about 24% in 1981 (see Figure 9.5).

The setting of a national minimum wage soon after the 1974 April Revolution was a decisive contribution to the narrowing of the earnings gap between the sexes, with significant increases in the lower wages groups where the women's labour force was predominant.

One can assess from Table 9.12 that in 1981 and in the whole of the manufacturing industries, the gap was close to 29%, a figure which was

Table 9.12   *Earnings gap between sexes by economic activities*

Economic activities	1974	1981
Fishing	66.7	44.9
Mining	−0.8	9.1
Manufacturing	38.2	28.6
Electricity, gas, and water	17.3	9.6
Construction	0.3	−8.7
Trade	30.1	19.3
Transport and communication	−2.3	−8.3
Financial institutions	22.2	19.2
Insurance	15.8	11.1
Real estate and business services	36.2	28.7
Personal services (household services excluded)	27.1	15.7
Total of non-agricultural activities	36.0	24.1

Source: Ministry of Labour, Statistics Department, Survey 'Level of Skills' to companies employing over 10 workers (agriculture, public administration, and some services branches are excluded) (1974, 1981).

higher for the food, paper, and electrical machinery apparatus industries. Since 1978 the gap in manufacturing industries has stayed unchanged. In the services, the branches with the biggest differentials are the real estate services (28.7%) and trade and banking (about 19%).

In the agricultural activities the gap between the two sexes was near to 36% in 1980; a figure which wasn't too far off the 41.4% of 1973, and this in spite of a tendency for the gap to close between 1974 and 1977 (30% in this latter year).

Notwithstanding the diversity of sources, one may generally conclude that women's wage discrimination is far higher in agriculture than in other activities. One also notices how pay differentials are smaller for the unqualified professionals: the smallest gap goes to the clerical workers (8.5%) and the unskilled blue-collar workers (14.7%) (see Table 9.13).

Some characteristics of women's earnings

The comparison between the percentage of women and men in the various wage levels illustrates the striking differences between the sexes. In non-agricultural activities, and by January 1982, 34% of women earned under 12,000 escudos, but only 8.6% of men were in such a situation. By that date the national minimum wage was 10,700 escudos.

Differences between the proportion of women and men in the lowest-earning brackets are of a lower dimension in the under-18 age groups, and they grow as age increases, showing how the chances of promotion for women throughout their working lives are far smaller than men's.

On the other hand, those differences are bigger among blue-collar workers (the proportion of women earning less than 12,000 escudos was about 52% against 11% of men in January 1982) than in the white-collar workers (4.3% of women and 2.8% of men).

The concentration of women in low-paid occupations and unskilled jobs, and the small amount of professional training given to them, including on-the-job training, can be pointed out as the main factor for this discriminatory situation. In spite of legislation granting equal pay for work of equal value, collective labour regulations still include important wage differences between men and women, especially implicit discriminations which are not easily detected. They most often occur in the occupational categories usually reserved for women, and are therefore underrated as far as wages are

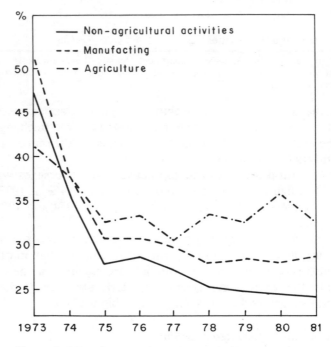

Figure 9.5 Earnings gap between sexes (*Source*: Ministry of Labour, Statistics Department and Planification Department (1981); Instituto Nacional de Estatistica, Agricultural Statistics.) *Note*: Data presented as earnings on Tables 9.12 and 9.13, and Figures 9.5 and 9.6 refer to wages and salaries before any deduction (for taxes, union dues, etc.) and exclude any complementary payments such as subsidies, awards, tips, payment of overtime work, etc. If a broader concept of earnings were to be used the gap would necessarily be widened, since the number of women with surplus types of payment is inferior to the number of men

conccrned; this being the case for those classified as 'semi-skilled' with a lower or similar wage than the 'unskilled' male. This type of discrimination exists above all in sectors such as agriculture, marble and granite quarries, bakeries, milling, textile, paper paste, chemicals, hotels, textile wholesale, chemical and pharmaceutical goods, paper storage, etc. (Moreira *et al.*, 1983)

Table 9.13 *Earnings gap by job status and level of skills*

	1973	1981
White-collar workers	38.9	26.1
Professional (managers)	40.1	26.7
Technical workers	23.1	16.5
Sales workers	54.3	32.5
Clerical workers	33.0	8.5
Blue-collar workers	51.1	28.3
Skilled	49.6	30.1
Semi-skilled	44.9	20.4
Unskilled	43.3	14.7

Source: Ministry of Labour, Statistics Department; Survey 'Level of Skills', to companies employing over 10 workers (agriculture, public administration, and some services branches are excluded) (1982)

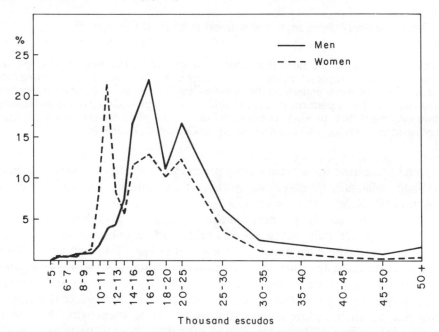

Figure 9.6 Percentage distribution of non-agricultural workers by earnings brackets (1982) (*Source*: Ministry of Labour, Statistics Department; Survey 'Earnings Brackets', to Companies Employing over 10 workers)

THE LEGAL SITUATION

The Constitution

The Constitution of the Republic in 1976 meant an historical change in the situation of women at large, and of working women in particular, by bringing about a process of change in Portuguese society which started in April 1974 and which also found its expression in new legislation.

The revision of the Constitution carried out in 1982 kept and improved all gains enshrined in 1976. The present Constitution enshrines the principle of all citizens' equality (Article 13), and clearly declares that no-one may be privileged, damaged, acquire or lose any right or be exempted from any duty, due to sexual discrimination.

The right to work is seen in the Constitution as a fundamental right of all citizens; this means the State has to enforce that right through carrying out economic and social plans. Among some of the state's obligations as regards the right to work, it is fair to stress the one referring to 'equal opportunities in choosing a job or occupation and no limits being established to having access to whatever position, job or professional category' (Article 59, No. 3b).

To all workers, both men and women is granted the right to

wages according to the quantity, nature and quality of the work performed, by observing the principle of equal pay for equal work, to grant a decent living; the organization of work under socially dignified conditions, so as to achieve personal success; work being performed under health and safety provisions; to rest and leisure, to a maximum time in working hours, to the weekly time-off and to regular paid holidays; to material subsidies when being unemployed (Article 60).

Special protection for women during pregnancy and after delivery is seen as a State obligation to ensure all workers their rightful working conditions (Article 60, N.2c).

As far as the family is concerned the Constitution says that 'all have the right to set up a family and be married under fully equal conditions' and also that 'man and wife have equal rights and duties regarding civil and political capacity and the upbringing and education of children'. 'Maternity and paternity are eminent social values' (Article 68, N.2) and 'fathers and mothers have a right to be protected by society and State in the irreplaceable task of bringing up their children, especially in educating them with the aim of sending them into professional life and preparing them to participate in the country's civil life' (Article 6, N.1).

As far as State duties regarding family protection are concerned, it is worth emphasizing 'the setting up of a national network of child-care institutions, of a network of creches and nurseries, and of basic structures in support of the family' (Article 67, No.2-b).

According to the Constitution, working women have the right to a period of leave, before and after delivering a child, without loss of pay or any other facilities (Article 68, No.3).

In reading out the Constitution it becomes clear that in its wording, women and men are equal. But the Constitution does not simply spell out equality principles, but goes well beyond that, by compelling the State to implement these principles through the setting out of concrete aims that permit personal and professional success and the participation of both men and women, on an equal footing in the country's civic life.

One can never overstress the importance of such items, since during the Fascist regime which existed before 25 of April 1974, Portuguese women were clearly in an inferior situation compared to that of men. Article 31 of the then existing National Labour Code expressly stated that 'women's work outside the home, will be regulated by special laws, under the principles of *moral*, physical defence of maternity, of *domestic* life and of *welfare*'. Consequently, some rights were limited for women, such as the possibility of marriage when working in certain occupations such as nursing and air hostesses; being a shopkeeper depended on a special authorization from the husband, and other positions and jobs were totally forbidden to them. Even the signature of a working contract could be opposed by the husband if he used sufficient 'powerful reasons'.

Therefore, the publication of the 1976 Constitution acted as an important contribution to profound changes in the family and labour laws, by adapting them to the constitutional principles.

Labour legislation

Since it follows the major constitutional principles, the labour legislation does not include rules that discriminate against working women. One should not consider as discrimination the so-called protectionist rules, such as those protecting maternity and those imposed by the need to correct existing inequality.

However, there are regulations for certain activities where women are dominant (for instance in agriculture and in household service), which establish a regime for women more unfavourable than the one existing for the rest of the workers; namely concerning wages, social security, dismissals, and working hours. This may also be applied to activities predominantly performed by women, where legal protection is non-existant (e.g. work at home).

Equal opportunities for jobs and non-discrimination resulting from marital status or family situation are granted at least in the law; the same goes for dismissals, since the law forbids the employer to dismiss a worker without a just motive. There are nevertheless exceptions in the law, such as whenever the nature of a particular job necessitates employing either a woman or a man (fashion, art, show business)

The guarantee of equal job opportunities and equal treatment at work

In admitting that working women are discriminated against at work and in their jobs the law (Law No. 392—20 September 1979) seeks to grant equal opportunities and treatment for both men and women, and even extends its application to cases where men are also discriminated against.

Discrimination is defined as 'any distinction, exclusion, restriction or preference based on sex, aiming at or having as a result, putting at stake the recognition and the exercise of all rights which are granted by the labour laws', but does not see as a form of discrimination 'temporary rules which establish a preference based on sex, but which are trying to correct an inequality or protect maternity while considered as a social value'. The law clearly forbids discrimination in access to jobs, to vocational training, to professional promotions, to wages, and to working conditions at large.

This is why the law sees as null and void all rules and regulations that may in any sense limit the access of women to whatever job, occupation, or position, with the exception, as previously indicated, of jobs which the law sees as having a real or potential risk for pregnant women. On the other hand, employers are compelled to grant full equality of opportunities and treatment both for women and men in vocational training. It is strictly forbidden, in all advertising related to job vacancies, to refer directly or indirectly to any preference based on sex, and recruitment must proceed on objective criteria.

Also made null and void, will be all contract rules which determine any occupations or categories specifically for one of the two sexes, as well as any that may set up lower wages for women working in the same or equivalent categories. Wages have to be determined according to equal jobs being done or producing equal value for the same employer, and wage variations should only be allowed when based upon objective criteria, but applied both to men and women.

In that same law, women have also a right to a professional career under the same conditions as men with access to all leading positions at work. As far as positive action is concerned, this diploma awards the State the obligation to 'promote, foster and co-ordinate actions related to vocational guidance and training for women' with special attention being given to the 14–19 and 20–24 age groups of unskilled youngers; to those not having basic education diplomas, and also to women who raise their children single-handed; and to those who, after a career break, want to reintegrate the labour market, namely through special re-training programmes.

On the other hand, the Minister of Labour is by law compelled to annually assess the number of women to whom the access to training courses is granted.

Any worker who feels he or she is being discriminated may, by himself/herself, or through his/her trade union, protest in Court, to enforce these legal rules, without being fired, punished, or damaged. In any case since the principle of equality was only recently adopted and the Law No. 392 only adopted in 1979, there has not yet been a significant number of Court decisions relating to this question.

To implement the enforcement of this diploma, a Commission was set up. It is called the Equal Work and Employment Commission, it is tripartite (government, trade unions, and employers), and it works within the scope of the Ministry of Labour. It may recommend that the Minister of Labour should adopt legal measures or other measures to enforce equal opportunities and to research on all questions related to the discrimination of women at work, and to give advice on concrete cases, as well as to publicize the Equality at Work Law.

However, this law does not apply to household workers, to jobs performed in individual homes, and to civil servants and local government officials.

Maternity protection

The law grants that women have a right to 'not working, during pregnancy and until 3 months after birth, in all kinds of duties which may be medically seen as non-advisable, and this without a cut in the wages', 'to take a 90–days' leave during the maternity period, and these days cannot be discounted for holidays, surplus old-age payments or retirement age'. During this period women have also the right to be paid the full wages (civil servants and public employees), or a benefit which is paid by Social Security. They also have the right to 'stop their work for two half-hour periods per day so as to feed the babies, without a cut in the wages or in the period of annual holidays', 'not working night shifts in factories, during pregnancy and until 3 months after delivery, and to medical and health care during pregnancy, delivery and after delivery'.

In spite of the fact that the law recognizes the social value of maternity and forbids discrimination against working women due to this reason, the truth is that maternity is an obstacle to the participation of women at work. In actual fact the ruling mentality is to bring almost exclusively upon women the duty of family responsibilities, and the fact that there are no social supporting bodies enhances this even further. As an example, we may see that in 1978 there were 1,026,118 children with ages ranging from 0 to 6 years and of these only 93,504 were being properly looked after and educated (9%). By 1980 the number of nurseries and creches was 2242 with 105,682 places. In 1979 only 24% of the pregnant women were seen by the Health and Mothercare medical services, and only 49% of babies were medically supervised. In spite of the growth in the number of deliveries in hospitals, in 1979 there were still 47,923 deliveries at home (31.5%) and 18,918 without any assistance.

These figures may give an idea of the existing difficulties as far as mothercare and protection are concerned, and the difficulties that women are facing who go to work and also have to accept family responsibilities at the same time.

In 1982 in Parliament, four Draft Laws were presented—Protection and Defence of Maternity, Family Planning, Sexual Education, and Voluntary Interruption of Pregnancy (Abortion law)—all of which attempted to respond to these problems. Parliamentary arrangements prevented the first two from being voted on, and the others were rejected.

The Draft Law on the Protection and Defence of Maternity, which clearly distinguished between what is the irreplaceable role of women in maternity and family responsibilities which should be embodied and shared by the mother and the father, set out a number of measures concerning health care (mother and child), concerning working conditions (maternity leave, leave of absence to assist the children, forbidden or limited jobs, regime of absences) and concerning social security. If it comes into force it will most certainly be an important step towards the alteration of the present situation for working women in Portugal.

CONCLUSION

After 25 April 1974, very important steps were taken in order to alter the situation of discrimination which women were facing in Portugal until then. These advances have mostly occurred in the Constitution and in the laws. However, these gains do not correspond to the same extent with the changes that took place in society. For that, it is essential to have the means to put the necessary mechanisms to work, so as to fully guarantee the true effectiveness of those gains.

REFERENCES

Nunes, Mido Carmo. (1981) *Women in the Labour Market*. Unpublished manuscript.
Instituto Nacional de Estatistica (1978) Education Statistics Lisbon.
Instituto Nacional de Estatistica (1982) Household Employment Survey Lisbon.
Ministry of Education (1979). Survey of the Department of Permanent Education. *Preparatory Studies for the National Literacy and Adult Education Plan,* Lisbon.
Ministry of Labour (1981). *Employees Maps*. Statistics Department, Lisbon.

Ministry of Labour (1982). *Survey of Employment in Companies Employing Over 10 Workers*. Statistics Department, Lisbon.
Moreira, I., Murteira, M., and Goulao, M. (1983). *Collective Labour Regulations—Some Features of its Evolution in the Last Few Years*. CISEP, Lisbon.
Instituto Nacional de Estatistica (1970) *Population Census*, Lisbon.

Part III

Women at Work: the Two Superpowers

Women at Work
Edited bt M.J. Davidson and C.L. Cooper
© 1984 John Wiley & Sons Ltd

Chapter 10
Women at Work in the USA

Laurie Larwood
Department of Management, University of Illinois at Chicago,
Chicago, USA
and
Barbara A. Gutek
Claremont Graduate School, Claremont, USA

INTRODUCTION

The 1970s were momentous years for American women, marking the turning point from non-paid to paid work. By the end of the decade 51.2% of American women over the age of 16 were working in part-time or full-time jobs. The labour force participation rates of women have increased steadily from 33.9% in 1950 to 50.0% in 1978 and 51.2% in 1980. These same years saw a steady decline in men's participation in the labour force, from a high of 86.5% in 1951 to 77.2% in 1980 (US Department of Labor, 1980). Women now constitute 42.5% of the US labour force, an increase from 29.6% in 1950.

The rapid influx of American women into paid work that really began in the late 1950s was not predicted. However, economists (e.g. Flaim and Fullerton, 1978) now project that women will continue to enter the labour force in increasing numbers at least through the 1980s. Thus, the traditional view that paid work is a male sphere, and the family is a female sphere (Parsons and Bales, 1955), is at least half wrong!

In this chapter we summarize the characteristics of women workers and women's work in the United States. We note changes and trends, many of which run counter to myths and stereotypes about working women. From this analysis we conclude that women at work experience discrimination on the basis of their sex and discuss the concept of discrimination. Then we discuss factors that maintain discrimination in the United States, focusing on current innovative research in this area. Since there is a great deal of work on the subject, we examine that which is theoretically interesting and relatively unique to the US. At the end of the chapter, we discuss trends for the future and offer a more complex view of discrimination.

A review of the literature is more meaningful if one understands the political context in which the research and theoretical debate occur. In the United States over the past 20 years, a variety of policies, regulations, and laws have been passed by the United States government in an attempt to provide 'equal opportunity' for women as well as minority groups. All of these laws have been passed since 1960 and have been the subject of much controversy. Later in the chapter we discuss some of the laws and regulations directly. Here we merely note the presence of such laws without commenting on their success or failure.

CHARACTERISTICS OF WORKING WOMEN

Age

American women of practically all ages are more likely to be working now than in 1950; only after age 65 has the rate of labour force participation declined since 1950. In 1950, 9% of women 65 and older were working; in 1980, 8.3% of women 65 and older were working. At all other ages, the percentage of women working has increased since 1950. For example, among 16- and 17-year-olds there is a 12% increase over 30 years, from 30% to 42% employed at least part-time. Almost 68% of women 20–24, and over 65% of women 25–34, the prime childbearing years, are in the labour force. In 1950, only 34% of women from 25 to 34 were in paid employment, 31% less than the percentage working in 1980. There is no longer any appreciable decline in rate of labour force participation during childbearing years. The labour force participation rate steadily increases until age 20–24 and holds fairly steady until age 54 when it starts to decline (US Department of Labor, 1980).

Education

Working women in the United States are more educated than ever and their educational attainment is now very similar to men's. In 1979, 48% of female high school graduates and 50% of male high school graduates were enrolled in college. The 50% figure represents a decline for men (from a high of 57% in 1965), while the 48% figure represents a new high for women (US Department of Labor, 1980). Their increased enrolment in college has had an effect on the educational level of working women. The median years of school completed is now the same for men and women—12.6 years—and has been essentially the same since 1965. However, working women are more likely than working men to have completed high school (77.3% vs. 73.6% for 1979) but less likely to have completed 4 or more years of college (14.9% vs. 19.6% for 1979) (US Department of Labor, 1980).

Marital status and presence of children

Previously, married women with a husband present were much less likely to work than women who were divorced or single. Now those differences are smaller. For example, in March, 1979 63% of the never-married women worked (up by 17% from 1950) and 74% of the divorced women worked (up by 2% from 1960 when such figures were first available). However, in 1979, 49% of married women with husbands present also worked, up by 27% from 1950 (US Department of Labor, 1980). The increase in labour force participation by married women with husbands present is one of the important changes in the female labour force.

In the case of divorced women, the probability that they will be working outside the home has not increased much in the past 20 years. However, the *number* of women who are divorced has increased dramatically so that there are now more divorced women than ever in the labour force. For example, the number of households headed by women has increased from 9.4% of households in 1950 to 14.6% of households in 1979.

These two findings—that married women are more likely to engage in paid work and that more women are divorced—means that more children have working mothers. In fact, one of the biggest changes in the female labour force in the United States has been in the number of mothers who are working. In 1950, less than 12% of women who had children under 6 years of age were in the labour force; in 1979, over 43% of women who had children under 6 were working outside the home (US Department of Labor, 1980). Just within the 1970s, the participation rate rose from 30% to 43%.

Thus, the characteristics of women workers have changed over the past 30 years. Working women are now a more diverse group than they were in 1950. A high percentage of working women today are also wives and/or mothers. They have dependants to support and family obligations to meet.

CHARACTERISTICS OF WOMEN'S WORK

Although the shifts in labour force participation rates by age, educational level, marital status, and presence or absence of children have been discussed and analyzed, these factors have not captured the imagination of the media and researchers like shifts in occupation. Much research and public attention has focused on women who have entered non-traditional (that is, male-dominated) occupations. Pictures and articles featuring professional, managerial, and blue-collar women are featured in newspapers and advertisements. While they serve the very useful function of showing that women can do those jobs, they also suggest, erroneously, that women are now prevalent in non-traditional work.

In reality, the occupations of working women in 1980 are not that different from the occupations of working women in 1950. In some respects, this is in contrast to the changes in characteristics of working women in terms of their age, marital status, and presence and age of children. Most women are entering the same few female-dominated occupations such as clerical work and some professional occupations. For example, a representative sample of working men and women in Los Angeles County in 1980 (Gutek, 1981; Gutek, in preparation), showed that 46.7% of working women were in clerical jobs; 63% of women under age 20 were in clerical work, and over 57% of women aged 20–24 were in clerical work.

Nationally, the percentage of women in clerical work rose steadily from 1950 to 1979. In 1950, 62% of clerical workers were women, in 1960, 68% of clerical workers were women, in 1970, women were 74% of clerical workers and in 1980 they were 80%. In 1950, 95% of the secretaries/typists in the United States were women; in 1979, 99% of the secretaries/typists were women (US Department of Labor, 1980).

Despite these figures, women have made some inroads into non-traditional jobs. For example, from 1950 to 1979, women engineers increased from 1.2% to 2.9%; women carpenters increased from 0.4% to 1.3%; women bus drivers increased from 1% to 8%; and women protective service workers increased from 2% to 9% (US Department of Labor, 1980). Overall, however, the bulk of the increase in female labour force participation is in a few job categories in which 70% or more of the workers are women.

Sex-segregated work

The above discussion suggests two conclusions: that women are clustered into relatively few occupations and that work is sex-segregated (see also Nieva and Gutek, 1981, chapter 1; Laws, 1979; Oppenheimer, 1968; Schrank and Riley, 1976; Coser, 1980).

The extent of sex-segregation is well-documented. For example, Coser (1980) reported that 'one-half of all female workers in America can be found in 21 occupations and male workers in 65 occupations' (p. 52). And Laws (1979) reported that 69% of men would have to change jobs in order to eliminate sex-segregated work in the United States.

The extent of sex segregation was demonstrated by Gutek (in preparation); she was able to correctly predict a worker's sex 80% of the time on the basis of just four sex-segregation variables: whether there were more men or more women in the subject's job, whether the worker's supervisor was male or female, the amount of work time spent with the opposite sex, and the percentage of women in the subject's occupation. In general, men work with men as colleagues, have male bosses, supervise other people, and spend relatively little time in work-related interaction with women. All of these results support the finding that work is sex-segregated.

Furthermore, according to data provided by Meyer and Maes (1983), that situation is likely to remain. In predicting the percentage of women *entering* an occupation, they found that the strongest predictor was the percentage of women *currently in* the occupation. In fact, it accounted for over 80% of the variance in percentage of new entrants that were women. These data suggest that interests, tastes, and preferences of women may not be very important in determining the kinds of jobs women get. They do show that women enter jobs in which women predominate.

Low-paid work

In addition to the fact that most women work in female jobs, that work is characterized by low pay. The 'feminization of poverty', a term that has been used in the past few years, captures the essence of the situation (Pearce, 1978). It is not surprising that probably the single most widely discussed and researched aspect of women's work is its relatively low pay.

Women continue to earn much less than men, even in occupations in which women predominate. For example, in clerical work, full-time women workers earn 64% of male clerical workers' salaries (US Department of Labor, 1980).

Overall, in 1978, the average women earned $0.59 for every $1.00 earned by the average man. This figure represents a decline from 1955 when the average woman earned $0.64 for every $1.00 earned by the average working man (US Department of Labor, 1980). The figures are less discrepant in some occupations than in others. For example, in full-time sales jobs, women earn only 51% of what the average salesman earns; whereas in the professional–technical occupations, women earn 71% of what the average man earns in those fields.

The pay discrepancies have been subject to much speculation and research. In general, the research shows that the discrepancies can be reduced, but not eliminated, by taking into account factors such as time on the job and relevance of educational background. For example, Suter and Miller (1973) showed that women earned only 62% of men's income, even after they took into account education, occupational status, differences in work status during the income year, and years in the labour force (see also Treiman and Terrell, 1975; Featherman and Hauser, 1976).

Short career ladder

Besides low pay and a preponderance of women, 'women's work' in the United States is also characterized by a short career ladder. The occupations tend to have relatively low ceilings; that is, there is limited opportunity for upward mobility within the occupation. Elementary school teachers and social workers tend to stay in the same positions; the same is true of female secretaries, waitresses, and receptionists. Furthermore, there is limited mobility across occupations or within careers. In other words, women's jobs do not have clear career paths that include advancement. Male-dominated professions such as engineering or finance are considered appropriate stepping stones to management positions. However, female-dominated professions such as elementary school teaching and nursing do not lead directly to positions in school administration or hospital administration.

The limited opportunities available in women's work are alluded to in Raelin's (1982) longitudinal analysis of young men's and women's careers. While men have multiple ways of achieving high occupational status and high earnings, the options for women are much more limited. For example, for men mobility is positively (although not strongly) related to increased earnings, but there is no relationship between mobility and earnings for women. When women change jobs, they generally do not earn more money. Nor do they 'advance' with job changes.

Personal characteristics

Although relatively little research has been done on the topic, it is possible to argue that women's work often depends on their personal appearance and their gender more than it does on their academic qualifications or work experience (MacKinnon, 1979, chapter 2). Linton (1936) made a useful distinction between ascribed characteristics (that come with the person and are not enhanced by effort or training) and achieved characteristics (that result from the actor's efforts and accomplishments). The extent to which women's work depends on their ascribed rather than achieved characteristics limits the ability of talented women to advance at work. Gutek's research (Gutek, 1981; Gutek and Nakamura, 1982) suggested that personal appearance and personality were more important factors in women's work than in men's work. Almost 60% of women said that physical attractiveness was at least somewhat important on their jobs, and a majority said that physical attractiveness affects the way they are treated by men at work. In addition, 58% said that having a good personality is *very* important in the way they are treated by men at work.

Indirect support for the view that a woman's physical attractiveness is important at work was provided by Levinson's (1975) research. He found that when men applied for traditionally female jobs such as receptionist in a physician's office, they were often told such things as 'I'm sure the doctors would rather have a woman', or 'we are just looking for a girl' (p. 537).

DISCRIMINATION AGAINST WOMEN IN THE WORKPLACE

As a result of her review of the literature, Almquist (1977) assessed the situation this way: 'I am arguing that employer discrimination is the chief factor which produces wage gaps between men and women' (p. 851). She is not alone in her assessment. Others, including some US government agencies, have concluded that women experience discrimination at work.

Social psychologists usually make a distinction between discriminatory behaviour (discrimination) and prejudicial attitudes (prejudice). Thus, women are discriminated against when they are treated differently from men. There is prejudice against women when people hold negative attitudes about women as a group. In theory, discrimination can occur in the absence of prejudice and prejudiced people do not necessarily behave in a discriminatory manner.

In the United States the cultural norms generally support efforts to eliminate discrimination but view prejudice as individual belief, appropriately outside the influence of government policy. Thus, researchers interested in public policy tend to be interested in documenting behavioural differences between the sexes, e.g. differences in pay, advancement, criteria for promotion (Abramson, 1979; Astin and Snyder, 1982).

Factors maintaining discrimination

After documenting and verifying the existence of discrimination, a next step is to identify the factors that maintain discrimination and examine ways to change them. In this section we examine three broad sets of factors that contribute to the generally unfavourable position of women workers relative to men. In each of these areas we will highlight some of the current research efforts of American scholars. First are structural factors in the work-place. We argue that the ways that organizations, occupations, and families are currently structured facilitate and support differential treatment of men and women workers. Here we focus on two structural factors that are attracting research interest: sex-ratios and sex-role spillover.

Second, we focus on interpersonal factors in the work-place. We argue that the ways that men and women behave as members of same-sex dyads or opposite-sex dyads contribute to differential treatment of men and women workers. Here we discuss two factors that are attracting research interest: sexual harassment and mentoring. We also mention networking, a topic that is widely discussed but not well researched yet.

Third, we focus on cognitive factors in the work-place. We argue that the beliefs held by men and women about themselves and the other sex contribute to differential treatment of men and women workers. Here we focus on three sets of beliefs that have engaged the interest of researchers: stereotype biases, attribution biases, and self-serving biases.

Structural factors

Sex-ratios

Earlier in the chapter we discussed the extent of sex segregation of work. The term 'sex-ratio' is used to describe the gender composition of an entity (e.g. group, department, organization, occupation). The sex-ratio of a group can be skewed (e.g. 90% male and 10% female) or relatively balanced (e.g. 55% male and 45% female). While the sex-ratios are themselves one indication of differential treatment of men and women, they also have been shown to contribute to differential treatment. Kanter (1977a,b) pioneered this research area by convincingly spelling out some of the probable consequences of being in the minority.

When a person's group is in the minority, that person may be assigned the difficult and onerous task of acting as a spokesperson/representative for her/his group (e.g. asking a woman for the 'women's point of view' (Taylor, *et. al.* 1978).

Another major effect of being in the minority is visibility.

Outside their traditional positions in the workplace, women are highly visible. Their presence is immediately noted, although this does not mean that their achievements are similarly prominent, since the attention directed at them arises from their deviant characteristic—their gender. As Kanter (1977a,b) notes, male colleagues would tend to forget information about a woman's credentials and expertise, while remembering her dress style and appearance (Nieva and Gutek, 1981, pp. 64–5).

Visibility often brings with it pressures to perform that are not felt by majority members. The minority person, if a woman, has to look good in order to justify her position, but if she looks too good or performs too well, she may arouse a backlash because she has stepped out of an appropriate feminine role.

A special class of research on sex-ratios concerns the solo or the token, terms used to refer to the only person of one kind in a group (Laws, 1975; Kanter, 1977b; Northcraft and Martin, 1982). The term 'token' according to Laws (1975) '. . . is a member of an underrepresented group, who is operating on the turf of the dominant group, under license from it' (p. 51). Northcraft and Martin (1982) use the term 'token' to refer to a solo who works in an organization that is pressured (usually by Federal regulation) to increase its representation of women and minorities. Their research (1982) has shown that token status is a case of double jeopardy; besides having all the pressures of being a minority, the token must face a work group who believes that the token was an inferior candidate, hired only to fulfill Affirmative Action regulations.

Sex-role spillover

Sex-role spillover refers to the 'carryover of other gender-based roles into the workplace' (Nieva and Gutek, 1981, p. 60). The 'stroking function' (Bernard, 1972) is one such aspect. Sex-role spillover occurs, for example, when women are expected to be more nurturant, sympathetic, and loyal than men in the same work roles.

Sex-roles spillover means that workers are treated or expected to behave in a manner that is more consistent with their sex-role than with their work role. These expectations may be held by both sexes, and by both actor and observer (Gutek and Morasch, 1982). For example, a man may expect a female worker to be a sex object and she may expect that she will be a sex object.

At least three influences underlie the occurrence of sex-role spillover (Gutek and Morasch, 1982). One is that gender is a more basic cognitive category than work role (Bem, 1981; Laws, 1979). Bem (1981) noted that gender-based cognitive processing is based on society's insistence that an individual's sex makes a difference in all areas of life. Laws (1975) is even more outspoken: 'Gender is a master status, which conditions all social interactions of the individual' (p. 53). A second reason for sex-role spillover is that women may feel more comfortable with traditional female roles in some circumstances at work, especially if they think men will accept them more readily if they behave that way. A third reason is that men feel more comfortable under some circumstances responding to a woman in familiar role relationships, such as parent, son, spouse, lover. For example, Gutek et. al. (1983) found that men were more likely than women to label sexually ambiguous interactions between a man and woman as appropriate for the work-place. The prevalence of sex-segregated jobs means that many men are not accustomed to interacting with women as colleagues and feel uncomfortable trying to do so (Gutek and Morasch, 1982).

The emphasis on sex-role to the neglect of work-role means that women's work accomplishments may be ignored whereas her hairstyle, for example, will be noticed. This lack of emphasis on the appropriate work-role behaviour of women serves to make their accomplishments invisible. Women may not be considered for certain jobs or promotions because their accomplishments are not publicly known.

Interpersonal factors

The interpersonal factors we examine—sexual harassment, mentoring, networking—are primarily interpersonal; that is, they occur between two or more people. However, the structure in which they occur influences the interpersonal events. For example, a mentor–protegé relationship may be quite different in a context of skewed sex ratios than it is in a sex-integrated organization.

Sexual harassment

The issue of sexuality in the work-place became visible, and was brought to public attention, in the form of sexual harassment. The first accounts of sexual harassment were journalistic reports and case studies (Safran, 1976; Lindsey, 1977; Pogrebin, 1977). The first large-scale, systematic analysis of the problem was Farley's *Sexual Shakedown: the sexual harassment of women on the job* (1978), a book that not only defined the concept but also provided numerous examples of harassment of women in a variety of jobs and life situations.

Farley's book was followed closely by MacKinnon's *Sexual Harassment of Working Women* (1979). MacKinnon, an attorney, was not interested in merely publicizing the existence of sexual harassment. Her goal was to provide a basis for legal action to combat sexual harassment. In a strong and convincing argument, MacKinnon contended that sexual harassment was primarily a problem for women, that it did not happen to men, and therefore it should be viewed as a form of sex discrimination. Viewing sexual harassment as a form of sex discrimination made available to victims of sexual harassment the same legal protection available to victims of sex discrimination.

Defining sexual harassment has been problematic for lawyers and researchers (as well as working women!). Should sexual harassment be limited to forced sexual relations? Should it be limited to situations of unequal power, i.e. supervisor–subordinate relationships? Can a worker harass a co-worker, or only a subordinate? How about touching, cornering, leering, staring, obscene gestures, comments, jokes? Can these constitute sexual harassment? As it turns out, some women and men consider all of these to be sexual harassment. A few do not consider any of these to be sexual harassment (Gutek *et. al.*, 1980; Gutek, 1981). In general, women are more likely than men to label any behaviour sexual harassment. For example, among Los Angeles County workers, 85% of women but only 55% of men said that sexual touching is sexual harassment (Gutek, 1981).

One commonly used definition of sexual harassment, *unwanted* sexual overtures, has the virtue of parsimony, but necessarily concerns intentions and motivation, not just overt behaviour. Defining sexual harassment as unwanted sexual overtures has the same problem that is inherent in defining rape as unwanted sexual relations. In practice, it becomes incumbent upon the woman to prove that the sexual relations or the sexual overtures were unwanted (Burt, 1981).

One strong early thrust of the literature on sexual harassment has been that of documentation. For example, one of the earlier representative surveys (Gutek, et. al., 1980) found that 11% of employed women in Los Angeles County reported that they were expected to engage in sexual relations in order to get or keep their job. Another 24% of women reported receiving sexual insults.

The United States Merit Systems Protection Board (1981) studied a representative sample of the entire federal work force to assess the amount of sexual harassment. They found that 9% of women reported experiencing pressure for sexual favours within the last 2 years at work. Twenty-six per cent of women reported deliberate sexual touching and 33% of women reported receiving sexual comments. The study concluded that, overall, 42% of women in the Federal work force were sexual harassed.

Another large-scale representative survey was done by Gutek (1981; in progress); this one included 827 working women in the Los Angeles area. She found that up to 53% of women have been sexual harassed at work. Nine per cent of women quit a job some time in their working lives because of sexual harassment. Altogether, over 30% of women have suffered some negative consequence of sexual harassment in their working lives. Together these studies demonstrated that sexual harassment is widespread and has significant consequences for working women.

Another thrust of the literature has been to examine the work environment. In choosing to focus on the work environment, researchers recognize that sexual harassment is not just an event that happens between two people. The norms, rules, and constraints of the organization profoundly affect the way people behave in that setting. The hierarchical nature of work organizations is also relevant. The rules and norms of managers apply to their subordinates and often extend to their subordinates' subordinates. Top management has the power to influence employees' work habits, style of dress, recreational interests, and social behaviour. When top management tolerates or condones sexual harassment of employees, that standard reverberates throughout the organization (Gutek and Nakamura, 1982). Thus, sexual harassment, like other forms of interpersonal behaviour in an organizational context, is strongly influenced by that context.

Mentoring

The terms 'mentoring' and 'networking' have become popular in recent years.

As used in the media, they refer to the establishment of informal and formal contacts that can be of assistance in furthering one's career and in furthering the careers of others of their group (Rosen *et. al.*, 1981; Atkinson *et. al.*, 1980; Blackburn *et al.*, 1981).

Mentoring refers to the specific relationship of a junior-level worker to a senior in which the junior—the protegé—is 'trained, developed, and given special advice, inside information, critical experiences, and social status by association with his mentors' (Nieva and Gutek, 1981, p. 57). In addition to providing access to information and contacts, the mentor functions as a role-model for the protegé, providing guidance on the correct way to behave in a variety of situations, what attitudes are appropriate, and what aspirations are appropriate.

Women are rarely sponsored in this manner (Epstein, 1970a, b; Warihay, 1980). Women often play the assistant role but mentors only infrequently see them as interested or worthy successors. In addition, women may not recognize the importance of having a mentor. For example, the female executive managers studied by Hennig and Jardim (1977) emphasized superior competence and technical ability as the true determinants of advancement. Similarly, Schreiber (1979) found that the biggest worry of women entering male-dominated technical jobs was whether or not they would be able to do the job. Nieva and Gutek (1981) pointed out that many men, on the other hand, 'are concerned with informal ties of loyalty and dependence that can make the critical difference in an employee's life and movement at work' (p. 58).

Networking

Whereas mentoring refers to a relationship of a senior-level person to a junior-level person, networking is used to refer to support groups among peers. Women's networks have sprung up in various cities and within a variety of occupations. Sometimes they are formalized, as in the American Psychological Association's division on women or the Academy of Management's Women in Management Division. Less formal women's networks exist within many large companies and universities as well. Relatively little research has emerged yet on the meaning or effectiveness of networking.

Cognitive biases

An additional factor maintaining discrimination appears to be that of cognitive biases concerning the processing of information regarding both one's own efforts and abilities and those of others. We consider this factor a failure in information processing because it is mistaken and, apparently, unintended.

Thus if men and women inaccurately assess their efforts, discrimination may arise based on these mistaken beliefs.

Three types of cognitive biases have been shown to be of importance with respect to women's work and discrimination: stereotype or socialization-based biases, attributional biases, and self-serving biases. These and the mechanisms for dealing with them are discussed in the sections below.

Stereotype and gender discount biases

Among the most pervasive biases in American culture are those pertaining to what males and females are capable of doing—and 'should' appropriately do. Very young children are taught to prefer toys, activities, and careers stereotypically appropriate for their sex and will avoid those which are inappropriate, even when they have not seen the toy and are aware only of stereotypic labelling (Fling and Manosevitz, 1972; Gettys & Cann, 1981; Stein et. al., 1971).

The general nature of these stereotypes suggests that women are warm and expressive, while men are competent (Broverman, et. al., 1972). Similarly, men are respected, while women are liked. By implication, work activities requiring competence are the province of the male, while others requiring nurturance are left to the female.

'Gender discount' bias shows how stereotyping works in practice. A variety of research studies have shown that women's performance and nurturant activities are rewarded less and are considered less valuable than men's, or activities assumed to require more competence (although we wonder if that would still be true if men were stereotyped as more nurturant). This has been termed the 'gender discount'—if a woman did it, whatever 'it' is, the result is worth less than if done by a man. Thus scholarly work written by women is rated as less competent and persuasive than the same work said to be written by a man (Goldberg, 1968), and a woman who irrefutably does perform well is considered exceptional (Abramson et. al., 1977; Pheterson, et. al., 1971).

Similarly, when subjects were told that specific occupations such as law and architecture would experience an influx of women, those occupations were rated as less prestigious than when the subjects were led to believe that men dominated or would continue to dominate the field (Touhey, 1974a, b). These studies and others (e.g. Deaux Taynor, 1973; Dipboye et al., 1975, 1977; Rosen and Jerdee, 1974; Lao et al., 1975) suggest that, at least under some circumstances, women and their accomplishments are valued less than men and their accomplishments.

A critical review of the literature by Nieva and Gutek (1980) showed that the gender discount is most likely to operate in three situations. First, gender bias is more prevalent when the evaluator has relatively little information about a woman and is required to make inferences about her performance or abilities. Thus there is more gender discount in evaluating a candidate for a job than in evaluating an employee who already works for the organization. In general, the greater the required level of inference or assurance on the part of the evaluator, the greater the gender bias. Second, bias occurs against those violating sex role expectations more often than against those behaving consistent with them. Finally, gender bias seems to be affected by the level of performance involved: when high competence is required, women are evaluated less favourably than men; when only low-level performance is needed, women are not penalized as much relative to men with objectively equal skills.

It should be noted that stereotyping also has consequences within particular professions. For example, women in the Air Force are viewed as incompetent and are overprotected, making it difficult for them to develop or display their abilities (Adams et. al., 1979; Woefel, 1981). Management is viewed as a men's profession, and men are stereotyped as being like managers, while women are viewed as unlike either men or managers (Massengill and Di Marco, 1979; Schein, 1975). Medical students of both sexes commonly avoid association with women medical students whom they stereotype as unqualified (Kutner and Brogan, 1981). It is not surprising therefore to find that women are discriminated against for entry into each of these professions and are held to a higher level of accountability once there (Larwood et. al., 1979).

The studies above are only a representative selection of several hundred related research articles concerning sex stereotyping and gender discount appearing in American research literature during the past decade. In contrast to this topic, the other forms of bias discussed below have received relatively less attention (Larwood and Powell, 1981).

Attributional biases

For the past decade, social psychologists have examined the process by which people attribute causality to events. Weiner, et. al., (1971) suggested that an event such as job success may be attributed in any of four ways. It may be ascribed internally to either effort or ability, or externally to task difficulty or luck.

The manner in which an individual attributes success or failure on a task can influence both willingness to try the task again, and what is learned from the outcome. For example, most of us are unwilling to try a task repeatedly on which we anticipate failure. Further, success which can be ascribed to our ability or effort provides information which may be useful to future behaviour, while success ascribed to luck offers few guidelines.

During the last decade, observers have frequently found that men and women attribute their successes and failures differently from one another but consistent with the general stereotyping described above. Men see their successes more as the result of their abilities, while women are more likely to view their successes as the result of good fortune (Bar-Tal and Frieze, 1976; Deaux and Farris, 1977; McMahan, 1982). In addition, men are more likely to attribute failure to luck, while women often see failure as a demonstration of their expected lack of ability.

The source of these attributional differences appears buried in the socialization history of American women in which they are taught that they are unlikely to succeed in non-traditional areas, and even that their success may be frowned upon or punished by others in society (Kahn, 1981; Larwood and Wood, 1977). The attributional differences have the unfortunate consequence of producing a 'low expectation cycle' (Jackaway, 1975; see also Gitelson et al., 1982), in which even repeatedly experienced success may fail to raise a woman's expectations concerning her task or problem-solving ability. Perhaps as a result of low expectations, women are more likely to over-prepare (such as through obtaining additional schooling) before making changes in the job market; men are more likely to obtain on-the-job training if they need it—or simply to make a change (Gurin, 1981).

It seems likely that women who deliberately select demanding professions such as management or medicine are less subject to these attributional biases. Nonetheless, evidence indicates that even highly achievement-motivated women are somewhat reluctant to view their successes as a result of ability, instead ascribing it to effort (Bar-Tal and Frieze, 1976), at least publicly (private sex differences in ascriptions are little studied).

Most evidence concerning this phenomenon has been gathered in artificial situations which do not resemble the actual work environment. A recent study of matched male and female supervisory employees in two firms shows how this is extended into work activities, however. Men evaluated themselves as performing better, doing more difficult jobs, and as being more intelligent. Women in both samples felt that ability was less important to their success than did men (Deaux, 1979).

Self-serving biases

For some time, educators and personnel evaluators have recognized that people often overstate their likelihood of success. While observers originally dismissed this as harmless optimism, more recent investigators have noted that overstatement can have some quite real and important consequences. For example, those biased in this manner may plan their futures in an unrealistic manner (Weinstein, 1980), overexpand their businesses (Larwood and Whittaker, 1977), or have difficulty in meeting their goals (Kidd & Morgan, 1969).

While several forms have been identified, it now appears that one type of self-serving bias is of particular concern to members of the work force. In this form, individuals selectively recall information which places them in a positive light relative to others or to objective reality. Unless they are faced with a confidence-shaking event which they cannot avoid recalling, they can maintain their high expectations despite minor setbacks. Major negative events force the individual to become realistic only with respect to activities similar to that on which difficulty was experienced, and do not broadly generalize to others (Larwood, 1978; Larwood and Whittaker, 1977).

As yet, there is little direct research concerning how this phenomenon affects women in the work force, and there is no reason to expect sex differences in self-serving bias. Nonetheless, it appears that women face a double problem with self-serving bias: that is, both they and their employers are subject to it. For example, a woman will probably overpredict her likelihood of avoiding discrimination (Northcraft and Martin, 1982). Meanwhile, her employer is likely to believe that he or she is different from other employers and does not discriminate against women. If this analysis is correct, neither the woman nor her employer sees any reason to change course—a course which may lead to substantial disappointment, under-utilization of resources, and discrimination.

Some existing evidence supports these conclusions. National probability samples of women workers have shown that up to 95% suffer actual financial discrimination relative to equally prepared men in the same jobs. Nonetheless, only 8% of women were aware of any discrimination against themselves in a 1969 study; several years later this figure had risen to 16%—but was still substantially below the actual level of discrimination (Levitin, *et al* 1971; Staines *et al.*, 1976).

What of employers? Self-serving bias predicts thay they feel they are doing well by women—despite the continuing discrimination. Indeed, this has been found. Fifty per cent of the firms in one study felt they had difficulty in recruiting acceptable women, 29% said they could not retain women, and 25% indicated that their policies were so favourable towards women as to incite fears of reverse discrimination on the part of other personnel (Larwood, 1982). Nevertheless, many large organizations have now been successfully sued on grounds of discrimination—although this has apparently produced little meaningful change (Miner, 1976).

Dealing with biases

The biases described above have been directly attacked by a series of federal (US nationwide) and sometimes state regulations, each attempting to prevent discrimination or eliminate some of its sources. The three most important groups of direct federal regulations are discussed here. The overall thrust of regulations against discrimination has been towards forcing employers to examine the entire work force potentially available for a particular activity, to train and promote fairly, and to pay both sexes equally for the same work. Further discussions appear in Ledvinka (1982), and Hall and Albrecht (1979).

1. The *Equal Pay Act* makes it illegal for a single employer with more than $250,000 per year in sales to pay men and women differently for 'substantially equal work' and allows women to sue for up to 2 years' back-pay and additional damages in the federal courts. While seemingly advantageous, the act relies on the enforcement efforts of those believing themselves discriminated against. Further, it allows exceptions to be made for instances of differing pay at different locations, or different levels of experience, seniority, or productivity. Thus it is useful in ending only the most obvious cases of pay discrimination.

2. In contrast, the *Equal Employment Opportunity Act* empowers a federal commission to actively attack sex discrimination in hiring, promotions, layoffs, transfers, fringe benefits, and training—as well as in pay. In recent years sexual harassment has also been viewed as unfair sex discrimination, and guidelines to define and eradicate sexual harassment have been added. To aid in enforcement, employers are required to file an annual summary of their employment by sex at each of nine organizational levels. The act nominally applies to all private and many public employers of fifteen or more persons. In practice, however, the enormous backlog of cases brought under this act (at one point over 150,000 cases pending, stretching back several years) has resulted in active prosecution of only the larger and more visible employers. After initial attempts at fact-finding and mediation, women may be empowered by the act to proceed with their suit by themselves (or sometimes on behalf of a 'class' of other women in their situation). The most frequent settlement is back-pay and the employer's agreement to refrain from particular discriminatory practices.

Although the act is stated in general terms, the federal commission enforcing it has been considerably more specific. For example, it has required that all employment tests which have a discriminatory result be shown to be good predictors of on-the-job performance. Where less discriminatory tests with only modestly less performance validity are available, employers are required to use the less discriminatory alternatives. In some cases employers have been required to change job specifications in minor ways to allow those with a smaller physical stature to perform them. The ladders used by telephone companies are now provided such that they can be obtained from company trucks with a minimum of brute strength.

3. Several US Presidents have issued 'Executive Orders' banning discrimination by the government itself or by those contracting with the government.

The orders have built compliance with equal employment opportunity into federal contracts, and require that both major contractors and government departments monitor their employment of women relative to the proportion available to assume major job categories (through recruitment, advancement, or training). Substantial imbalances are to be redressed through 'affirmative action programmes' in which the employer sets down plans to obtain a higher proportion of women over an extended period of time. In fact, however, affirmative action plans are frequently unenforced, and few organizations have been threatened with suspension of their government contracts.

What is the effect of the legal attack on bias? Some discriminatory procedures have been changed. For example, many employers have dropped discriminatory employment tests (Lancaster, 1976), and the requirement for affirmative action has sensitized both men and women to the general problem of discrimination (whether or not they apply it to their particular situation). Holding employers responsible for sexual harassment has alerted many women to their rights and made obvious sexual threats much more difficult and risky.

The results are often contradictory and difficult to fully evaluate, however. For example, a study of women in higher education (Astin and Snyder, 1982) found that women's proportion of new PhDs increased from 13.6% in the 1967–72 period to 26.0% in 1975–80 . . . at least partly in response to regulations prohibiting sex discrimination in education and to the new opportunities perceived by women in the academic job market. Nonetheless, women were still underrepresented among new PhDs being hired by major institutions, taught more hours than men, had a growing but lower amount of research support, and were increasingly but still less likely than men to publish. Women academics in 1980 earned 77% of what men earned—an identical discount to that of 1972—although the gap was smaller with increased research productivity and rank with women full professors earning 90% of the salaries of men at that level. The proportion of tenured men increased by 17.7% between 1972 and 1980, while the proportion of tenured women increased by only 13.4%, and women were less likely to be promoted. A part of this problem may be attributed to the shrinking academic job market necessarily less receptive to keeping and promoting those without experience than others who had already obtained some status.

In contrast to the position of women in higher education, the overall position of working women relative to men has become worse since the onset of regulation (US Commission on Civil Rights, 1978), and there is little overall policy difference between firms which have been successfully prosecuted or sued and those which have not been (Miner, 1976). This pessimistic view is tempered by several other factors, however. For one, the overall legal position of women has been changing rapidly with the result that many more opportunities are open than previously. Rather than being regarded as legal and economic chattel of their husbands, women have equal and independent property rights in most states. Banks have recently been prohibited from discriminating against women seeking financing and can no longer require a male cosigner or disregard a woman's income in issuing loans. Further, despite a period of general economic turmoil, an unprecedented proportion of women have entered the work force—many for the first time or without directly related prior experience that would justify an advanced position with high pay. Thus it may be that the worsening job conditions reported by the Commission on Civil Rights has ignored many important related issues. The situation of women might be substantially worse without the regulations concerning discrimination, harassment, and the overall economic status of women. Still, there seems little reason to judge them an unqualified success.

In contrast, there is evidence that the regulations may be a counter-productive means for attacking bias. Researchers are finding that men fear the possibility of reverse discrimination (Larwood, 1982). Also, strong legal sanctions against discrimination may cause employers to react negatively against the restraints on their hiring freedom (Rosen and Mericle, 1979) or to evaluate women as less capable than men (Siegfried, 1982). Men labour under the assumption that women and minorities would not have been employed were it not for affirmative action—that is, that they are less competent and less suitable for further promotion than a man would be in the same job (Chacko, 1982; Northcraft and Martin, 1982). It appears that underlying stereotypes cannot be effectively changed with the legal mechanisms developed to date. Political reactions against affirmative action will be considered later in this chapter.

Government regulation is but one means of changing stereotypes and attributional biases. An alternative means is through gradual change in educational and work force patterns. Women are now obtaining over half of the college degrees in the United States—and close to half of advanced degrees in some professions such as business administration (compared to less than 5% in 1970). This change in aspirations may account for the steady increase in women's scores on tests of achievement motivation, motivation to manage, and commitment to work; women's scores are now equal to or higher than those of American men (Korn/Ferry International, 1982; Miner and Smith, 1982). Interestingly, the early studies finding attributional differences between men and women have become increasingly difficult to replicate (Sohn, 1982; Travis, 1982). Both women and men with high achievement motivation react attributionally with the traditional male pattern, while both sexes with low achievement motivation react with the former traditional female pattern (Levine et al., 1982).

Self-serving biases may be more difficult than other forms of bias to change because they provide comfortable 'bubbles' in which neither party need acknowledge the true situation. While biases resulting from faulty information processing may be remedied by providing irrefutable information, self-serving biases are intensely personal. Providing employees with information that the organization discriminates does not tell them that *they* discriminate. Thus their confidence remains intact, and there is little reason for them to change. It appears that techniques must be found to make each decision-maker responsible for his or her own actions. From the point of view of women workers, it might be similarly valuable to launch programmes aimed towards identifying where their individual careers are relative to those of comparable men.

TRENDS IN THE FUTURE

The discussions above have already suggested some of the trends for the future of women at work in the United States. The increase of women in the work force and the political backlash to affirmative action, for example, can be reliably projected into the future. These and other trends regarding the position of women, important cultural and political side-effects, and the development of theory are examined in depth in this section.

Position of women

A temporary increase of women among the American work force is not unusual. Wartime, for instance, typically brings women into jobs formerly held by men; at the end of the war, the men return to the jobs and the women return home. Following the Second World War, the services of many women in the military were not acknowledged, while men were given the opportunity for free education. Further, legislation was passed requiring civilian women workers to give up their jobs to men returning from the war.

The current influx of women into the work force seems unlikely to be temporary and is distinguished from previous increases in several ways. Instead of being discouraged by regulations, it is encouraged. Rather than being accompanied by a period of national military emergency, it is accompanied instead by personal economic emergency in which two earners are needed by many families to maintain their expected level of income. At the same time, the women's movement and reliable family planning have helped bring women into the work force and sustain them once there.

Educational institutions have actively cooperated in seeking women students for most professions because they are facing a steadily declining number of young men to fill their classes. Proportionately fewer men are attending college, with the result that half of the college population is female for the first time. While women have been slower to enter many professional

graduate programmes, this is also changing. For example, women now constitute over 40% of those seeking master's degrees in business at many leading
universities—up from less than 5% in 1970 (Scherrei, 1979).

Education is one of the accepted routes to career success in North
American society (Larwood and Wood, 1977; Nieva and Gutek, 1980).
Eighty-eight per cent of the single women in a study at York University in
Toronto said they planned a career (Greenglass and Devins, 1982); 95% of
women at Barnard College in New York planned to work or have careers,
while 16% planned careers without children (Komarovsky, 1982). On this
basis we can anticipate that the change in women obtaining educational
degrees will translate to larger numbers of women obtaining entry level
professional jobs—in addition to entry level non-professional positions.

The population bulge of children born during the war and postwar periods
is now at or approaching mid-career (Barabba, 1981). In the past this group
may have acted as a block to the success and advancement of new women
workers by absorbing positions itself, but a dramatic decline in the proportion
of young adults in the next decade will result in labour scarcity at a time
when women have the skills and education to take advantage of it.

Time is required for advancement to occur and for those who now have
entry level positions to progress beyond them. Since those who are more
successful or who have more investment (time, education, or commitment)
are less likely to leave the labour market for long periods, we anticipate that
women now in the labour market will remain . . . and that their numbers
will continue to grow. Further, their success, so far difficult to document,
should gradually become more apparent.

Cultural side-effects

Since the past long-term standard has been the male-breadwinner, single-
earner family, we can anticipate considerable cultural change as a result of
women becoming a joint or, in many families, the only, wage-earner. Children are socialized to a different standard and in a different way. Families
must cope with the loss of 'free' time on the part of the woman who might
previously have performed as a housewife.

One of the questions examined closely by researchers has been that of
how children accept having their mothers working. Early warnings by tradi-
tionalists suggested that girls would grow up confused and boys would
become more often involved in disciplinary problems. We now have solid
research on these points which shows that the changes to be expected are
much more modest—and optimistic. Several studies have found that a
mother's working has no direct effect on self-concept, aspirations, or maturity
of children of either sex (Rosenthal and Hansen, 1981; Wise and Joy, 1982).
Daughters develop attitudes towards work and liberation of women similar

to those held by their mothers (Rollins and White, 1982), and may resist stereotyping themselves if their mothers behave in a non-stereotypic manner (Urberg, 1982; see also Hoffman, 1979 for a review of this literature).

Dual-work or dual-career couples have to work out a non-traditional pattern of family activities (Nieva and Gutek, 1981, chapter 4). Early research found that each $1000 increase in a woman's income led to a 2% increase in the divorce rate—although the implications of that finding were unclear (Johnson, 1975). Evidence is now accumulating that fathers in dual-career families participate with their children to a greater extent than do fathers who are sole-earners (Baruch and Barnett, 1981). Weingarten (1978) found that husbands who have similar employment histories to their wives do a greater portion of family work than other husbands. It is also of interest to note that men who are feminist perform more housework, child care, and related activities than other men (Perucci, *et al.*, 1978). A recent review of research has indicated that women in dual-career families are actually happier than women who are housewives. Overall marital satisfaction is likely to increase unless the couple holds the view that a wife's work signals the husband's failure to be able to support the family (Yogev, 1982).

There are still major cultural problems to be resolved. The extent of a husband's involvement in family activities is still substantially less than the involvement of the wife—and this limits her discretionary personal and career development (Berk and Berk, 1979; Nieva and Gutek, 1981, chapter 4). Quality day care centres are still expensive or unavailable to most working women; most employers have not yet reached the point of viewing day care for children as a valuable mechanism for increasing worker performance. Nonetheless, it appears that the change under way to dual-earner couples and dual-involvement families is healthy and increasingly supported by social expectations and custom. We anticipate that this change will gather force in the decade ahead.

Political side-effects

The political concomitants of the movement of women into the labour force are substantial, both at the level of the employer and of the federal government. This section discusses just three aspects of this movement: organizational backlash, the sidelining of affirmative action, and the organization of women in politics.

Organizational backlash

As noted earlier, some research has indicated that affirmative action programmes can have undesirable results: those employees who are not covered by such programmes may themselves fear discrimination, and women who obtain key positions are viewed as less capable than the comparably-skilled men who otherwise would have those jobs. The painfully slow change in the proportion of women in meaningful positions may partly reflect these two effects.

Because of the legal implications of direct discrimination, some organizations appear to have become more covert in their means of discrimination. This is not to suggest a conspiracy. Instead, employers deliberately select the personnel whom they feel are best, but their beliefs may be swayed by attributions of inability stemming from the regulations. Individual organization members who otherwise favour equal rights may go along with the misattributions or cover them from outside investigation. Their behaviour is justified by their fear of personal reverse discrimination or their belief that the misattributions square the imbalance created by legislation. The result is that affirmative action programmes can become paper exercises without real meaning or impact. This analysis notwithstanding, it should be recognized that there is necessarily little systematic evidence in this regard—although individual cases have been widely reported in the press.

Sidelining of affirmative action

Affirmative action is also being attacked in a more direct manner. The present President and his administration are anxious to demonstrate that they are friendly to the needs of business and other work organizations, and to dispose of unneeded paperwork and governmental inhibitions on performance. As it happens, the exercise of constructing and carrying out an affirmative action programme is the single most intensive function of personnel administrators in many organizations (Astin and Snyder, 1982) and often one of the most misunderstood—thus it becomes an ideal target of governmental attack.

Without changing the regulations themselves, different administrations can alter their effect by, for example, limiting the resources available for investigation, or promulgating changes in the rules concerning who will be investigated. Both of these alternatives have been undertaken by recent administrations; the Reagan administration has recently suggested that smaller organizations should consider themselves exempt from many requirements concerning equal opportunity and affirmative action. In a case presently being litigated, the federal Justice Department argued that previously court-approved affirmative action is illegal reverse discrimination and should be abolished. The Equal Employment Opportunity Commission, which had not been consulted by the Justice Department, was forced to withdraw from the case by pressure from the Attorney General (*Wall Street Journal*, 1983).

Political organization of women

One result of the regulations, and of the women's movement in the US, has been an increasing awareness on the part of women of the opportunities which should be open to them in the labour market. This has not only increased the numbers of working women and their career preparedness, but has also meant that a growing number are discovering discrimination and becoming concerned with their underrepresentation in meaningful positions (Staines, *et. al.*, 1976).

Aside from guarding their right more carefully in the work-place, the growing awareness has begun to transform women into a potent political voting block. While the block cannot yet be considered solid, women have moved steadily towards candidates sensitive to the problems of the working woman and who profess their interest in advancing women's rights. Work has become a feminist issue with women counting the number of women and feminist men who vote in favour of equal rights in state and federal legislatures. It seems likely that women will be even more strongly politically organized in the future, and that this block will be directly counterposed to others sidelining affirmative action or attempting to rebuild the previously traditional family relationship with the male as sole bread winner.

Development of theory

The subject of women at work has been the object of a wide-ranging group of theories extended largely from the three disciplines of sociology, psychology, and economics. Each of these social sciences has attempted to apply its analytical techniques and framework to explain observed phenomena. For example, some economists have addressed pay differentials in terms of equilibrium market conditions by suggesting that the pay of men and women fairly reflects the values of their different levels of performances (Lloyd and Niemi, 1979). Psychologists and sociologists are concerned with how sex differences in ability, differences in role socialization, and differences in status affect situation in the work-place and subsequent performance.

Despite the obvious utility of these theories, it has been shown that they explain some work phenomena only with difficulty. To cite one example, the economic argument above runs counter to the finding that women are paid less than men irrespective of their experience and productivity (Sommers, 1974; Staines, *et. al.*1976). Similarly, addressing the difficulties pointed out by the perspectives of these theories is not sufficient to promote the opportunities of women to the level of those for men.

Two changes in theory-building seem necessary. The first is that theorists must develop dynamic, or action-oriented, theories capable of predicting the effect of changes in policy and social values. These can replace the current static theories which operate with the hidden assumptions of past social tradition (Larwood and Lockheed, 1979). We need to know, for example, what changes to make in affirmative action policy, and what will occur as a consequence. Will a loosening of restrictions improve or degrade the opportunities open to women—and in what ways? A part of the reason for the lack of such theories may be that 'policy' is not considered a discipline by American researchers, and thus discipline-related theory development is accorded a premium.

A second change must be in the direction of developing organizational theories related to women at work. Organizations and management have become a strong area of research interest, yet little research or theoretical development has been directed towards understanding the thought and decisional processes of organization members who advance or discriminate against women. One possible such theory has been offered recently by Larwood *et. al.*. (1983). Their theory of 'managerial discrimination' explains how employers may discriminate irrespective of a lack of personal bias and despite understanding that women and men have the same organizational performance capabilities. According to the model, employers react to actual or assumed pressure from powerful others. In order to satisfy these others, including customers and superiors, employers behave as they believe the others would like. Since discrimination is widely practised in society, it may be appropriately assumed that the powerful others prefer discrimination unless there is evidence to the contrary. If supported by direct research evidence, this model not only indicates why discrimination is difficult to eradicate in organizations, but provides a new suggestion for coping with it (demonstrating to subordinates that equal employment opportunity is important).

Despite the evident importance of policy and organizational theory in the area of women at work, their development and testing remain tasks for the future. At this point it is possible only to determine that research interest appears to be moving in this direction. It seems likely that the continued movement of women into the work force and the development of these new areas of research will stimulate one another, although the dimensions of this interaction have still to be determined.

REFERENCES

Abramson, J. (1979) *Old Boys, New Women: the politics of sex discrimination.* Praeger Publishing, New York.

Abramson, P. R., Goldberg, P. A., Greenberg, J. H. and Abramson, L. M. (1977). 'The talking platypus phenomenon: Competency ratings as a function of sex and professional status,' *Psychology of Women Quarterly*, **2**, 114–124.

Adams, J. R. Lawrence, F. P., and Cook, S. J. (1979). 'Analyzing stereotypes of women in the work force,' *Sex Roles*, **5**, 581–594.

Almquist, E. M. (1977), 'Women in the labor force', *Signs*, **2**, 843–855.

Astin, H. S., and Snyder, M. B. (1982). 'Affirmative action 1972–1982: A decade of response', *Change*, July-August, 26–31, 59.

Atkinson, C. Alberts, R. and Belcher, F., *et. al.* (1980). 'Management development roles: coach, sponsor, and mentor, *Personnel Journal*, **59**, 918–921.

Barabba, V. P. (1981). 'Demographic change and the public work force', *The Changing Character of the Public Work Force*, 134–59–7. Office of Personnel Management, Washington, DC.

Bar-Tal, D., and Frieze, I. (1976). 'Achievement motivation and gender as determinants of attribution for success and failure'. University of Pittsburgh Learning Research and Development Center, Pittsburgh.

Baruch, G. K., and Barnett, R. C. (1981). 'Fathers' participation in the care of preschool children,' *Sex Roles*, **7**, 1043–1055.

Bem, S. (1981). 'Gender schema theory: a cognitive account of sex typing, *Psychological Review,* **88**, 354–364.

Berk, R. A. and Berk, S. F. (1979). *Labor and Leisure at Home: content and organization of the household day*. Sage, Beverly Hills, CA.

Bernard, J. (1972). *The Future of Marriage*. World Books, New York.

Blackburn, R. T., Chapman, D. W. and Cameron, S. W. (1981). 'Cloning' in academe: mentorship and academic careers', *Research in Higher Education*, **15**, 315–327.

Broverman, I. K., Vogel, S. R., Broverman, D. M., Clarkson, F. E., and Rosenkrantz, P. S. (1972) 'Sex-role stereotypes: a current appraisal', *Journal of Social Issues* **28**, 59–78.

Burt, M. R. (1981). Results of the national survey of federal workers by the U.S. Merit Systems Protection Board. In S. Tangri (Chair), 'Sexual harassment at work: evidence, remedies, and implications'. Symposium presented at the annual meeting of the American Psychological Association, Los Angeles.

Chacko, T. I. (1982). Women and equal employment opportunity: some unintended effects.' *Journal of Applied Psychology*, **67**, 119–123.

Coser, R. L. (1980). 'Women and work'. *Dissent*, **27**, 51–55.

Deaux, K. (1979). 'Self-evaluations of male and female managers', *Sex Roles*, **5**, 571–580.

Deaux, K. and Farris, E. (1977) 'Attributing causes for one's own performance: The effects of sex, norms and outcome', *Journal of Research in Personality*, *11*, 59–72.

Deaux, K. and Taynor, J. (1973). 'Evaluation of male and female ability: bias works two ways', *Psychological Reports*, **31**, 20–31.

Dipboye, R. L., Arvey, R. B. and Terpstra, D. E. (1977). Sex and physical attractiveness or raters and applicants as determinants of resume evaluations', *Journal of Applied Psychology*, **62**, 288–294.

Dipboye, R. L., Fromkin H. L., and Wiback, J. K. (1975). Relative importance of applicant sex, attractiveness, and scholastic standing in evaluation of job applicant resources', *Journal of Applied Psychology*, **60**, 39–43.

Epstein, C. (1970a). 'Encountering the male establishment: sex-status limits on women's careers in the professions', *American Journal of Sociology*, **75**, 965–982.

Epstein, C. (1970b) *Woman's Place: options and limits in professional careers*. University of California Press, Berkeley, CA.

Farley, L. (1978) *Sexual Shakedown: the sexual harassment of women on the job*. McGraw Hill, New York.

Featherman, D. L. and Hauser, R. M. (1976). 'Sexual inequalities and socioeconomic achievement in the U.S., 1962–1973', *American Sociological Review*, **41**, 462–483.

Flaim, P. O. and Fullerton, H. N. (1978). 'Labor force projections to 1990: Three possible paths', *Monthly Labor Review*, December, 225–235.

Fling, L. B. and Manosevitz, M. (1972). 'Sex typing in nursery school children's play interests', *Developmental Psychology*, **7**, 146–152.

Gettys, L. D., and Cann, A. (1981). 'Children's perceptions of occupational sex stereotypes', *Sex Roles*, **7**, 301–308.

Gitelson, L. B., Petersen, A. C. and Tobin-Richards, M. H. (1982) 'Adolescents' expectancies of success, self-evaluations, and attributions about performance on spatial and verbal tasks', *Sex Roles*, **8**, 411–419.

Goldberg, P. A. (1968). 'Are women prejudiced against women?', *Trans-Action*, **5**, 28–30.

Greenglass, E. R. and Devins, R. (1982). 'Factors related to marriage and career plans in unmarried women', *Sex Roles*, **8**, 57–71.

Gurin, P. (1981). 'Labor market experiences and expectancies', *Sex Roles*, **7**, 1079–1092.

Gutek, B. A. (1981). 'Experiences of sexual harassment: results from a representative survey', In Tangri S. (Chair), 'Sexual harassment at work: Evidence, remedies, and implications'. Symposium presented at the annual meeting of the American Psychological Association, Los Angeles, CA.

Gutek, B. A. *Sexuality at work: Experiences, reactions, attitudes* (In preparation).

Gutek, B. A., and Morasch, B., (1982). 'Sex-ratios, sex-role spillover, and sexual harassment at work', *Journal of Social Issues*, **38** (4), 55–74.

Gutek, B. A., Morasch, B., and Cohen, A. G. (1983). 'Interpreting social-sexual behaviour in a work setting', *Journal of Vocational Behavior*, **22**, 30–48.

Gutek, B. A., and Nakamura, C. Y. (1982). 'Gender roles and sexuality in the world of work', in Allgeier, E. R. and McCormick, N. B. (eds.), *Changing Boundaries; gender roles and sexual behavior*. Mayfield Publishing, Palo Alto, CA.

Gutek, B. A., Nakamura, C. Y., Gahart, M., Handschumacher, I., and Russell, D. (1980) 'Sexuality in the workplace', *Basic and Applied Social Psychology* **1**, 255–265.

Hall, F. S., and Albrecht, M. H. (1979) *The Management of Affirmative Action*. Goodyear Publishing, Santa Monica, CA.

Hennig, M. and Jardim, A. (1977). *The Managerial Woman*. Anchor Press/Doubleday, New York.

Hoffman, L. W. (1979) 'Maternal employment: 1979', *American Psychologist*, **34**, 859–865.

Jackaway, R. (1975). 'Achievement attributions and the low expectation cycle in females'. Paper delivered at the annual meeting of the American Psychological Association, Chicago.

Johnson, S. B. (1975). 'The impact of women's liberation on marriage, divorce, and family life-style', in Lloyd, C. B. (ed), *Sex, Discrimination, and the Division of Labor*. Columbia University Press, New York.

Kahn, A. (1981). 'Reactions of profeminist and antifeminist men to an expert woman', *Sex Roles*, **7**, 857–866.

Kanter, R. M. (1977a). *Men and Women of the Corporation*, Basic Books, New York.

Kanter, R. M. (1977b). 'Some effects of proportions on group life: Skewed sex ratios and responses to token women', *American Journal of Sociology*, **82**, 965–990.

Kidd, J. B., and Morgan, J. R. (1969). 'A predictive information system for management', *Operational Research Quarterly*, **20**, 149–170.

Komarovsky, M. (1982). 'Female freshmen view their future: career salience and its correlates', *Sex Roles*, **8**, 299–314.

Korn/Ferry International. (1982). *Korn/Ferry International's Profile of Women Senior Executives*. Korn/Ferry International, New York.

Kutner, N. G., and Brogan, D. R. (1981). 'Problems of colleagueship for women entering the medical profession', *Sex Roles*, **7**, 739–746.

Lancaster, H. (1976). 'Job tests are dropped for many companies due to antibias drive', *Wall Street Journal*, 3 September pp. 1, 19.

Lao, R. C., Upchurch, W. H., Corwin, B. J., and Crossnickle, W. F. (1975). 'Biased attitudes toward females as indicated by rating of intelligence and likeability', *Psychological Reports*, **37**, 1315–1320.

Larwood, L. (1978). 'Swine flu: a field study of self-serving biases', *Journal of Applied Social Psychology*, **8**, 283–289.

Larwood, L., (1982). 'The importance of being right when you think you are: self-serving bias in equal employment opportunity', in Gutek, B. A. (ed), *Sex Role Stereotyping and Affirmative Action Policy*. Institute of Industrial Relations, University of California, Los Angeles.

Larwood, L., Gutek, B., and Gattiker, U. E. (1983). 'Perspectives on institutional discrimination and resistance to change'. Paper delivered at the annual meeting of the Academy of Management, Dallas.

Larwood, L., and Lockheed, M. (1979). 'Women as managers: toward second generation research', *Sex Roles*, **5**, 659–666.

Larwood, L., and Powell, G. N. (1981). 'Isn't it time we were moving on?: necessary future research on women in management', *Group and Organization Studies*, **6**, 65–72.

Larwood, L., Rand, P., and Der Hovanessian, A. (1979). 'Sex differences in response to simulated employee discipline cases', *Personnel Psychology*, **32**, 539–550.

Larwood, L., and Whittaker, W. (1977). 'Managerial myopia: self-serving biases in organizational planning', *Journal of Applied Psychology*, **62**, 194–198.

Larwood, L., and Wood, M. M. (1977) *Women in Management*. Lexington Books, Lexington, M.A.

Laws, J. L. (1975). 'The psychology of tokenism: an analysis', *Sex Roles*, **1**, 51–67.

Laws, J. L. (1979). *The Second X: sex role and social role*. Elsevier, New York.

Ledvinka, J. (1982). *Federal Regulation of Personnel and Human Resource Management*, Kent Publishing, Boston.

Levine, R., Gillman, M.-J., and Reis, H. (1982). Individual differences for sex differences in achievement attributions?' *Sex Roles*, **8**, 455–466.

Levinson, R. M. (1975). 'Sex discrimination and employment practices', *Social Problems*, **22**, 533–543.

Levitin, T. E., Quinn, R. P., and Staines, G. L. (1971). 'Sex discrimination against the American working woman', *American Behavioral Scientist*, **15**, 237–254.

Lindsey, K. (1977). 'Sexual harassment on the job', *Ms.*, November, pp. 47–48.

Linton, R. (1936). *The Study of Man*. Appleton-Century, New York.

Lloyd, C. B., and Niemi, B. T. (1979). *The Economics of Sex Differentials*. Columbia University Press, New York.

Massengill, D., and Di Marco, N. (1979). 'Sex-role stereotypes and requisite management characteristics: a current replication', *Sex Roles*, **5**, 561–570.

MacKinnon, C. (1979). *Sexual Harassment of Working Women*. Yale University Press, New Haven.

McMahan, I. D. (1962). 'Expectancy of success on sex-linked tasks', *Sex Roles*, **8**, 949–958.

Meyer, P. J., and Maes, P. L., (1983). 'The reproduction of occupational segregation among young women', *Industrial Relations,* **22** (1), 115–124.

Miner, J. B., and Smith, N. R. (1982). 'Decline and stabilization of managerial motivation over a 20-year period', *Journal of Applied Psychology*, **67**, 297–305.

Miner, M. G. (1976). *Equal Employment Opportunity: programs and results.* Personnel Policies Forum Survey #112. Bureau of National Affairs, Washington, DC.

Nieva, V. F. and Gutek, B. A. (1980). 'Sex effects on evaluation', *Academy of Management Review*, **5** (2), 267–276.

Nieva, V. F., and Gutek, B. A. (1981). *Women and Work: a psychological perspective,* Praeger Publishing, New York.

Northcraft, G. B., and Martin, J. (1982). 'Double jeopardy: resistance to affirmative action from potential beneficiaries', in Gutek, B. A. (ed.), *Sex Role Stereotyping and Affirmative Action Policy.* Institute of Industrial relations, University of California, Los Angeles.

Oppenheimer, V. (1968). 'The sex-labeling of jobs', *Industrial Relations,* **7**, 219–234.

Parsons, T., and Bales, R. F. (eds.), (1955). *Family, Socialization, and Interaction Processes.* Free Press of Glencoe, New York.

Pearce, D. (1978). 'The feminization of poverty: women, work, and welfare', *The Urban and Social Change Review,* **11**, (1 and 2), 28–36.

Perucci, C. C., Potter, H. R., and Rhoads, D. L. (1978). 'Determinants of male family role performance', *Psychology of Women Quarterly,* **3**, 53–66.

Pheterson, G. I., Kiesler, S. B., and Goldberg, P. A. (1971). 'Evaluation of the performance of women as a function of their sex, achievement, and personal history', *Journal of Personality and Social Psychology,* **19**, 114–118.

Pogrebin, L. C. (1977). 'Sex harassment: the working woman'. *Ladies Home Journal,* June, p. 24.

Raelin, J. A. (1982). 'A comparative analysis of female-male early youth careers'. *Industrial Relations,* **21**, 231f.

Rollins, J., and White, P. N. (1982). 'The relationship between mothers' and daughters' sex-role attitudes and self-concepts in three types of family environment', *Sex Roles*, **8**, 1141–1155.

Rosen, B. and Jerdee, T. H. (1974). 'Influence of sex role stereotypes on personnel decisions', *Journal of Applied Psychology,* **59**, 9–14.

Rosen, B., and Mericle, M. F. (1979). 'Influence of strong versus weak fair employment policies and applicant's sex selection decisions and salary recommendations in a management simulation, *Journal of Applied Psychology*, **64**, 435–439.

Rosen, B., Templeton, M. E. and Kichline, K. (1981). 'The first few years on the job: women in management'. *Business Horizons,* **24**, (November/December), pp. 26–29.

Rosenthal, D., and Hansen, J. (1981). 'The impact of maternal employment on children's perceptions of parents and personal development', *Sex Roles,* **7**, 593–598.

Ross, M., and Sicoly, R. (1979). 'Egocentric biases in availability and attribution', *Journal of Personality and Social Psychology,* **37**, 322–336.

Safran, C. (1976). 'What men do to women on the job: a shocking look at sexual harassment', *Redbook* (November), **149**, 217–223.

Schein, V. E. 'Relationships between sex role stereotypes and requisite management characteristics among female managers', *Journal of Applied Psychology,* **60**, 340–344.

Scherrei, R. A. (1979). 'Changes in career aspirations of women entering college', in Gutek, B. A. (ed.), *New Directions for Education, Work and Careers: enhancing women's career development.* Jossey Bass, San Francisco.

Schrank, T. H., and Riley, J. W. (1976). 'Women in work organizations', in Kreps, J. M. (ed.), *Women and the American Economy*. Prentice-Hall, Englewood Cliffs, NJ.

Schreiber, C. (1979). *Changing Places*. MIT Press, Cambridge, MA.

Seigfried, W. D. (1982). 'The effects of specifying job requirements and using explicit warnings to decrease sex discrimination in employment interviews', *Sex Roles*, **8**, 73–82.

Sohn, D. (1982). 'Sex differences in achievement self-attributions: an effect-size analysis', *Sex Roles*, **8**, 345–357.

Sommers, D. (1974). 'Occupational rankings for men and women by earnings', *Monthly Labor Review*, **97** (8), 34–51.

Staw, B. M. (1980). 'Rationality and justification in organizational life', in Staw, B, and Cummings, L. (eds), *Research in Organizational Behavior*, vol. 2. JAI Press, Greenwich, CT.

Staines, G. L., Quinn, R. P., and Shepard, L. J. (1976). 'Trends in occupational sex discrimination: 1969–1973', *Industrial Relations*, **15**, 88–98.

Stein, A. H. Pohly, S. R., and Mueller, E. (1971). 'The influence of masculine, feminine, and neutral tasks on children's achievement behavior, expectancies of success, and attainment values', *Child Development*, **42**, 195–207.

Suter, L. E., and Miller, H. P. (1973). 'Income differences between men and women', *American Journal of Sociology*, **78**, 962–974.

Taylor, S. E., Fiske, S. T., Etcoff, N. L., and Ruderman, A. J. (1978). 'Categorical and contextual bases of person memory and stereotyping', *Journal of Personality and Social Psychology*, **36**, 778–793.

Touhey, J. C. (1974a). 'Effects of additional men on prestige and desirability of occupations typically performed by women', *Journal of Applied Psychology*, **4**, 330–335.

Touhey, J. C. (1974b). 'Effects of additional women professionals on ratings of occupational prestige and desirability', *Journal of Personality and Social Psychology*, **29**, 86–89.

Travis, C. B. (1982). 'Sex comparisons on casual attributions: another look at the null hypothesis', *Sex Roles*, **8**, 375–380.

Treiman, D. J., and Terrel, K. (1975). 'Sex and the process of status attainment', *American Sociological Review*, **40**, 174–200.

US Commission on Civil Rights (1978). '*Social Indicators of Equality for Minorities and Women*. Washington, DC August.

US Department of Labor (1980). *Perspectives on Working Women: a databook*. US Department of Labor, Bureau of Labor Statistics, Washington, DC. October.

US Merit Systems Protection Board (1981). *Sexual Harassmen in the Federal Workplace: is it a problem?* US Government Printing Office, Washington, DC.

Urberg, K. A. (1982). 'The development of the cncepts of masculinity and feminity in young children', *Sex Roles*, **8**, 659–668.

Wall Street Journal (1983). 'EEOC reverses stand on New Orleans suit due to pressure from Justice Department', 7 April p. 14.

Warihay, P. D. (1980). 'The climb to the top: is the network the route for women?'- *Personnel Administrator*, **25** (April), 55–60.

Weiner, B., Frieze, I., Kukla, A., Reed, L., Rest, S., and Rosenbaum, R. M. (1971). *Perceiving the Causes of Success and Failure*. General Learning Press, New York.

Weingarten, K. (1978). 'The employment pattern of professional couples and their distribution of involvement in the family', *Psychology of Women Quarterly*, **3**, 43–52.

Weinsten, N. D. (1980). 'Unrealistic optimism about future life events', *Journal of Personality and Social Psychology*, **39**, 806–820.
Wise, P. S., and Joy, S. S. (1982). 'Working mothers, sex differences, and self-esteem in college students' self-descriptions', *Sex Roles*, **8**, 785–790.
Woelfel, J. C. (1981). 'Women in the United States Army', *Sex Roles*, **7**, 785–800.
Yogev, S. (1982). 'Happiness in dual-career couples: changing research, changing values', *Sex Roles*, **8**, 593–605.

Women at Work
Edited by M. J. Davidson and C. L. Cooper
© 1984 John Wiley & Sons Ltd

Chapter 11
Women at Work in the USSR

Lynne Attwood
and
Maggie McAndrew
University of Birmingham,
Birmingham, UK

INTRODUCTION

The Soviet Union was the first country in the world to declare the equality of men and women, and to commit itself to a series of policies to ensure this equality. Involvement in productive work was the base on which women's emancipation was to be erected. This commitment, and the route to its achievement, stemmed from the Marxist—Leninist ideology which inspired the October Revolution and defined the agenda for Soviet development. For Marx and Engels, women's inequality and oppression were caused by their exclusion from the sphere of public production—the world of paid, socially recognized work—and their confinement to private production and reproduction in and for the individual family. The transition from the private to the public sphere was thus the motor of women's emancipation; in the words of Engels, 'the first condition for the liberation of women is to bring the whole female sex back into public industry' (Engels, 1977, p. 117). Lenin similarly argued that: 'The position of women, as long as they are engaged in domestic labour, will necessarily be constrained. In order to achieve the full emancipation of women and their genuine equality with men, a socialized economy is necessary, and women must participate in general productive work. Then women will occupy the exact same position as men' (Lenin, 1963b, p. 201).

The necessary condition for women's emancipation was the abolition of private ownership. For Engels, the socialization of property meant that '. . . the single family ceases to be the economic unit of society. Private housekeeping is transformed into a social industry' (Engels, 1977, p. 139). Lenin stressed the importance of liberating women from the 'unproductive, petty, nerve-wracking, stupefying and choking drudgery of household chores'

(Lenin, (1963), p. 24), and the 1919 Party Programme committed itself to the future replacement of privatized domestic work by public institutions which would satisfy the daily needs of the family (Triska, 1962).

According to economistic interpretations of Marxism there is, then, a direct relationship between women's activity in the work force and their emancipation. Social phenomena such as the oppression of women are seen as inevitable features of class society, destined to disappear with the dissolution of classes.

If there is such a causal link between women's employment and their equality with men, current Soviet statistics would suggest that the goal of securing this equality has been attained. Approximately 90% of Soviet women of appropriate age are engaged in full-time work or study (*Work and Family Life*, 1980); they constitute 51% of the work force (*Vestrik Statistiki*, 1982).

By any standards these are extremely high participation rates. However, the extent to which women participate equally with men, and to which their participation has led to sexual equality in other spheres of life, requires further exploration. More detailed statistics present a picture of low levels of skill, mobility, wages, and ambition amongst women workers, which interact with problems of domestic overburdening to affect the health and well-being of working women and contribute to the increasing divorce rate and decreasing birth rate. It has become clear to Soviet sociologists and policy-makers that, instead of a unified world of work, with men and women participating on equal terms, their experience of work is quite different; and this difference seems on many indicators to be to women's detriment.

In this chapter we will be looking at women's experience of work in the Soviet Union, and its costs and benefits to both women themselves and to the Soviet state.

PRE-REVOLUTIONARY RUSSIA

Before we look at women and work in the Soviet period, we should be aware of the position prior to the Bolshevik Revolution in 1917.

Industrialization began in Russia in the nineteenth century, but lagged way behind that of Western Europe or the United States. As historians have demonstrated, the family or household of pre-industrial societies represented the basic economic unit, and the work of its members—including women—was essential (Scott and Tilly, 1976). As well as arable and livestock work, women also derived a subsistence from cottage industry, though this had declined by the late nineteenth century. At the same time, an increase in the use of machines facilitated women's employment in factory work; as Engels suggested, machines not only rendered male strength irrelevant to factory work but actually made men less suited to it than women and children, whose supposedly greater dexterity was more appropriate than men's better-developed arm muscles (Rashin, 1958). By 1897 women formed 15% of the total industrial work force and were employed in all industries except construction. Their distribution was far from even, however. They were particularly well represented in the tobacco industry (constituting 61.3% of the total number of workers in Russia by 1897), the textile industry (41.4%), and the chemical industry (26%). On the other hand their participation in industries such as mining, metal smelting, and metal and wood processing was slight (5.4%, 5.8%, 1.6% and 3.9% respectively) (Rashin, 1958).

The proportion of women workers continued to grow, though there is some evidence that women workers were considered the most expendable in periods of economic decline (Sacks, 1976). By 1901 women constituted 26.1% of the total work force in the Russian empire; by 1914 this figure had risen to 31.7%. The increase was particularly marked in textiles; in 1902 women formed 47.8% of the industry's workers, and by the beginning of 1914 they accounted for 56.2% (Sacks, 1976).

In Russia, as elsewhere in Europe, the First World War produced a sharp increase in female employment. By January 1917 women constituted 40% of the total work force (Sacks, 1976). Other countries endeavoured to return women to their former lives of domesticity at the end of the war. In Russia, however, war was followed by Revolution, and the Bolsheviks embraced a commitment to drawing women into the work force rather than expelling them from it. As we have seen, this commitment did not initiate, but rather supported, a process which preceded the Revolution by several years, a process linked to the onset of industrialization in Russia.

THE EARLY SOVIET PERIOD

Bolshevik thought on woman's participation in socialist society, and the attainment of her complete equality with men, dictated two simultaneous processes: her entry into productive labour, and her liberation from privatized domestic work. The latter was to be achieved by, in effect, nationalizing the family; its various functions would be placed in the hands of state institutions such as dining rooms, laundries, creches, and kindergartens, hence freeing women from the need to provide such services on a privatized basis and paving the way for their mass entry into the labour force. In 1919 a women's department (Zhenotdel) was established within the party to tackle this problem. However, it was allotted vastly inadequate resources to cope with its various tasks, which were not limited to solving the 'Woman Question' but included such diverse concerns as looking after the hordes of abandoned and orphaned children, organizing health care and food distribution, and supervising education and housing programmes. Gail Lapidus suggests that the task of securing women's equality was never intended to be its main function; its chief object was to draw women into the political community and secure their support for the new regime (Lapidus, 1978a). Even if this were not the case, and the Zhenotdel was in fact the visible expression of a continued dedication to women's equality, the impediments against its success in this period would have been insurmountable.

The early years of Soviet rule were characterized by mass poverty and unemployment. Nonetheless, in this climate of general shortage there were movements towards equality of employment. Legislation in 1917 and 1918 established women's equal right—indeed, obligation—to work, and to equal pay for such work. From 1919 to 1922 wage differentials were narrowed so that the wages of skilled workers could not exceed those of unskilled workers by more than 175% (Holt, 1980). Given that the majority of working women were unskilled, the effect of this was to reduce male/female wage differentials. However, there were simply not enough jobs to go round. Certain restrictions on female employment were introduced at the same time, with the intention of protecting women from hazardous work conditions; women were banned from night work, overtime, all underground work, and a number of other occupations listed by the Labour Commissariat (Dodge, 1966). However, this served to decrease women's access to work by convincing employers, who could pick and choose from the vast ranks of the unemployed, that men were a sounder employment proposition. By 1928 the female proportion of the work force had dropped to less than a third of the total (Stites, 1978), despite the loss of manpower which war-deaths had produced. Those who did find jobs were not, in fact, protected by the legal restrictions, which were constantly flouted; and, glad to be employed at all, they were hardly likely to complain to the authorities. Indeed, the state itself repealed the restrictions temporarily whenever it deemed this necessary (Dodge, 1966).

While most women were denied the economic independence of full-time work, male abuse of the liberalization of divorce laws also cost them, in a vast number of cases, the economic protection of their husbands. Some men, knowing that the contract could be easily terminated, seem to have married merely for sexual gratification, and abandoned their hapless wives in the event of pregnancy, or when a new challenge came along (Stites, 1978). Others, according to Trotsky, outgrew marriages contracted before the Revolution; men were more likely than women to flourish in the new conditions created by the Revolution, and frequently divorced wives who, trapped within the stultifying atmosphere of the family, had had no such opportunities for self-development. In Trotsky's words:

One of the very dramatic chapters of the great book of the Soviets will be the tale of the disintegration and breaking up of these Soviet families where the husband as a party member, trade unionist, military commander or administrator, grew and developed and acquired new tastes in life, and the wife, crushed by the family, remained on the old level. The road of the two generations of the Soviet bureaucracy is sown thick with the tragedies of wives rejected and left behind. (Sacks, 1976, p. 25)

Many women, unable to procure financial support from their ex-husbands, were forced to seek employment in the 'oldest profession' which, despite the Zhenotdel's efforts to stamp it out, grew to alarming proportions (Stites, 1976). The New Economic Policy (NEP) of 1921 had reinstated small-scale private enterprise as a temporary emergency measure to deal with the ravages of war; this, in creating a new monied class of owners and managers, provided ample customers for prostitution. Partly in response to the increase in prostitution, some of the restrictions on women's work were relaxed in 1925 in an effort to increase their legitimate employment (Sacks, 1976).

Legislation was also introduced in the years immediately following the revolution aimed at helping women combine work and motherhood, and protecting them and their offspring from the detrimental effects of heavy or unhealthy work during pregnancy and the period of breast-feeding. From the fifth month of pregnancy a woman could refuse to be sent on a business trip. She was not permitted to work nights during pregnancy or while breast-feeding. If engaged in physical work, she was to be granted leave of absence, with state benefits equal to her average earnings, for 8 weeks before and 8 weeks after the birth of her child. For a white-collar worker this figure was reduced to 6 weeks before and 6 weeks after. An employer who did not release a woman from work during the stipulated period was liable to a heavy fine (from 1000 to 3000 rubles), or even imprisonment for a period of 1-3 months. The woman worker was, in addition, to receive an allowance while breast-feeding (12.5% of the average local salary), plus a lump-sum payment (50% of the average salary) to purchase a layette. During the breast-feeding period she was to receive a break from work at least every 3½ hours, for the minimum duration of ½ hour, which was to count as part of her working day (Dodge, 1966). Such legislation certainly represented a major advance for women; however, like the other restrictions on female employment, it was likely to deter employers from hiring women.

Like women's entry into productive work, the socialization of the domestic economy did not proceed according to plan. The period of civil war and communism led to a disruption in supplies and hence a breakdown of urban domestic life; with little available in the shops, most people ate in canteens rather than preparing food at home (Holt, 1980). With the onset of the NEP, even this limited move towards a socialization of house-work was reversed. The envisaged network of public domestic institutions failed to materialize in more than a rudimentary fashion. This was partly due to the resurrection of private industry in the NEP period; as Geiger notes, the new breed of entrepreneurs which emerged 'were reluctant to invest in such uneconomic ventures as creches and restaurants' (cited by Sacks, 1976, p. 43). However, the government also failed to prioritize women when it came to the distribution of scarce resources, relying on the unpaid work of women in the home. Lenin, in a speech to women workers in 1919, acknowledged that there were deplorably few such institutions, due to the terrible post-war conditions in which the Soviet state found itself. The ultimate responsibility lay with women themselves, however:

We say that the liberation of workers must be the cause of workers themselves, and in just the same way, the liberation of women workers must be the cause of women workers themselves. Hence women workers themselves must see to the development of such institutions, and this action on the part of women will lead to a complete overturn of their old position in capitalist society (Lenin, 1963, pp. 202–203).

Given the low level of resources allotted to the project, this was hardly a practicable proposition—unless women were expected to fund such institutions themselves and staff them with voluntary workers. It also indicates that domestic work was still seen as a female occupation; the 'overturn of women's old position in capitalist society' amounted to their engaging in this work now on a collective rather than an individual basis.

The achievement of women's equality in the early Soviet period was doomed to failure. As Louise Luke notes, women's transition from the domestic sphere to the productive sphere 'depended upon an economic base not yet laid in the NEP period' (Luke, 1953, p. 46). It also depended on a change in attitude towards male and female roles, which was not promoted and failed to emerge.

THE STALINIST PERIOD

By the beginning of the 1930s the situation had changed radically. Stalin's intensive industrialization programme, the first Five-Year Plan, begun in 1928, demanded a massive supply of labour; suddenly women were in demand as workers. From 1928 to 1932 the number of women workers more than doubled (Holt, 1980). Between 1930 and 1937, 82% of new recruits to the work force were women; by 1937 women constituted 40% of industrial workers (Lapidus, 1978a). The motive force behind this vast mobilization of women was more one of expedience than ideological commitment to women's equality. Although frequent references were still made to the latter, Lapidus (1978a) suggests that these functioned as a *post-hoc* legitimization of policies based on economic grounds. Most obviously, 7 years of war had taken their toll on the male population, to the extent that there were now too few to conduct an industrialization programme on the scale and at the speed envisaged. This deficit grew still larger throughout the following years as a result of collectivization, the purges, and the Second World War. Many women were thus left without male partners; hence their entry into the labour force, as well as providing essential additional labour, enabled them to support themselves (at least, after a fashion) and their dependent children, rather than living off state benefits.

For those women whose husbands had survived, employment was also often a financial necessity. Rapid industrialization led to high inflation and a reduction in real wages. Women's employment removed the necessity of making men's salaries sufficient to support wives and families, or of paying out increased benefits.

Lapidus (1978a) also suggests that female employment reduced the number of rural migrants needed to work on urban industrial enterprises, hence saving the cost of extra housing. While the provision of public domestic institutions was still recommended, it was done so more in terms of the cost to society of privatized domestic labour—i.e. the number of potential work-hours thus squandered—than the cost to women of performing tedious, repetitious, stultifying domestic tasks. Citing one contemporary Soviet calculation that every member of the population squandered an average of 700 hours per year on unproductive domestic labour, Lapidus (1978a) concludes that 'the development of a wide network of communal institutions to replace household tasks was now urged not merely to free women from drudgery but to release a vast pool of labour from the expanding Soviet economy' (p. 126).

The need to draw women into the work force resulted in a spate of decrees in the early 1930s designed to facilitate this process. This was the first major legislation concerning women's employment in almost a decade, since the 1922 Labour Code reiterated the restrictions on female employment which were laid down in 1918. The emphasis of the new decrees was completely different, in tune with the different economic conditions. In the 1920s the involvement of women in production was somewhat theoretical; now it was a pressing reality in the face of rapid industrialization. A Central Committee resolution of 1930 discussed the urgent need for more workers. This led to a decree establishing quotas for women in various industries and directing training institutions to take quotas of women in various specialisms (Lapidus, 1978b). Hence while female labour was essential for rapid and intense industrialization, there was an attempt to divert the new influx of women workers, as far as possible, into certain occupations—those which reflected their traditional domestic roles. This decree, in urging that 'the use of female labour should be greatly expanded' (Dodge, 1966, p. 63) in certain specified occupations, served to officially sanction the idea of a sex-differentiated employment policy.

Legislation also defined areas from which women's labour was to be excluded for their own protection. The 1932 'List of especially strenuous and

hazardous jobs and trades in which women cannot be employed' prohibited
women from certain jobs in the metallurgical, metal working, chemical,
leather, textile, paper, and printing industries, and in transport, construction,
and utilities (Sheptulina, 1982). Another 1932 decree, 'On limiting norms
for handling loads by adult women', limited the maximum load women could
carry to 20 kilos. There is evidence that such legislation did not exercise
much influence on the treatment of women workers. A greater impact was
had by the new 'discovery' that underground work, contrary to previous
opinion, was not harmful to women (Dodge, 1966), and women were allowed
to form a quarter of the workers in iron ore mining, coal mining, and steel
and iron production by November 1939 although the protective legislation
of the 1920s was not formally repealed (Lapidus, 1978b).

Distinct areas of male and female employment emerged in the 1930s.
Women were well represented, for example, in the public dining industry;
in 1930 they constituted 55.5% of workers in this field, with this figure
increasing to 64.2% by 1935 and 67% by 1940. Public health was even more
predominantly female; in 1930, 67.1% of its employees were female, rising
to 71.2% by 1935 and 76% by 1940. In the textiles and clothing industry
women constituted 64.2% in 1936, and 72% in 1940. On the other hand,
they were badly represented in construction and mechanical work. In the
construction industry women formed 9.6% of the work force in 1930, rising
to 19.7% by 1935 and 20.6% by 1937. In transport they represented 9.7%
in 1930, rising to 24% by 1940. Among workers on machine and tractor
service stations, female representation remained low throughout the 1930s;
the figure of 7% in 1933 had increased only to 11% in 1940 (Dodge, 1966).
The decade of the 1930s saw a huge transformation in women's lives. In 1928
women constituted 24% of the work force, with 2,795,000 women at work.
By 1940 this figure had multiplied to 13,190,000 or 39% of a hugely increased
labour force (Lapidus, 1978b).

Attention was pledged to the improvement of domestic services in order
to free women for the work force. However, the concentration on heavy
industry meant that the resources directed to such services remained inadequate, especially given the increased number of working women; and the
majority of women continued to carry out at home domestic services which
the state had intended to take over, as well as holding down full-time jobs.
The double-burden of work plus family obligations which was thus established in the 1930s continues to this day.

Legislation concerning the maternity rights of working women was also
revised in the 1930s. As from 1932 the two categories of women
workers—those engaged in physical work and those in mental work—were
merged into one for these purposes, and were granted 16 weeks' maternity
leave (which previously only physical workers had received). However only
women who were trade union members, and had worked for a minimum of

3 years, 2 of them at the same work-place, were now eligible for grants equal to their full salaries. Other women received reduced amounts. While the allowances for nursing mothers and for the purchase of a layette were previously contingent on average local salaries, in 1932 a fixed amount was introduced for both; a woman was now to receive 32 rubles for the layette, and 45 rubles nursing allowance (divided into nine monthly instalments of 5 rubles). These allowances were raised in 1936 to 45 rubles for the layette and 90 rubles (or 10 rubles per month) nursing allowance (Dodge, 1966).

However, these amounts were rarely paid in full. Just as legal restrictions in women's working conditions were easily flouted, so too were laws concerning maternity leave and benefits.

In 1936 additional financial assistance was also awarded to large families, in the form of annual grants of 2000 rubles for a period of 5 years for the seventh and each additional child up to the eleventh; the 11th child and all subsequent children received a single grant of 5000 rubles at birth, and an annual allowance of 3000 rubles for 4 years beginning from the first birthday (Dodge, 1966). The aim of these benefits was to provide a financial incentive to have large families, though it could hardly have been a very effective one since the benefits began only with the seventh child. Families would be unlikely to suffer the poverty induced by six children in order to benefit from the seventh.

The Family Law of 1936, making abortion illegal and restricting divorce, was an attempt to assert traditional family values and roles, after the dislocation of the immediate post-revolutionary period and its subsequent fall in the birth rate. The needs of a rapidly industrializing state, together with an awareness of military threats, chiefly from Germany, led to a pro-natalist policy. The cult of motherhood called upon women to fulfil their true natures by a combination of multiple maternity and employment, a demanding combination of old and new roles, unsupported by state investment in social or domestic services (Evans, 1981).

Despite the evident lack of respect amongst managers of laws governing female employment, another was introduced in 1937 which ruled that women in arduous jobs should be given less demanding work during pregnancy, with no loss of salary. This, like those before it, was often ignored (Dodge, 1966).

The Second World War, like the one before it, produced a chronic labour shortage, both because of the large numbers of male workers recruited into the Red Army, and the need for a rapid increase in the production of weapons and other military goods. In anticipation of this shortage, legislation which debarred women from work in certain occupations began, as early as 1938, to undergo modifications. From November of that year women were permitted to work as railway engineers and engine stokers. In June 1940 they were granted access to work on river transport (although they were still not permitted to become steamship stokers or sailors on cargo ships). From

October of the same year they could legally work underground, although the harsher aspects of mining work—coal cutting, digging, and shovelling—were still not permitted (Dodge, 1966).

The media urged women to take part in the war effort, and large numbers responded. By 1945 they constituted 55% of the total industrial labour force, as opposed to 40% in 1937 (Ladipus, 1978). In the initial phase of the war much of this mobilization took place on a voluntary basis, though some regions did introduce labour conscription towards the end of 1941, and the nation as a whole followed suit in 1942 (Tupper and Evans, 1981).

Despite the scale of female entry into the industrial labour force during the war years, and the legal changes which permitted them entry into some former male bastions, a marked sexual division of labour was retained in industry. The majority of women were still to be found throughout the war in secretarial and service positions, and light industrial work. This may partly have been due to the persistence of traditional notions about women's work, which Stalin's pro-natalist policies of the 1930s, in attempting to foster an image of the dignity of Soviet motherhood which was none too compatible with heavy physical work, did little to dispel. The war itself, while encouraging an increase in women's employment, also placed barriers against its dissemination into all areas of the economy. For example, the military's policy of drawing its soldiers primarily from agriculture and light industry, considered less essential areas of the economy in the current situation, meant that many new recruits were injected into these areas rather than into heavy industry. Also most female entrants into the work force were rural women with little formal education or work-training; this rendered their assimilation into light, unskilled industrial work easier than into more complex heavy industry. Since there were inadequate public facilities to care for the children of these new recruits, older female relatives often had to stay at home with the children of younger women workers. Women workers thus tended to be much younger than their male colleagues, who were mostly men beyond military-service age. The latter had, for the most part, had jobs prior to the war, and hence were more experienced and skilled than the new female workers. This also served to accentuate the sexual division of labour at work (Tupper and Evans, 1981).

When the war ended, the need to replenish the lost population became as acute a problem as the labour shortage. Measures were taken once again to persuade women to reproduce. Maternity rights and benefits, which had been reduced during the war years, were now restored to something approaching their pre-war level. Before the war, women had received 16 weeks' maternity paid leave, 8 weeks before and 8 weeks after the birth. During the war this was reduced to 5 weeks before and 4 weeks after the birth. In 1944 the post-birth leave was extended to 6 weeks, while the 5 weeks prior to the birth remained unchanged. Layette allowances were increased dramatically, from 45 to 120 rubles; nursing benefits were also doubled, to

20 rubles per month (a total of 180 rubles). Child benefit allowances for mothers of large families were also increased and extended. Whereas the 1936 allowances had provided only for the seventh and any subsequent children, the birth of a third child now merited a lump-sum allowance, and all further children received a lump sum plus a monthly allowance beginning from the first birthday and extending till the fifth. These allowances must, as Dodge (1966) notes, have made a considerable difference to the family income, especially since they went hand-in-hand with tax exemptions for large families. In addition, a large family was likely to have more than one child under five, and hence receive several allowances concurrently. Evidently the benefits accrued to the state in the form of additional citizens did not justify the expense, however. In 1947 the allowances were cut by half (Dodge, 1966).

A series of medals was also introduced in 1944 for mothers of several children, designed to encourage a psychological climate in which motherhood was seen as patriotic and prestigious. This system continues to the present day. The 'Medal of Maternity, 2nd degree' is awarded to a mother giving birth to, and rearing, five children; the 'Medal of Maternity, 1st degree' goes to a mother of six children. Mothers of seven, eight and nine children are awarded medals of 'Maternal Glory' of the 3rd, 2nd and 1st degree respectively. The highest accolade goes to a mother of ten children; she receives the title 'Mother-hero', along with the Order of the Mother Hero and a certificate from the Supreme Soviet. Between 1944 and 1973, 183,000 women became 'Mother-heroes'; 3,572,000 received 'Maternal Glory'; and 9,788,000 received the 'Medal of Maternity'. The same legislation reiterated the illegality of procuring or performing an abortion (abortion was outlawed until 1955, when the high number of illegal abortions forced a liberalization of the law), as well as making it a criminal offence to insult or humiliate the dignity of mothers! (Rumyantseva and Pergament, 1975).

The most recent wave of female recruitment to the labour force occurred as a result of the post-war economic reconstruction and the overall development of the economy, particularly the tertiary service sector, against the background of a male deficit. The female work force almost doubled in the period from 1955 to 1970, from 23 million to 45.8 million, or from 46% to 51% of the total work force (*Narodnoe Khozyaistvo*, 1979). This percentage has remained constant since.

The shortage of skilled and male labour led to a continued redistribution of existing labour resources into skilled work and the absorption of the new female untrained and unskilled work force into low-skilled blue-collar jobs. The greatest increases in female employment were registered in occupations such as cook and salesperson. Nearly a million new women workers took up jobs as office cleaners, janitors, porters, gatekeepers, and cloakroom attendants (Kostakov, 1982). The number of women specialists, that is those with higher or further education, more than trebled in the same period, from

3.1 million in 1955 to 9.9 millimn in 1970 (*Vestnik Statistiki*, 1982).

There is now very little in the way of untapped labour reserves available, hence the current urgency of the attention the Soviet government is devoting to resolving the conflicts in women's roles as both workers themselves and the providers of future workers.

THE PRESENT DAY

In quantitative terms the Soviet Union has accomplished its goal of drawing women into the work force; they now have the highest rate of paid female employment in the world. Approximately 90% of women between the ages of 16 and 54 are in full-time employment or study. Women form 51% of the nation's workers and employees (statistical categories broadly identifying manual and non-manual work), while they constitute 53% of the population. Overall sex-specific participation rates show that 88% of men and 82% of women, of appropriate age, are in work (*Vestnik Statistiki*, 1982). That the female participation rate so closely approximates the male rate is especially interesting given that women take leave from their employment in order to have children. It is clear that female participation has reached the demographic maximum.

The level of participation varies according to region and nationality group (see Table 11.1).

Table 11.1   *Percentage of women amongst workers and employees, by republic, 1981*

USSR	51	Lithuania	52
Russia	52	Moldavia	51
Ukraine	52	Latvia	55
Belorussia	53	Kirgizia	49
Uzbekistan	43	Tadjikistan	39
Kazakstan	49	Armenia	47
Georgia	46	Turkmenia	41
Azerbaijan	43	Estonia	54

Source: *Vestnik Statistiki* No. 1 (1983).

In the European republics women are far more likely to work outside the home than are women in the Central Asian republics. Further examination shows that of those women in the Central Asian republics who do work outside the home, the vast majority are immigrants from the European areas rather than the indigenous population. In Turkmenistan in 1973 only 12% of the employed women were Turkmenian and of these, less than a quarter were involved in industry or construction (Lapidus, 1978a). In a country the size of the USSR (8 million square miles), which comprises 15 republics with 92 major nationality groups and a population of 267,700,000 there is a great deal of cultural diversity which is reflected in the lives of women (Khozyai-stvo, 1980). The influence of Islam on cultural traditions and expectations has a great effect on women's lives. Many young Central Asian, Georgian, and Armenian women marry early and settle into domestic life immediately after school, without any vocational training or work experience. There is a tendency towards large families (70–80% of women engaged in full-time household duties in the Central Asian republics have three to six children; some have even more), and a history of women's exclusive domestic activity, which is reinforced by the fact that the number of places available for pre-school child care is half the national average. This chapter deals mainly with the experience of work for women in the European areas of the USSR, as it is in these areas that the majority of the work force is located. It should be noted, however, that Soviet Central Asian women are presenting dilemmas for policy-makers, who are trying to resolve the problems of an overall decreasing birth rate and a current, as well as a speculated future, labour shortage.

Unlike the situation in many Western industrial countries (described in the previous chapters), where women's right to work outside the home has received little or no social sanction or state support, Soviet women workers are highly visible and receive considerable ideological and material backing. As has been seen, the Marxist–Leninist ideology which has structured the Soviet approach to women as a social group was in fortunate coincidence with the needs of the rapidly expanding Soviet economy after a series of demographic disasters had decimated the male workforce (the First World War, the Civil War and its accompanying famine, Collectivisation and more famine, the Purges, and the Second World War). Since the Soviet Union has been committed ideologically to the emancipation of women via their incorporation into the socially productive labour force for almost as long as the processes of modernization, urbanization, and industrialization have been under way, it is difficult to distinguish between the two sets of factors as influences on policy affecting women. What is undoubtedly true is that work outside the home is regarded as the norm, and women's right to work and the obligation of the state to ensure the conditions for securing this right are included in the Constitution of the USSR.

Women and men have equal rights in the USSR. Exercise of these rights is ensured by according women equal access with men to education and vocational and professional training, equal opportunities in employment, remuneration, and promotion, and in social and political, and cultural activity, and by special labour and health protection measures for women; by providing conditions enabling mothers to work; by legal protection, and material and moral support for mothers and children, including paid leave and other benefits for expectant mothers and mothers, and gradual reduction of working time for mothers with small children.
Article 35 of the 1977 Constitution (Fundamental Law) of the USSR. (*Konstitutsia SSSR*, 1977).

Resolutions from Party Congresses and from the Trade Union Central Committee, and the guidelines for the Five-Year Plans, include measures to improve the working and living conditions of women. In his report to the 26th Congress of the Communist Party of the Soviet Union, Brezhnev acknowledged the problems women face in combining motherhood and socially productive work, and reaffirmed the duty of the state to assist women to fulfil these roles:

We are talking about the introduction of partially paid leave for the care of children up to one year, about part-time work for the mothers of young children, about the broadening of the network and the improvement of the quality of children's preschool institutions, extended-day schools and domestic services. We are providing increased grants for children, especially second and third children.

This is only the most recent expression of a tendency, increasingly evident since the death of Stalin, for the state to intervene to reduce the tensions between women's productive and reproductive roles by extending the maternity rights and benefits of working women.

Pregnant women are now entitled to a transfer to lighter work during pregnancy if this should be necessary, with no loss of salary or any of the rights connected with length of service in their usual job. The need for such a transfer is decided by a doctor, who also signifies what type of work the woman may do, or, alternatively, what improvements could be made in her work conditions to enable her to continue in her usual job. In some industries in which women predominate, such as textiles, clothing manufacture, and leather goods, lists have been compiled jointly by the government and the Trade Union Central Committee of alternative jobs which pregnant women may be offered. They might also be permitted to continue with their usual work, but with lowered norms (Rumyantseva and Pergament, 1975).

Mothers who are breast-feeding, or have children less than 1 year old, are also entitled to a transfer with no loss of salary if they cannot perform their usual work. This might be, as in the case of pregnant women, because of the conditions of work (and again, medical confirmation is required). Alternatively a woman may be transferred without medical confirmation if her normal work is incompatible with the demands of a small child—for example, if it does not permit her to take the required breaks for feeding (Rumyantseva and Pergament, 1975).

It is prohibited to dismiss a pregnant woman, a woman who is breast-feeding a child, or a woman with a child less than 1 year old. Similarly these three categories of women cannot be employed on night work, overtime, public holidays, or other days on which they would normally be free. (If a woman breast-feeds her child for more than a year she must produce confirmation of this from a doctor or children's clinic in order to retain her benefits) (Rumyantseva and Pergament, 1975).

A woman who is breast-feeding or has a child less than 1 year old is entitled to a 30 minute break every 3 hours, in addition to her usual lunch break. If 30 minutes is not long enough due to special problems with the child's health, or because the mother lives too far from her work-place, these breaks might be extended. If a woman has two or more children under the age of 1, the breaks will be extended to a minimum of 1 hour each. If the child has health problems which require more frequent feeding, additional breaks can be arranged with medical confirmation of their necessity, (Rumyantseva and Pergament, 1975).

The paid period of maternity leave has, since 1956, been fixed at 112 days (56 days before and 56 after the birth). Women can, if they like, take an additional period of leave without forfeiting their jobs; this was extended in 1981 from a maximum of 1 year to a maximum of 18 months. Partial payment was also introduced in 1981 for the first year, which varies according to region. In the Far East, Siberia, and the northern regions—areas considered particularly inhospitable, but where there is a need to attract labour for work on industrial enterprises—the figure is 50 rubles per month; elsewhere it drops to 35 rubles. A woman is also permitted paid leave from work to tend a sick child under the age of 14. This extends for the duration of the illness or a maximum of 7 days (whichever is the shorter period), or 10 days in the case of single parents. If a mother must accompany her sick child to hospital, she receives payment for the duration of the hospitalization period. Mothers of two or more children were also granted in 1981 an additional 3 days' paid leave per year (*Pravda* and *Izvestiya*, 6.9. 1981). Such legislation is now generally observed, and supervised by factory Trade Union Committees, although breaches are occasionally criticized in the press.

Child benefit allowances were introduced in 1944 for mothers of three or more children. These were extended in 1981 to cover all mothers. These take the form of one lump-sum payment after the child's birth. Large families receive an additional monthly allowance per child, from the fourth child onwards; these begin from the child's first birthday and continue for four years. The amounts are listed in Table 11.2

The allowance for single mothers also increased dramatically in 1981. Previously, if no support was forthcoming from the child's father, the woman received 5 rubles per month for a first child, 7.50 for the second, and 10 rubles for any subsequent children. This grant continued until the child reached the age of 12. However, she now receives 20 rubles for each child, until the child reaches the age of 16 or, in the case of full-time students who are not in receipt of a government student grant, the age at 18 (*Pravda* and *Izvestiya*, 6.9. 1981).

Despite the increase in child benefit allowances, when one compares them with the average industrial wage (currently 172.5 rubles per month), or with the figure taken as the necessary minimum amount on which to live (51

Table 11.2   *Child benefit allowances according to the decrees of 1936, 1944, 1947 and 1981*

	1936		1944		1947		1981	
Child	Lump sum at birth	Annual	Lump sum at birth	Monthly	Lump sum at birth	Monthly	Lump sum at birth	Monthly
1	–	–	–	–	–	–	50 (500)	–
2	–	–	–	–	–	–	100 (1000)	–
3	–	–	400	–	200	–	100 (1000)	–
4	–	–	1300	80	650	40	65 (650)	4 (40)
5	–	–	1700	120	850	60	85 (850)	6 (60)
6	–	–	2000	140	1000	70	100 (1000)	7 (70)
7	–	2000	2500	200	1250	100	125 (1250)	10 (100)
8	–	2000	2500	200	1250	100	125 (1250)	12.50 (1250)
9	–	2000	3500	250	1750	125	175 (1750)	12.50 (1250)
10	–	2000	3500	250	1750	125	175 (1750)	12.50 (1250)
11	5,000	3000	3000	300	2500	150	250 (2500)	15 (150)

The amounts for 1936 to 1947 are given in old rubles. The 1981 figures are in new rubles (following the 1961 currency reform). Old rubles are shown in parentheses. (The exchange is 1 new ruble for 10 old rubles.)

The 1936 annual figure was for 5 years from birth, apart from the figure for the eleventh child, when the annual allowance started from the child's first birthday and ran for 4 years. Monthly allowances from 1944 onwards run for 4 years starting from the child's first birthday.

Source: Dodge, (1966), p. 24; Rumyantseva and Pergament (1979), p. 139; *Pravda* and *Izvestiya*, 6 July 1981, p. 1.

rubles per person per month), it is evident that they are still far from sufficient (Rzhanitsyna, 1977; *Vestnik Statistiki*, 1982).

In the European republics of the Soviet Union, one child has now become the norm for urban families. This is seen as a major demographic problem and is frequently discussed in the press, along with possible methods of persuading women to increase their reproductive output to two or even an optimum three children. (There would appear to be a racist element here. The birth rate in Soviet Central Asia remains high, and the local press there exhorts women to take a more active role in economic life rather than stressing their maternal function. A fear that the Slavic races could lose their numerical supremacy in the Soviet Union seems a likely explanation for this.) The contribution unmarried mothers make to society is now discussed—an interesting development for a society which generally preaches a Victorian-type morality of 'knightly chivalry' and 'maidenly honour'. As one Soviet scholar notes, there is a permanent imbalance in the sex ratio since even in peace-time the death rate is higher for men than for women; hence not all women will be able to find husbands.

And if a woman has already reached a certain age, and if all her fellow workers are women, and if by nature she is reserved and reticent, her chances are limited. She ought to be aware of this, and she also ought to be aware that motherhood sometimes brings more joy (or in any case, no less) than matrimony, especially if matrimony is not accompanied by mutual love and respect. (Urlanis, 1982, pp. 10–11).

This appears to promote not only single parenthood, but also loveless sex for the purpose of procreation.

Measures are also under way to ease the physical burden of combining work and motherhood, and to create a psychological climate where two or more children are seen as the norm. As Severina (director of Moscow's Department of Marriage and the Family, established in 1980) said:

Both in public opinion and in the consciousness of individual people, we must heighten the prestige of the family with two or three children, employing to this end the most diverse means: practical help, propaganda and upbringing. It is especially importance to correctly orientate young people (Prelovskaya, 1982, p. 30).

The latter takes its most prominent form in a school programme (so far in an experimental stage in a limited number of schools) on the preparation for family life, which stresses the joys of parenthood. An article in *Komsomolskaya Pravda*, the organ of the Communist Youth League, talks of the psychological benefits all family members derive from living in large families (the children, for example, learn to be more modest and less self-centred, develop a love of work and a spirit of communalism; alcoholism is very rare amongst adults in large families; and a happy and festive atmosphere is ever-present) (Mnogodetnaya Sem'ya, 1981). While the original Bolshevik idea was to relieve women of domestic drudgery through a network of public domestic institutions, the stress now is on helping the individual woman cope more successfully with a privatized domestic setting. Hence improvements in domestic commodities are recommended, and priority treatment in shops for mothers with several children, or even free deliveries to their homes. An experimental programme in Moscow also allows working mothers with three or more children special privileges at work, in the form of priority service in the canteens, shops, and order departments (Prelovskaya, 1982).

The Soviet Union retains its commitment to the provision of preschool child care institutions; the increase in the number of places offered in such institutions over the years is frequently cited in articles and books as evidence of the party's concern for women and children. However, the availability of places and the quality of the institutions is still vastly inadequate. While the number of creches and kindergartens increased from 46,000 in 1940 to 125,400 in 1979 (*Zhenschchini v SSSR*, 1981), a 1971 study showed that only one in 16 children attend a creche in their first year, and that 50% of all children under the age of 3 are cared for by their grandparents while their mothers work. Despite the large waiting list for creches and kindergartens in most urban areas, many women prefer not to use them if at all possible.

The quality of supervision is often lacking (the job of 'upbringer', as creche and kindergarten attendants are called, receives low pay and status, which inhibits the incumbents' good will and patience with their charges). The ratio of upbringers to children is extremely low, making creative, personal involvement with each child an impossibility. Creches are generally breeding-grounds for childhood infections, especially those of the respiratory tract, a problem exacerbated by the fact that a woman may not be able to find one near her home and must then take the child long distances by public transport in often harsh weather. The loss of worktime incurred by women staying home to care for sick children is an area of current concern. (CDSP, 1982a). The partial payment for 1 year's leave may persuade more women to stay at home for the child's first year.

A letter published in *Izvestia* (a national daily newspaper) from women workers in Orenburg complained of the shortage and inadequacy of kinder-gartens and nurseries. Local authorities devoted their attention to housing and industrial construction while child care facilities were neglected. The ninth Five-Year Plan for their area had included 19 children's institutions, but none had been built, and 3190 children in that area alone were without places. The result of this could be counted in lost production, inefficiency, and high turnover rates of harassed women workers (CDSP, 1982b). *Izvestia* took up the issue, with the result that the Council of Ministers of the Russian Republic published a Resolution on the need to 'expand the network and strengthen the material base of pre-school institutions and to establish condi-tions that will allow more women to participate in social production' (CDSP, 1982c). It is accepted that provision is still inadequate to meet the demands: currently there are places for 40% of children under school age (i.e. the age of 7). This is subject to regional variation; there are more facilities in urban areas than rural, and more in the Baltic and Slavic republics than in Central Asia. About 70% of these institutions operate throughout the year, providing 9, 12, or occasionally 24 hour care (Rzhanitsyna 1980).

Some schools operate an extended-day system for children of lower and intermediate age groups, in order to ease the problems families may face because of the overlap of the school and working day, and to avoid the 'latchkey child' syndrome. The children are given a hot meal after the day's lessons are finished; the youngest sleep for a while, and the rest of the time is organized by a teacher to include outdoor activities, indoor games, and homework (*Education in the USSR*, 1977).

The rebirth of Soviet empirical sociology in the 1960s, with the brief of providing practical recommendations towards the building of communism and the strengthening of the Soviet family, focused attention on women. Reasons for this include the visibility of women as subjects of social problems; Second World War deaths had left a population ratio of 73 men per 100 women in the 15–49 age group in 1950. (More recent figures are 86.3 to 100.) (Scott, 1976). The fact that this was having a considerable influence on the birth rate led to a recognition of the difficulties encountered by women who had both to actively participate in the labour force themselves and produce enough children to satisfy future labour needs. It was acknowledged that the 'woman question' had not been solved (Buckley, 1982); that although women had been drawn into the work force in equal numbers with men, they were not attaining equal success; and that their experience and perception of the world of work was significantly and disadvantageously different from that of men.

Women's attitude towards work has become one area of interest within sociology. Sociological studies show that the majority of women intend to work in social production for most of their lives, and regard their work and their families to be of equal moral value to them. Motivations to work include the desire to participate in socially useful work, the wish to be a member of a collective, and the desire for economic independence. Most women say they would continue working even if their material standard of living were otherwise guaranteed. They feel that work outside the home asserts their prestige in the eyes of husband and family. Women who do not work are also portrayed in the media as less developed members of society, whose families can have little respect for them (Novikova et. al., 1978).

Material incentives are also important. When listing their motivations to work, many women, particularly those at the lower end of the income scale, place financial need first. The existing wage structures mean that a family needs two incomes. The minimum expenditure in a family of two adults and two children was estimated by Soviet economists to be 51 rubles per month in 1977 when the average wage was 159.9 rubles. At that time 40.6% of Soviet workers were described as low-income earners. No definition was provided of what a low income might be; however, we can get some idea from the fact that the minimum wage in 1975 was 70 rubles per month, and social security payments to bring income up to the minimum averaged 30–40% of the aggregate income of low-income families (*Narodnoe Khozyaistvo*, 1979).

Of the 290 major occupations listed in the 1970 Census, there are almost none in which women do not work, and in 156 of them women comprise the bulk of the work force. (Yankova, 1975). Table 11.3 gives an indication of the location of the female work force. Most working women are found in the industrial sector, agriculture takes second place, and professions related to the humanities come third.

Female labour is subject to highly discernible patterns of horizontal and vertical segregation. Discriminatory horizontal segregation effectively exists in so far as there are certain sectors of the economy which have extremely high levels of female participation and which are poorly paid in relation to those in which male workers predominate. Vertical segregation refers to the tendency of women workers to cluster at the lower end of the occupational hierarchies and diminish in number further up the ladder. This occurs even

Table 11.3   *Women's employment by sector, according to 1970 Census (percentage of total female work force)*

Branch	1970
Material production	72.4
Industry	27.9
Construction, transport, mail, and communications	9.3
Agriculture and forestry	25.2
Trade, public catering, procurement, material supplies	10.1
Other branches	0.6
Non-production branches	27.6
Heath, sports, social security, education, science, art	20.7
Public housing, utilities and services, administration, banking, finance, public organizations	6.5
Unclassified	0.4

Source: V. G. Kostakov, 'The Development of Female Employment' in Lapidus, (1982), p. 52. Reproduced by permission of M. E. Sharpe, Inc.

in those occupational areas in which women are numerically predominant. Table 11.4 shows the relationship between wages and levels of female participation in some sectors of the economy. We would not wish to suggest a crude causal relationship but it is clearly noticeable that in all the sectors in which women predominate, wages are below the average. The following figures make this clear. While the average industrial wage is 189 rubles per month, male-dominated industries often pay much more than the average; transport workers receive around 204 rubles, construction workers 215, and workers in the fuel industries get as much as 276. In the service and light industry sectors where women predominate (forming around three-quarters of the work force), wages fall way below the average, however; workers in retail and catering get approximately 140 per month, in health services 128, in education 136, and in light industry 155 (*Vestnik Statistiki;* 1982).

Wages under Soviet socialism, as indeed elsewhere, are supposed to perform the dual economic function of providing a powerful material incentive to work, and at the same time serving as a source for consumption.

The principle of *khozraschet,* or enterprise self-financing, is used for the calculation of industrial wages. Through this mechanism the wage fund is related to the successful fulfilment of planned output, which in turn is related to production costs and profit. At the individual level, basic wage rates and skill demands are established for every job. All workers are assigned a skill grade, and increased skills correspond to increasingly complex jobs and hence higher rates. More than 45% of industrial workers are on piece rates supplementing the basic wage. There arc a variety of other inducement and bonus payments which are formally linked to over-the-norm production, but which managers often used as a sweetener for the work-force and to discourage high labour turnover (Rzhanitsyna, 1977).

Economic and political priorities also play a part in determining the wage scales in the different sectors. Those industries deemed to have greater political or economic significance are correspondingly better remunerated; hence jobs requiring equivalent skills and training receive better pay in the high-priority producer goods (or heavy industry) sector than in the consumer (or light industry) sector. Hence an engineer in the food, garment, textile, or leather industry will be on a lower pay scale than an engineer in coal or ore extraction, oil refining, or metallurgical industries (Chapman, 1978).

Female labour is generally located within this low-priority sector. This is partly because the tertiary sector—which includes retail, services, social security and administration—was a major growth area at the time of the last large-scale wave of female labour recruitment. It is also due to the persistence of the sex-typed occupational stratification which began in the thirties. This will be discussed in more depth later in the chapter.

As Table 11.4 shows, almost three-quarters of women workers are found

Table 11.4 *Distribution of women and wage scales in various sectors of the economy*

	Percentage of women in workforce	Average monthly earnings (rubles)
Overall average	51	172.5
Industry (production workers)	49	189.6
Workers	48	190.2
Engineering—technical workers	41	214.4
Employees	84	148.2
Agriculture	44	153.1
Transport	24	204.3
Communications	68	148.1
Construction	29	209.4
Retail, public catering, material, and technical supply and sales	76	140.7
Housing and communal services	53	135.8
Health, physical culture, and social security	84	128.5
Education	73	136.7
Culture	70	112.8
Art	46	136.5
Science and scientific services	49	183.2
Credit and social insurance	80	166.8
State, economic, and social administration	64	158.1

Sources: Percentage of women in workforce: *Zhenshchini v SSSR*, Moscow, 1975, pp. 32, 33, 39, figures are for 1974. Average monthly earnings: *Vestnik Statistiki*, No. 8, 1982, p. 78.

in branches of the economy directly concerned with production, and a quarter in non-productive branches. Productive work is generally more highly paid than non-productive work. Not all workers in the production sector are productive workers, however, since it includes auxiliary and white-collar workers. The majority of women workers are segregated in 'female' professions; that is, those in which the majority of the work force are women. This tendency has increased over the past 20 years (McAuley, 1981).

Table 11.5 indicates that the majority of women industrial workers (approximately one-third) are found in machine-building. They constitute 65–67% of precision instrument makers and radio-industry workers, occupations requiring an attention to detail which, according to Soviet opinion, is exhibited more often by women than men (Novikova et al., 1978).

Table 11.5 *Percentage of women in personnel categories in some branches of industry, 1974*

	All productive personnel	Workers	Engineering– technical workers	Employees
Industry as a whole	49	48	41	84
Machine construction	45	44	42	88
Electronics	51	50	46	85
Instrument making	53	52	48	87
Light industry	77	77	70	85
Textiles	72	72	62	84
Garments	86	86	85	86
Food industry	57	58	49	78
Meat	60	59	55	80
Dairy products	62	62	62	83

Source; *Zhenshchini v. SSSR*, Moscow, 1975, p. 39.

Light industry occupies second place. It is highly feminized and generally regarded as a woman's sector. This is particularly true of the garment and textile industries. Table 11.5 shows that, even in those industries in which women predominate, they constitute a relatively low proportion of the highly skilled group of engineering–technical workers, and a higher proportion of employees (the white-collar category). According to the 1970 Census, 44% of engineering–technical workers in all industries were women (Tsentralnoye Statisticheskie Upravleniye, 1973).

Agricultural occupations demonstrate similar patterns of sex differentiation. Soviet agriculture is heavily dependent upon large numbers of unskilled, older women workers. In 1970 over 40% of female agricultural workers were in the 40–54 age group. Women predominate in low-paid, manual, and often seasonal work. In 1972 two-thirds of all women agricul-

Table 11.6   *Wages (rubles) of different personnel categories in some branches of industry, 1981*

Machine construction	191.7
Workers	193.6
Engineering–technical workers	206.4
Employees	148.7
Light industry	152.8
Workers	155.3
Engineering–technical workers	180.3
Employees	133.0
Food industry	170.3
Workers	167.0
Engineering–technical workers	215.1
Employees	137.4
Fuel industry	277.5
Workers	276.5
Engineering–technical workers	325.4
Employees	180.8

Source: *Vestnik Statistiki*, No. 8, 1982, Table 4, pp. 79–80.

Table 11.7   *Distribution of workers in the '23rd Congress of the CPSU' collective farm, by type of employment, 1970*

Occupational group	Percentage of total work force	Percentage of male work force	Percentage of female work force
Machine operators, including tractor drivers	9.4	18.8	1.2
Livestock workers	8.4	7.4	8.5
Crop workers	66.3	50.4	82.1
Construction workers	3.5	6.3	0.2
Service workers	1.3	0.8	2.0
Administrative/management personnel; agricultural specialists	11.1	16.3	6.0
Total	100	100	100

Source: N. M. Shishkan, *Trud zhenshchin v usloviakh razvitogo sotsializma*, Kishenev, 1976, p. 55.

tural workers were engaged in crop farming, where the proportion of mechanized labour was 1.9% (Fedorova, 1982). Table 11.7 gives the occupational distribution by sex on a Moldavian collective farm.

The highly paid agricultural occupations are mechanized and male-dominated. Young women have been leaving the countryside in increasing numbers over the past two decades, creating a population imbalance which means not only that the female work force is older and less educated, but also that there are not enough brides for the male specialists. There have been campaigns in recent years to encourage young rural women to train in agricultural–technical specialisms in an attempt to halt their migration, as well as improve the quality of the work force. A Resolution of the Council of Ministers called for the establishment of special training courses to train women as tractor drivers, machine operators, electricians, and in other technical skills. The same Resolution lowered work norms by 10% for women machine operators working in agriculture, and doubled the annual leave of women tractor drivers. It further directed that women machine operators should receive the newest and most comfortable machines (*Soviet Legislation on Women's Rights*, 1978). This attempt to reduce rural migration and increase women's qualifications has met with little success, at least partly because of rural male prejudice (*Women in Eastern Europe*, 1982). Young women are dissatisfied with the low quality of life and opportunities available to them in the countryside, and are reluctant to return after their training.

Women workers, both manual and mental, are less skilled than men and far less likely to ascend the promotion ladder or to be in supervisory or management positions, even in occupations where they form the majority of the work force. As skill level is one of the elements determining the wage, this is yet another factor in pay differentials.

In industry women are far less likely to be in mechanized, automated work than men. Female labour and manual labour have almost become synonymous; when a work process becomes mechanized, it often becomes male. Some of the reasons for this are rooted in the history of female work force recruitment. Between 1962 and 1969 women were 96% of all new manual labourers (Shishkan, 1982). We have already seen that this wave of recruitment drew from former housewives who had no specific professional training; and it would appear that there has been little in the way of subsequent training. In the age group 30–39, 62.1% of male industrial workers are in the higher skill grades, but only 7.1% of female industrial workers (Kotliar and Turchaninova, 1982). Women constitute 70–80% of the workers in the lowest skill grades (Shishkan, 1982).

In machine building, where most women industrial workers are found, 67% of workers who occupy the two lowest skill grades are women, while 23% are men. Whereas only 5.5% of women machine builders are in the highest grades, over half of male machine builders are located here. According to the same study, women in this sector account for 96% of assemblers, a job which rates 1.9 on the 1–6 skill rating system. It was concluded that 'the predominance of female labour in manual, low skilled jobs is indicative of inefficient use of female labour, low mechanisation in largely female jobs, and, furthermore, a lack of concern for such problems as raising skill levels on the part of factory managers and public organisations' (Kotliar and Turchaninova, 1982, p. 83).

In textiles, where the majority of the work force are women, they similarly constitute only 5% of workers in the highest skill grade, while 44.5% of male textile workers are found in that grade. Male textile workers are employed in equipment maintenance and set-up operations; those involved in production line work are likely to be assistant foremen (Kotliar and Turchaninova, 1982).

In short, then, women form the vast majority of low-skilled workers in all sectors. Not even in the most highly feminized occupational sectors are there as many highly skilled women as men. This concentration of women workers in the manual, unskilled and often heavy work is giving rise to concern.

One Soviet economist offers the following reasons for the failure of women to figure more prominently in higher industrial grades. Higher skill grades correspond to increased levels of mechanization, and women tend not to be in mechanized work. The type of work they do is generally unstimulating, and does not provide them with the incentive to increase their qualifications. Any attempt to do so is also complicated by interruptions in their careers for child-bearing, and the consequent huge reduction in their available free time (Shishkan, 1982).

There is a positive correlation between the number of children women have and the continuation of their education. Shishkan argues that shortage of time is the main obstacle to women's advancement to managerial positions. The failing of technical training schools is also a factor. The proportion of women trainees is often less (and never more) than a third of the total. Male prejudice is another problem: 'Women's advancement to more skilled jobs and, especially, managerial positions is still blocked by remnants from the past in approaching women as housewives and viewing their participation in social labour as a temporary and passing phenomenon' (Shishkan, 1982, p. 129).

Almost one-third of women workers are engaged in predominantly mental work, and two-thirds in predominantly physical. Women comprise 46% of physical workers and 59% of mental workers. The latter covers professional and semi-professional workers, so we see that women are well represented in jobs requiring further or higher educational training. The number of women engaged in physical work increased by 4% in the period between the 1959 and 1979 Census, whereas the number engaged in mental work increased by 84.3%. This differential increase may be explained partly by the development of the service and administrative sector during this period. For instance, almost 2 million new women workers took up jobs in planning and accounting (Tsentralnoye Statisticheskie Upravleniye, 1973).

Women are involved in professional and semi-professional work to a far higher degree than in any Western economy, although, apart from the notable exception of engineering, they tend to cluster in similar recognizable occupational areas. Their high level of participation in such work is a reflec-

Table 11.8   *Women in non-manual occupations, 1970*

Occupation	Percentage
Physicians	74
Dentists	77
Midwives, medical assistants	83
Pharmacists	95
Nurses	99.1
Kindergarten heads and workers	99.5
Primary and secondary teachers, primary school heads, careers teachers	72
Publishing personnel	74
Librarians and chief librarians	95
Telephonists	96
Managers of shops	64
Managers of public dining establishments	69
Economists and planners	82
Accountants	85
Statisticians	95
Typists	99
Secretaries	95
Cultural workers	65
Technicians	59
Engineers	40
Designers and draughtspersons	57
Juridicial personnel	38
Agronomists	35
Livestock specialists	45
Veterinary surgeons	31

Source: Tsentralnoe statisticheskoe upravlenie, SSSR, *Itogi vsesoiuznoi perepisi naseleniia 1970 goda*, Tom 6, Moscow, 1973, pp. 167–169.

tion of their high numbers in education, as shown in Table 11.9. This table also indicates that occupational segregation at the professional level can be expected to continue as greater numbers train for careers in the humanities than for industrial careers. In both mental and manual work, women engage principally in what are acknowledged as 'women's professions', and which can be identified as extensions of domestic functions: cooking, cleaning, caring, clothing, and child-rearing.

There are exceptions, however. Women are well represented in engineering, accountancy, economic planning, and legal and technical specialisms, none of which are professions traditionally associated with women. Forty per cent of engineers, for example, are now women. The process of female entry into this profession was initiated by a quota system in industrial training schools which began in the 1930s, and has proceeded with government support. Traditional conceptions of female work are still reflected in this profession to the extent that women are far more likely to specialize in

Table 11.9   *Percentage of women studying in higher and further education institutes,*
1981–82

	Higher educational institutes	Further education institutes
Overall percentage of women students	52	57
Industry, construction, transport, and communication	42	44
Agriculture	34	36
Economy and law	68	85
Health, physical culture, and sport	58	90
Education, art, cinema	69	86

Source: *Zhenshchini v SSSR,* Moscow, 1983, p. 15.

food-product or consumer goods technology than in mining, transport, or machine building, and that 67% of women engineers are in the lowest grades and only 1% in the highest. Nonetheless, the high number of women in engineering can still be seen as an indicator of relative success in the intersection of ideology with economic imperatives in the transformation of women's lives (Dodge, 1978; Jancar, 1978).

   Table 11.10 shows the percentage of women in leading positions in industry for 1973, and indicates a severe under-representation of women in managerial positions.

Table 11.10   *Percentage of women in leading positions in industry, 1973*

Enterprise directors	9
Deputy directors, chief engineers, and other chief specialists	10
Workshop supervisors and deputies	16
Department chiefs	26
Forepersons	24

Source: Zhenshchini v SSSR, Moscow, 1975, p. 80.

In the white-collar professions there is a similar absence of women at senior and supervisory levels, and a noticeable negative correlation between high levels of female participation and positions of skill responsibility, status, and high income. If we look at the structure of the medical profession we see that 89% of all health workers are women. Women constitute 99% of nurses, as well as 83% of medical assistants, 74% of doctors, and 53% of chief doctors (i.e. heads of hospitals, research institutes, and departments). In other words, men make up 11% of all health personnel and take 47% of the most responsible posts. Statistically speaking, the relatively small number of men entering medicine stand a better chance of promotion than the women who form the bulk of the profession's staff. (Tsentralnoye Statisticheskie Upravleniye, 1973).

Education is another professional area where women are represented in large numbers. Women form 71% of the teaching profession. Again there is a discernible professional status hierarchy, and an inverse relationship between high female numbers and responsible, higher-status posts. Almost all kindergarten teachers are women, as are 77% of the directors of elementary schools and 80% of secondary school teachers. Women comprise 38% of the directors and 63% of the deputy directors of 8-year secondary schools (that is, the equivalent of schools without a sixth form), and 34% of the directors and 69% of the deputy directors of 10 year secondary schools (*Zhenshchini v SSSR,* 1983); 43% of university lecturers are women (Tsentralnoye Statistiches Upravleniye, 1973). In the rest of the academic world, women comprise 52% of the higher education students, 30% of postgraduate students, 28% of Candidates of Science (a Soviet higher degree located somewhere between the British Masters degree and doctorate), and 14% of Doctors of Science (*Vestnik Statistiki,* 1983). They constitute 50% of junior research associates, 24% of senior research associates, 22% of associate professors, and 10% of academicians and professors (Lapidus, 1978).

Why have women persisted in clustering in certain occupational sectors? Why have they failed to ascend the skills and promotion ladders? All Soviet schools are coeducational and follow a common curriculum. Formally boys and girls receive the same education, with one major exception, that of workshop training. For most of a child's school career she will have a weekly session of work education. This is a combination of careers guidance and practical experience of some work processes. Many schools have arrangements with enterprises in their locality which take groups of pupils for a period each week. This lesson is sharply segregated. Boys study woodwork, metalwork, basic mechanics, and so on; girls often spend the workshop session learning skills 'that will be useful to them in later life'—cookery, homecare, dressmaking (personal visits, 1979, 1982). This reinforces the traditional stereotypical images of male and female activity presented in children's readers (Rosenham, 1978) and also serves to compound their home experience where they may have noticed their mothers spend over 22½ hours a week on cooking, washing up, cleaning the apartment, and attending to clothes and shoes, in comparison to the 1 hour and 40 minutes similarly spent by their fathers (*Molodaya Sem'ya,* 1977).

That domestic work in general is still seen as a predominantly female function is evident from the studies on the domestic division of labour between husband and wife. Although men are exhorted by the Soviet media to help their wives more in the home, there is still a sharp imbalance in the contribution made by each, as Table 11.11 shows.

Table 11.11 *Weekly work-load of adults in a working family (in hours), from 1923 to 1970*

	1923–24		1967–70	
	Housework	Housework and professional work combined	Housework	Housework and professional work combined
Professional men	13	50	10	51
Professional women	34	78	27	65
Housewives	70	70	52	52

Source: A. G. Kharchev, *Brak i sem'ya v SSSR*, Moscow, 1979, p. 282.
Note: The decrease in time spent by both men and women on housework is the result of labour-saving devices introduced since the 1920s, minimal as they have been.

After school young men are more likely than young women to embark upon a course of professional training at a vocational-training institution; this training is likely to equip them for a career in industry. Less than a quarter of young men go straight into a job from school but more than half of young women are likely to do so. This means that many young women receive on-the-job training as apprentices which rarely leads to the acquisition of complex technical skills, whereas young male workers, after 2 years in industrial training schools, are equipped with the practical and theoretical knowledge which allows them to move up the occupational grade ladder more swiftly (Shishkan, 1982).

The female school-leavers who do progress to vocational training courses comprise 30% of the students in urban schools and 10% in rural. The vast majority are trained for women's jobs in the low-paid female-saturated occupations. One study of a professional training school showed that young women filled 90% of the places on dressmaking, plastering, and painting courses and 10–15% of the places on machine adjuster and repair courses, and were absent altogether from courses for specialized machinists, construction engineers, railway workers, and electric welders (Sacks, 1976).

One of the reasons for this is the fact that women are ineligible for certain of the courses offered in industrial training schools by virtue of the protective legislation which excludes them from certain occupations deemed harmful to their health. A new list of such occupations was drawn up by the State Committee of the Council of Ministers and the Trade Union Central Council in 1978 and circulated to all enterprises (*Soviet Legislation on Women's Rights*, 1978). There are indications that a number of women do work in these prohibited professions, that there is often not a great deal of logic or consistency in the selection of those professions which are 'arduous and hazardous', and that by no means all women are in favour of legislation which serves to exclude them from many of the highest-paying jobs (Rzhanit-syna, 1982).

Evidence indicates that boys and girls absorb social messages as to sex-appropriate occupational choice quite early. When asked to rank occupations in order of attractiveness, school girls have consistently ranked teaching, medical and cultural occupations higher, while boys have put engineering and technical specialisms first (Lapidus, 1978b).

Research on entrants to teacher training colleges, where there is a ratio of one male student to every ten female, indicated that the female students were more strongly motivated towards a teaching career than the male. There was a clearly perceived sexual division of labour amongst the trainees, boys preferring to work in further education and girls preferring to work with pre-school children. In response to the question 'Why do you think there are more girls than boys in teacher training colleges?', the most common replies were to the effect that teaching was a women's profession; girls had a natural talent for teaching; girls were more attracted to children; exams were easier at teaching colleges and so girls were more likely to gain places; boys would be ashamed of doing such work, and boys did not regard it as serious work. Before the Second World War teaching in the Soviet Union was a prestigious and male-dominated profession. It has since become feminized, relatively more poorly paid and unprestigious, and now occupies one of the bottom places on boys' list of job preferences—and is usually amongst the highest on girls' lists (Belyaev *et. al.*, 1969).

Although, as we have seen, Soviet women regard work as an important aspect of their lives, their attitude to this work often differs from that of men, in that many appear to want convenient jobs rather than challenging careers. Women evaluate their jobs in terms of relations with colleagues and conditions of work rather than in terms of the content of the work (*Zhensh-china, Trud i Semya*, 1978). When listing their reasons for professional satisfaction, women concentrate on factors such as nearness to home, a guaranteed kindergarten place, and convenient shifts, rather than factors connected with the work itself (Kharchev and Golod, 1971). Men give career-related reasons for changing their jobs, such as lack of job satisfaction and lack of facilities for increasing qualifications. Women give personal reasons such as lack of child care facilities, personal health, distance between home and work, and family difficulties. (*Problemi Ispolzovaniya Rabochei Sili v Usloviakh Nauchno-tekhnicheskoi Revolutsii*, 1973).

Where do women acquire such atttitudes? What is it that teaches girls from an early age that certain types of work are suitable for women?

A study of heroes and heroines in fiction in two of the most popular magazines for young people throws some light on this. First of all, men appear as main characters more than twice as frequently as women. Whereas almost all of the male characters are discussed in terms of their occupations, no such information is provided in the case of almost half of the women characters. Thus, '. . . it is almost impossible to imagine a man without a profession, but the same cannot be said about women. This does more than just reflect the traditional imaginary stereotype: it fixates it.' (Kon, 1975, pp. 655–665).

Certain jobs are indeed seen as specifically women's jobs, to which women will be attracted and in which they will be 'naturally' competent due to their psycho-physiological attributes. Some writers stress that 'equality' does not mean 'identity'; to be equal, men and women do not need to be represented in equal numbers throughout the economy. Indeed, given that women are not as strong as men, a mathematical notion of equality would be to women's disadvantage. The lowering of production norms for women in industrial occupations has been discussed throughout the 1970s, but so far only implemented for agricultural machinery operators. Although sex, according to the Constitution, is not a factor allowed to influence pay, it has been suggested that sometimes it is necessary to be 'unfair' in order to be fair.

There is much familiar talk of women's deftness and attentiveness to detail that makes them good at assembly work, but relatively little mention of sex-differentiated socialization patterns on the influence of available models of female behaviour. (The survey of male and female characters in fiction, cited above, is an enlightening exception.) No Soviet writer would talk of women's inferiority in the work force, but of their 'difference'. This difference is biological, stemming from women's child-bearing functions and ensuing maternal responsibilities. (The concept of paternity leave does not exist in the Soviet Union.) It is acknowledged that the tensions between women's two social roles, as mothers and as workers, have not been totally resolved, in spite of a considerable amount of state intervention for the legislative protection of women's jobs during pregnancy and maternity leave, and the provision of nurseries and kindergartens. It is recognized that domestic work falls almost exclusively on the shoulders of women. The original blueprint for women's emancipation in the Soviet Union included the removal of housework from the home and the withering away of the family as a unit of consumption. The establishment in the 1930s of the 'socialist family', almost identical in form and content to the bourgeois family, meant that the private domestic economy was maintained as the means of satisfying a whole series of needs through the use of women's unpaid labour. The Soviet family is the focal point of childcare and upbringing, of the organization and satisfaction of consumer needs and individual well-being (Yankova, 1975).

Women's emancipation in the Soviet Union has meant the integration of full-time professional work with the traditional responsibilities associated with women's roles in the home, as wife, mother, and housewife. The over-burdening involved in the attempt to fulfil both roles has caused mutual negative reinforcement. That is, women underperform in both functions.

Their family and domestic responsibilities cause them to take less demanding jobs than men and to demand less of them, in terms of satisfaction or promotion. They are frequently tired, specially if engaged in shift work (25% of women industrial workers are on a shift system that includes night shifts) and often ill. Research indicates that the average woman's overall work-load is 15–20% greater than the average man's. (Kotliar and Turchaninova, 1982).

As women's free time is almost wholly absorbed by housework and child care, they have considerably less time and energy than men to devote to increasing their qualifications. There is a negative correlation between the number of children a woman has and the likelihood of her studying. Twenty-eight out of 100 childless women study, whereas the proportions for women with one, two, three, and four children are 13, 9, 7 and 0.6 respectively. Of students at evening classes, 35–50% are not married men, while only 2–8% are married women.

It was supposed that bringing women into the public world of work would lead to greater equality and democracy within the family and hence to greater stability. In fact, increased education and labour participation by women have gone hand in hand with lower rates of marriage, later marriage, increased divorce, and lower birth rate. Family relations have not been democratized, in so far as housework still takes up the majority of women's 'non-working' time and little of men's.

The government is concerned about women's position; it is accepted that not all the contradictions between women's professional and family roles have been resolved. Principal shortcomings are noted in the lag of women behind men in levels of occupational skill and, hence, wages, and their longer aggregate working day as a result of domestic work (Sonin, 1982). From the mid-1970s there has been an annual nationwide 'Examination of the conditions of work, everyday life and rest of working women', conducted by the trade union organization in association with enterprise managements. The wide-ranging scope of these examinations includes: the raising of sanitary standards through increased ventilation and decreased dust, noise, and air pollution; the reduction of the number of women engaged in heavy, unqualified, and dangerous work, chiefly by raising their qualifications and encouraging them to retrain for new jobs; the overall increase in the number of women studying and increasing their qualifications; the improvement of services at enterprises which would lighten women's domestic work, such as facilities for ordering food, shoe repairs, laundry, etc.; and the increased availability of child care (*Sbornik Postanovlenii*, 1975). These examinations lead to the production of annual reports which are well publicized in the national press, and awards for those enterprises which have taken significant steps towards the improvement of conditions for women workers. Enterprises and sectors of industry which fail to promote improvements in women's working conditions are also publicly criticized. In the Report of 1980 it was noted that in the forestry, wood-processing, metals and alloys, tractor, and agricultural machine building industries not enough had been done towards the improvement of women's working conditions or freeing them from heavy or dangerous work. (*Sbornik Postanovlenii*, 1980).

One of the most significant recent initiatives to help women combine work and family has been the commitment to the reduction of the working week for women with children. Experiments were conducted in the 1960s and 1970s which reduced both the working day and week for women, with the expectation that the extra time would enable them to participate more in public affairs or increase their qualifications. However, results showed that the extra time was in fact spent on housework and child care rather than women's personal needs. Now part-time work is an accepted means of keeping women in the work force at specific times during their lives, when family responsibilities are particularly great. It is an acknowledgment of the accepted norm in Soviet life than child care is a woman's province (*Zhenshchini na Rabote i Doma,* 1978; *Literaturnaya Gazeta,* 1979).

It has also been suggested that women with small children be permitted to work from home. This is surprising, from a society pledged to collective, social work activity. In justification, advantages are indicated both to society and to the women themselves. The former gains additional work-days which are currently lost by mothers taking time off work to look after sick children, while women benefit from not having to resort to public child care institutions, nor to withdraw from productive life completely, which can result in lost opportunities for improving qualifications and hence a slower pace of promotion. (*Zhenschini na Rabote i Doma,* 1978). One Leningrad factory with a large proportion of female workers began organizing work at home in 1967, with considerable success; the number of people opting for such work rose from 16 to 346 in 1975 (or from 1.8% to 30.5% of the factory's work force). 68% of these were mothers with small children. It is also suggested that women with chronically ill, invalid, or elderly relatives could benefit from such a work arrangement. It is automatically women who are seen as responsible for the care of such relatives.

Much is written about the need to increase women's qualifications as a necessary part of the process of their transfer from manual to mechanized work, and it is one of the briefs of the annual inspection of women's labour to oversee this process. However, given the fact that the time women have available for the necessary study is severely curtailed, it is difficult to see how this can be accomplished at present. Some writers suggest that such training should be done during women's paid working time, and the experimental implementation of this approach has been successfully reported in a Leningrad shipyard (Rzhanitsyna, 1982). It may well be that such a scheme is being operated on a trial basis prior to its wider introduction.

CONCLUSIONS

A somewhat negative view of women's experience of work in the Soviet Union has emerged from the discussion presented in this chapter. As shown at the outset, women's entry into productive work was thought to be the basis of their emancipation; however, the Soviet experience indicates that it is not the sole factor in the development of women's equality. Early Soviet theorists acknowledged the importance of freeing women from privatized domestic labour in order to ensure their equal participation in social production, but this has yet to be accomplished. If anything, its likelihood becomes increasingly remote, since Soviet policy now concentrates more on providing commodities and services to help women perform their domestic tasks in a privatized setting (though these are still at a very low level), rather than promoting the socialization of these tasks. It becomes clear that there has been no basic redefinition of male and female roles in Soviet society; for Soviet women emancipation has meant the acquisition of a supplementary role, that of full-time paid worker, on top of their traditional roles of wife, mother, and housewife. The right—indeed, obligation—to work, without accompanying alterations in domestic roles, has imposed a great burden on them.

Nonetheless, the positive achievements of the Soviet Union in this sphere should also be acknowledged. Soviet women are more active in the economy, and in a wider range of occupations, than their counterparts in any other country in the world. They do not have to make a choice, as their Western counterparts often must, between work and motherhood, but are expected to experience both. Although at present this combination presents myriad difficulties, at least the government acknowledges its duty to ensure the possibility of such a combination.

REFERENCES

Anikeeva, L., and Schochina, L. (1978). 'Zhenshchini s det'mi i nadomnii trud', in *Zhenshchina na rabote i doma*, Moscow, pp. 48 and 49.

Atkinson, D., Dallin, A., and Lapidus, G. W. (1978). (eds). *Women in Russia*. Harvester Press London.

Belyaev, E. V. *et. al.* (1969). 'Sotsialni prestizh pedagogicheskoi professii i motivi yeyo vibora vipusnikami schkol' in *Chelovek i Obshchestvo*, vyp. 6, Leningrad, pp. 66–77.

Buckley, M. (1982). *'Women, Ideology and the Soviet State'*. Paper given to Political Science Association women's group conference.

CDSP (*Current Digest of the Soviet Press*) (1982). vol. 34, no. 30.

CDSP (1982b). Vol. 28, no. 15.

CDSP (1982c). Vol. 28, No. 18.

Chapman, J. (1978). 'Equal pay for equal work?' in D. Atkinson, A. Dallin, and G. W. Lapidus (eds), *Women in Russia*. Harvester Press, London, p. 228.

Dodge, N. T. (1966). *Women in the Soviet Economy*, Johns Hopkins University Press, Baltimore.

Dodge, N. T. (1971). 'Recruitment and the quality of the Soviet agricultural labour force', in J. R. Miller (ed.) *The Soviet Rural Community*. University of Illinois Press, Chicago, pp. 180–189.

Dodge, N. T. (1978). 'Women in the professions', in D. Atkinson, A. Dallin, and G. W. Lapidus (eds), *Women in Russia*. . Harvester Press, London, pp. 215–217.

Engels, F. (1977). *Origin of the Family, Private Property of the State*. Lawrence & Wishart, London.

Education in the USSR (1977). Progress, Moscow.

Evans, J. (1981). 'The Communist Party of the Soviet Union and the women's question: the case of the 1936 decree, in defence of mother and child. *Journal of Contemporary History*, **16**, 757–775.

Fedorova, M. (1982). The utilisation of female labour in agriculture', in G. W. Lapidus (ed.) *Women, Work and Family in the Soviet Union*. Sharpe, New York, p. 42.

Holt, A. (1980). 'Bolshevik theory and practice in the 1920s,' in T. Yedlin (ed), *Women in Eastern Europe and the Soviet Union* Praeger, New York, p. 92.

Jancar, B. W. (1978). *Women Under Communism*. Johns Hopkins University Press, Baltimore

Kharchev, A. G. and Golod, S. I. (1978). *Professionalnaya Rabota Zhenschchin i Semya*. Leningrad.

Kon, I. S. (1975). 'Women at Work': equality with a difference?' in *Revue International du Science Sociale*, **27** (4), 655–665.

Kostakov, V. G. (1982). 'Features of the development of female employment', in G. W. Lapidus (ed.), *Women, Work and Family in the Soviet Union*. Sharpe, New York, p. 42.

Konstitutsia SSSR, (1977). Moscow, pp. 16–17.

Kotliar, A. E., and Turchaninova, S. Y. (1982). The educational and occupational skill level of industrial workers', in G. W. Lapidus (ed.), *Women, Work and Family in the Soviet Union*. Sharpe, New York, p. 89.

Lapidus, G. W. (1978a). 'Sexual equality in Soviet policy: a developmental perspective', in D. Atkinson, A. Dallin, and G. W. Lapidus (eds). *Women in Russia*. Harvester Press, London, pp. 119–124.

Lapidus, G. W. (1978b). *Women in Soviet Society*. University of California Press, Berkeley.

Lapidus, G. W. (ed.) (1982). *Women, Work and Family in the Soviet Union*. Sharpe, New York.

Lenin, V. I. (1963). 'Velikii pochin (o geroizme rabochikh v tylu po povodu 'kommun- isticheskikh subbotnikov')' 28 June 1919, and 'O zadachakh zhenskogo dvizheniya v sovetskoi respublike' 23 September 1919, in *Polnoe Sobranie Sochinenii*, 5th edn. vol. 39, Moscow.

Literaturnaya Gazeta (1979). 16 May p. 12.

Luke, L. E. (1953). 'Marxian women – Soviet variants', in E. J. Simmons (ed). *Through the Glass of Soviet Literature*, Columbia University Press, New York, p. 46.

McAuley, A. (1981). *Women's Work and Wages in the Soviet Union*. Allen & Unwin, London.

Mnogodetnaya Sem'ya (1981) in *Komsomolskaya Pravda*, 30 October 1981, p. 3

Molodaya Sem'ya (1977). Moscow, p. 37.

Narodnoye Khozyaistvo SSSR v 1979 g., Moscow, 1980, pp. 391 and 394.

Narodnoye Khozyaistvo SSSR v 1980 g., Moscow, 1981, p. 7.

Novikova, Ye., Yazikova, V. S., and Yantiova, Z. A. (1978). *Zhenshchina, Trud, Sem'ya*. Moscow, p. 16.

Personal visits to Soviet schools and discussion with Soviet teachers (1979, 1982).

Prelovskaya, I. (1982). 'Sluzhba sem' i', in *Izvestiya*, 27 January, 1982.

Problemi ispol'zovaniya rabochei sili v usloviakh nauchno-tekhnicheskoi revolutsii (1973). Moscow.

Rashin, A. G. (1958). *Formitovaniye Rabochego Klassa Rossii*. Moscow.

Rosenham, M. S. (1978). 'Images of male and female in children's readers', in D. Atkinson, A. Dallin, and G. W. Lapidus (ed.) *Women in Russia*. Harvester Press, London, pp. 243–305.

Rumyantseva, M. S. and Pergament, A. I. (1975). *Spravochnik Zhenshchini-Rabotnitsi*. Moscow.

Rzhanitsyna, L. (1977). Soviet Family Budgets. Progress, Moscow.

Rzhanitsyna, L. (1980). 'Zabota o zhenschchine-trudzhenitse i materi', in *Sotsialisticheskii Trud*, **2**, p. 105.

Rzhanitsyna, L. (1982). G. W. Lapidus (ed). *Women, Work and Family in the Soviet Union*. Sharpe. New York, p. 11.

Sacks, M. P. (1976). *Women's Work in Soviet Russia*. Praeger, New York.

Sbornik Postanovlenii V.Ts. S.P.S. (1975). April–June, p. 97.

Sbornik Postanovlenii V.Ts.S.P.S. (1980), April–June, p. 57.

Scott, H. (1976). *Women and Socialism*. Alison and Busby, London.

Scott, B. and Tilly, R (1976). cited by M. P. Sacks, *Women's Work in Soviet Russia*. Praeger, New York, p. 14.

Sheptulina, N. N. (1982). 'Protection of female labour', in G. W. Lapidus (ed.), *Women, Work and Family in the Soviet Union*, Sharpe, New York.

Shishkan, M. M. (1982). 'Raising the skill levels of women workers', in G. W. Lapidus (ed.). *Women, Work and Family in the Soviet Union*. Sharpe, New York.

Sonin, M. Ya. (1982). 'Socio-economic problems of female emloyment', in G. W. Lapidus (ed.), *Women, Work and Family in the Soviet Union*. Sharpe, New York, p. 23.

Soviet Legislation on Womens' Rights (1978). Resolution 'On a more extensive employment of women in skilled labour in agriculture'. Progress, Moscow, pp. 94–95.

Stites, R. (1978). *The Women's Liberation Movement in Russia*. Princeton University Press, New Jersey.

Triska, J. F. (ed). (1962). *Soviet Communism, Programs and Rules*, 1919 Program of the All Russian Communist Party (Bolsheviks). Chandler, San Francisco.

Tsentralnoye Statisticheskie Upravleniye (1973). *Itogi Vsesoyuznoi Perepisi Naseleniya 1970 goda*, tom 6, Moscow.

Tupper, S., and Evans J. (1981) 'The Impact of the War upon the Participation of Women in the Industrial Workforce' (1936–42). Paper given at the West European Conference on Soviet Industry and the Working Class in the Inter-war years, 3–6 June, pp. 8–9.

Ubaidullaeva, R. A. (1982). 'The twenty-fifth Congress of the CPSU and current problems of employment of female labour in the Republics of Central Asia', in G. W. Lapidus (ed.), *Women, Work and Family in the Soviet Union*. Sharpe, New York, p. 148.

Urlanis, B. (1982). A wanted child, *Current Digest of the Soviet Press* (CDSP), **32**, (49), 10–11.

Vestnik Statistiki (1982). No. 1, Moscow.

Vestnik Statistiki (1983). No. 1, Moscow.

Work and Family Life (1980). ILO, Geneva.

Women in Eastern Europe (1982). The heirs of Pasha, (5), 5–7.

Yankova, Z. A. (1975). Razvitie lichnosti zhenshchini v sovetskom obshchestve', in *Sotsiologicheskiye Issledovaniye*, (no. 4), 44–45.

Zhenshchina na Rabote i Doma (1978). Moscow, p. 47.

Zhenshchina, Trud i Semya (1978). Moscow, p. 25.

Zhenshchini v SSSR: statisticheskie Materiali (1981, 1983). Moscow.

Index

abortion, 157
access to employment, 108
affirmative action, 71
age of the female workforce, 88
AnCO special programmes, 57

biases
  attributional, 250
  dealing with, 252
  self-serving, 251
  stereotype and gender discount, 249

care of the aged, 157
changes in men's roles, 201
child benefit allowances, 284
child care facilities, 78
company nurseries, 79
cultural side-effects, 257

day care, 19
decision to work, 127
'divided' labour market, 64
divorce, 161

education system, 10
employment rights, 29
Employment Equality Agency, 42
employment equality legislation, 42
equal pay, 43
Equal Pay Act, 35
equality legislation, 160
equality promoting projects, 162

factors maintaining discrimination, 243
family planning, 157
family work conflict, 74
feelings about work, 198
female earnings, 47
female home industry workers, 96
'female' jobs, 130
female stereotype, 125
Finland, 183–208
flexitime, 75
further education training, 69

Germany (Federal Republic of), 63–81
Great Britain, 3–38
Greece, 123–150

health insurance, 155
Holland, 83–102
hours of work, 47
household duties, 199

Ireland, 39–62
Italy, 103–122

job sharing, 26, 76
job splitting, 26

labour legislation, 229
labour market policy, 98
legal perspective, 133
legislation, 40
low-paid work, 241

maternity
  leave, 31, 77
  pay, 30
  protection, 43, 231
  rights, 29
media, 175
mentoring, 247
Minimum Wage Law, 91
mothers at work, 3

networking, 248
nightwork, 111

organization of work, 53
organizational backlash, 258

part-time work, 21, 75
paternity leave, 156
paternity provision, 29
pay differentials, 66
personal characteristics, 242
political and union life, 173
Portugal, 209–233

position of Swedish women in the 1980s,
    177
positive achievements of the Soviet
    Union, 302
positive action programmes, 7
positive discrimination, 116
promotion, 131
protective legislation, 145

responsibility of women for child care,
    50
right to return to work, 31

segregation
    between male and female
        occupations, 90
    by occupation, 169, 220
    job, 5, 65
Sex Discrimination Act, 35
sex-role spillover, 245
sexual harassment, 246
short career ladder, 241
sickness benefit and parental insurance,
    55
sidelining of affirmative action, 259
social security systems, 101
social welfare, 55
staff training programmes, 165
structuring of the working day, 74
Sweden, 153–181

taxation, 54
Trades Union Congress, 8
training, 12, 56

under-valuation of 'women's jobs, 14
unemployment, 66, 88, 132, 214
unfair dismissal, 29
university and tertiary education, 165

USA, 237–267
USSR, 269–304

vocational education, 67

wages, 130
women
    amongst workers and employees in
        the USSR, 280
    and education, 51, 222
    and trade unions, 50
    and wage scales in various sectors of
        the economy, 289
    as managers, 167
    as reproduction workers, 189
    hierarchical position of, 188
    in decision-making occupations, 49
    in engineering, 58
    in management, 58, 195
    in non-manual occupations, 294
    in the labour force, 44
    who do housework, 95
women's
    degree of qualification, 221
    earnings, 224
    employment by sector, 288
    family role, 114
    occupations, 6
    working lives, 16
work
    attitudes towards women at, 53
    character and quality of women's, 93
    contacts and the quality of, 190
    number of hours women work, 93
    outside the home, 199
    patterns, 64, 216
    protection of working women, 144
    where women work, 45